*K
3157
E5
F58*

93675

PELICAN BOOKS

FIVE CONSTITUTIONS

Professor Samuel Edward Finer was born in 1915, and
educated at Holloway School in London and Trinity
College, Oxford. He received his B.A. in 1937 and his M.A.
(Oxon.) in 1946. From 1946 to 1950 he was at Oxford,
first as Lecturer in Politics at Balliol, and then as Junior
Research Fellow. After twelve years at Keele University
he became Deputy Vice-Chancellor there (1962–4). Later
he was Professor of Government at the University of
Manchester (1966–74) and Chairman of the Political
Studies Association of Great Britain (1965–9). Professor
Finer is presently Gladstone Professor of Government
and Public Administration at the University of Oxford.
Professor Finer is the author of numerous articles and
books in his field. *Comparative Government* and *The Man
on Horseback: The Role of the Military in Politics* are
both published in Penguins.

FIVE
CONSTITUTIONS

*

EDITED, WITH AN
INTRODUCTION, BY
S. E. FINER

PENGUIN BOOKS

CONTENTS

PREFACE AND ACKNOWLEDGEMENTS

THIS volume was conceived and is designed to serve as a handbook for all those involved, whatever the way, in the study of modern government. Its core consists of the full texts of the constitutions of the United States of America, the Federal Republic of Germany, the Fifth French Republic and the two constitutions of 1936 and 1977 respectively of the Union of Soviet Socialist Republics.

In the course of a lifetime's teaching comparative government I have become increasingly dismayed and, finally, frustrated by students' ignorance of the text of the constitutions of the countries they are examining, and I am convinced that the principal reason for this is that these texts are, relatively speaking, inaccessible. There are, of course, two great publications which reprint the text of every constitution in the world, namely, A. J. Peaslee (ed.), *The Constitutions of the World* (New York, Justice House, 1977), and the more recent A. P. Blaustein and G. H. Flanz (ed.), *Constitutions of the Countries of the World*. But the first of these runs to seven and the second to fourteen volumes and, invaluable as they are to the researcher, they do not serve the purpose I have in mind. Briefly, I wanted to supply, and I think I have done this, a text which will always be at hand.

The student can sometimes find the text of the constitution required at the end of a textbook on the country concerned and this is particularly so for textbooks about the USA. However, it is not common where other states are concerned. The only alternative then is to write to the embassy of the country in question. Teachers and researchers may undoubtedly go to this length but students simply do not. This volume, then, contains the full texts of the constitutions of the four countries most widely studied in the western world.

These are the essential core of the book, but to assist the student further I have added two features of my own.

The first consists of the two Indexes. I have laid out both of them with the demands of comparison in the forefront of my mind. Also, I have used a 'see-at-a-glance' format for the reference to Sections, Articles and Clauses. The first Index is analytical; that is to say, the components of government are broken down into the major categories commonly used by political scientists, and the contents of the five constitutions

7

are cross-indexed accordingly. The second Index is traditional: topics are listed in alphabetical order – but here again, in such a way that instant cross-comparison between the constitutional provisions of the four countries is possible.

The second feature is designed for overseas students. British students are usually taught the rudiments of the British Constitution and in any case have easy access to excellent texts on British constitutional law. Overseas students have always been handicapped by the fact that our constitution is unwritten. Since Britain is a state whose constitution is always studied throughout the western world, I decided to offer a précis of its main features, and I have incorporated this in my Introduction. In drafting it – using layman's language of course – I allowed myself to be guided by what the written constitutions printed here single out as matters of such high importance as to qualify as 'supreme' or 'fundamental' or 'basic' law of the land.

The order in which the constitutions appear caused me a difficulty. My first intention was to cite them in the order of historical appearance so that the USA would always appear first and France last. However, the Soviet Union then decided to promulgate a new constitution, in 1977. My problem was whether to place this immediately after the earlier, Stalin Constitution (which makes comparison very easy between the two texts), or to be a purist and put it into its strict chronological slot, i.e. last in the list. The first alternative seemed to make things easier to the user of this book, and I have followed it although it marred my intention of presenting the texts in their historical order.

Turning now to the text: in the cases of the Soviet Union and the Federal Republic of Germany I have used the official translations of the constitutions of these countries, and wish to acknowledge the permission their governments have given me to use these in this edition. I regret that the semi-official English-language version of the Constitution of the Fifth French Republic is thoroughly unsatisfactory and accordingly I have presented a translation of my own.

Friends and colleagues have given me indispensable assistance. I would first like to thank Mr John Weston of the Foreign and Commonwealth Office and Visiting Fellow of my college, together with Mr M. B. Nicolson also of the FCO (Soviet Section of the Research Department) for their cooperation in getting me the Russian and English texts of the new 1977 Constitution of the USSR within two days of its promulgation, thus saving weeks of delay. Next I offer thanks to the help and encouragement of Mr John Simmons, Codrington's Librarian, for valuable bibliographical advice, help on questions of indexing and the facilities of the library itself; and in this context I would like to express thanks and appreciation for the patient help of the Assistant Librarians, Mr Brittan and Miss Potter.

Most of the preliminary indexing was carried out while I was Visiting Professor at the European University Institute, San Domenico, Florence; I am grateful for the facilities afforded me there and particularly for the help of my old friend and colleague Professor Hans Daalder, the Chairman of the Institute's Politics Department.

I wrote the Introduction after I returned from the Institute and here I received invaluable help from friends and colleagues. I am particularly grateful to Eric Barendt, Fellow of St Catherine's College; to Tony Honoré, Regius Professor of Civil Law at the University of Oxford and Fellow of All Souls; to Patrick Neill, the Warden of All Souls; to David Yardley, the Barber Professor of Law in the University of Birmingham; and last, for the most honourable and most obvious reason, to my former teacher and also my predecessor in the Chair I occupy, Sir Kenneth Wheare, Fellow of All Souls – the pioneer and also the doyen of all those, everywhere, who study constitutions. Individually and collectively, all these gave me great encouragement, and also picked out a number of errors, some of which were so gross that I blush. I hope the final text is now free of them. If it is, it is due to them. If it is not, it is I who take the full responsibility.

All Souls College, Oxford, March 1979

Introduction

THE FIVE CONSTITUTIONS AND THE BRITISH CONSTITUTIONAL FRAMEWORK

1. ON THE COMPARATIVE STUDY OF CONSTITUTIONS

THE classic purpose of studying constitutions, from Lord Bryce to Sir Kenneth Wheare, has been to define, by comparative examination, what is meant by the term 'constitution' and to explore its role in the political process.[1]* This broad path is not the one I follow here although occasionally I find I must travel some of it. My purpose is the simple and utilitarian one of presenting the constitutions of a limited number of states in order to assist our understanding of the way in which these are governed. Five constitutions appear in this volume, those of four countries, namely the USA, the USSR (1936 and 1977), France (the Fifth Republic) and the Federal Republic of Germany (which I shall henceforth simply refer to as Germany, *tout court*). The selection of these constitutions and no others was not decided for the purpose of throwing light on the nature and role of constitutions as such but because the four countries concerned (along with Britain) are the ones studied most widely in the comparative-government courses in western universities and other institutes of higher learning. By good fortune, however, the selection turns out to be very representative. It contains the oldest written constitution – the American – as well as the youngest, the Brezhnev Constitution of the USSR (1977). It illustrates the full presidential form (the American), the semi-presidential form (that of the Fifth French Republic), the parliamentary-cum-cabinet form (Germany) and the collegial form (the USSR). Again, three of these constitutions are federal; one is unitary. In one, the American, the 'separation of powers' is a supreme constitutive principle, in another (the Soviet) this principle is deliberately rejected. Three of the constitutions envisage political competition for public office, and one (the Soviet) eschews it. In three – the former, 'competitive' class, comprising the USA, France and Germany – the practice of politics does not widely diverge from

*References are printed on page 86 below.

13

the guidelines in the constitutional texts; in the fourth, the USSR, it does, and grossly. So, this selection of constitutions is in fact highly defensible on strictly academic grounds – except for one major omission: Britain. We are in the same fix as the fabled American Congressman in a Congressional inquiry who became so furious at the praises lavished on British government that he bellowed to the committee clerk: 'File me a copy of the British Constitution!'

The fact that no such single document exists is what has determined the scope and the object of this introduction. I propose to make good the deficiency by using the texts of the five constitutions as a background against which I shall outline those features of British law, convention and custom which seem to me salient enough to qualify as the Constitution of the United Kingdom.

2. ON WHETHER CONSTITUTIONS MATTER

CONSTITUTIONS are codes of rules which aspire to regulate the allocation of functions, powers and duties among the various agencies and officers of government, and define the relationships between these and the public.

Nowadays a good many political scientists reject the study of constitutions or accord it a low priority and, surprisingly, a fair number of public lawyers seem to share their view. They argue – and in this they are perfectly right – that these codes are highly incomplete guides to actual practice, i.e. to what is often called the 'working constitution' or the 'governance' of a country. Rules which are included in one constitution may be omitted from others, so that each individual constitution is *pro tanto* incomplete. Furthermore, the extra-constitutional organizations which generate and conduct the political process, like the political parties, the churches, the pressure groups, the bureaucracy and conceivably the armed forces also, find the scantiest mention in some constitutions and are entirely absent in others.

But although constitutions are not textbooks on the governance of a particular country, it does not follow that such textbooks should, or even can – without peril – ignore the constitution of that country. A constitution resembles a sharp pencil of light which brightly illuminates a limited area of a country's political life before fading into a penumbra where the features are obscured – even if that surrounding darkness may conceal what are the most potent and significant elements of the political process.

To this argument about incompleteness, others have added one concerning the ineffectiveness of constitutions. Almost every state in the world today possesses a written constitution. Yet, the vast majority of these are either suspended, or brazenly dishonoured, or – if neither of these – are constantly and continually torn up to make room for new ones. Moreover – so this line of argument goes – Britain, New Zealand and Israel do not possess written constitutions but nevertheless follow what constitutional rules they do have with remarkable consistency and continuity. Hence – it is concluded – constitutions are dispensable: if the powerholders exercise self-restraint, the written constitution is unnecessary and if they do not then no written constitution will check them. The last contention is quite correct: the great majority of states today are either in the throes of revolution or have powerholders who are indifferent to legal norms – or both – and in these cases the constitution is otiose. But this is not a sound reason for rejecting the study of constitutions, rather for pursuing it with sensitivity and common sense: otherwise one might just as well deny the usefulness of door locks. These are clearly unnecessary to honest people who pass the door, and equally are useless against the determined burglar. But they can and do deter the casual stroller who might otherwise come in and help himself.

Nor is this all. For unless we know what the rules are, we cannot know whether anybody is in breach of them, and the breach of a rule can be as informative as its observance. The answers to questions such as 'Who has broken this rule? Why? With what effect?' tell us important things about the quality and temper of political behaviour in the country in question and, indeed, usually point out to us the *active* sources of political power.

But in any case it is perfectly clear from the most superficial comparative survey that not all constitutions are dishonoured all the time and that certain parts of certain constitutions are honoured most of the time. Just as no one constitution is an entirely realistic description of what actually happens, so precious few are one hundred per cent unrealistic fictions, bearing no relationship whatsoever to what goes on. Most constitutions fall between the two extremes, in that they contain fictive or decorative passages as well as omitting many of the powers and processes met with in real life. They are best subdivided into the entirely or largely non-fictive and the partially non-fictive class. The constitutions of the USA, France and Germany fall into the former, that of the USSR into the latter category. In both cases there are strong reasons for close study of the texts: but, corresponding to the difference in kind, so the reasons for studying them are not identical.

The reason for studying the first category, the 'realistic' constitutions, is that these documents affect the political process and our knowledge of it in at least three ways. First, in so far as these constitutions are 'realistic', they channel and to that extent constrain the scope and the direction of the power of government in general and the various organs of government in particular. For instance, the Constitution of the USA states that 'Congress shall make no law . . . abridging the freedom of speech or that of the press' – and accordingly the United States government was forced to allow the *New York Times* to publish articles and comments based on the Pentagon Papers (*New York Times* v. *USA*, 403, US713 (1971); *USA* v. *The Washington Post*, 403, US713 (1971)). Second, such constitutions provide an exact knowledge of what happens, or who does what where and when, on highly important occasions. We know from the United States Constitution for instance that every four years the electors will vote for a President and Vice-President. Third, and as an implication of what has been said so far, constitutions of this 'realistic' class supply their respective publics with firm predictions about what will happen in certain circumstances. Suppose the President of the French Republic is incapacitated, or declared insane, or resigns? Who verifies these situations? Who takes over from the President for the time being? What happens after that? Or, suppose the President has dissolved the National Assembly and dislikes the result of the subsequent elections – can he dissolve the assembly again and hold new elections? To this the answer is plain: 'No, not until one year has elapsed.'

When we turn to the part-fictive constitutions, the first question that presents itself is *why* they depart from the reality of political life. This may occur, in the first place, because extra-constitutional conventions or activities modify the constitutional provisions so greatly. For instance, in the USSR the two Houses of the Supreme Soviet consist of picked candidates, meet only for a few days each year, and sit together, not separately; hence the 1977 provisions relating to disagreements between the two Houses

(Article 115) are otiose and, to the extent that they suggest that such disagreements occur, misleading.

Second, it may be that what the constitution grants in one place it takes back in another. For instance Article 72 of the new Soviet Constitution asserts the right of every Union Republic freely to secede from the Soviet Union. But Article 3, which establishes the principles of 'democratic centralism' as a constitutive principle, stipulates that 'lower bodies' must 'observe the decisions of higher ones', whence it follows that the Union Republics must fulfil the decisions of the Union government.

Third, it may be that the government of a state may be entirely indifferent to provisions of the constitution and blandly act as though these never existed. The freedom of religious worship guaranteed by Article 124 of the Stalin (1936) Constitution of the USSR was notoriously restricted and impaired.

For all that, the study of these part-fictive constitutions may prove very rewarding for a number of reasons. In the first place, and at the very lowest level of political understanding, these constitutions do identify the main legal authorities in a state. That the USSR consists of fifteen Union Republics is a basic piece of information and although it is mentioned in the most rudimentary accounts of USSR government (e.g. in the summary in *Whitaker's Almanack*, which boldly states that 'The USSR is composed of 15 Union Republics'), the sole source for this information is the constitutional text. Second, where a gap is observed between the constitutional stipulations and the practice of politics, this generates the inquiry: 'What really happens, how and through whom?' For instance, take the contradiction between Article 125 of the Stalin (1936) Constitution of the USSR, which stipulates 'freedom of the press', and what was widely known to be the state monopoly of printed material. Inquiry into this discrepancy would have revealed, first, the restrictive interpretation of the Article as concerning publications that conform to 'the interests of the working people' and are written for the purpose of 'strengthening the socialist system' which occurs earlier in this Article, and is held to govern its application; and second, the extra-constitutional provisions of the Civil Code under which possession of any press or duplicating machine requires official sanction, to say nothing of the Glavlit (censorship) or of the monopoly over publication exercised by the (official) Writers' Union, or, finally, the pre-selection and placement of editors throughout the entire Union by the Nomenklatura office of the Communist Party of the Soviet Union. And finally, constitutional provisions, however dishonoured in practice, can and often do become the operative ideal for citizens determined to close the gap between law and reality: in just such a way Vladimir Bukovsky and other dissidents held a demonstration in 1967 for the repeal of Article 70 of the Civil Code of the RSFSR on the grounds that this violated the freedom of expression and of street demonstrations permitted under Article 125 of the constitution.

It would be improper to conclude this recital of the rewards to be gained from the study of the actual texts of constitutions (instead of the study of what scholars have made of these texts – which is what ninety-nine out of one hundred students in Britain do today) without referring to what is arguably the most important single factor that has made for the neglect of constitutional texts. I refer to American 'behaviouralism', which began in the fifties. This movement was both timely and wholesome in so far as it reacted against the formalism and literalism of much earlier political science and stressed that constitutional law might conceal more than it revealed political realities. Where it went wrong – at least in the form expressed in the pages of some of its most enthusiastic champions, whose names I will simply omit to disclose out of vicarious shame – was its crass philistinism in substituting the term 'political system' for 'state' and 'rule' for 'law'. Even more crass was its failure to observe that popular support of the law, and the law's felt and effective constraint upon the public, are not only behavioural facts but *the* behavioural fact: the one that is central and primordial in constituted political organizations. A state, implying an authoritative political organization, is not the same as just any 'political system', an amorphous term for an amorphous thing – as it might be, 'the Atlantic community'. A law, with its connotation of supreme authority, its very special sanctity as the embodiment in some way or other of the community, is not the same as just any rule, a term which could include the by-laws of the East Willesden Tennis Club. It is right to distinguish legitimacy and legalism; but these share a common ground with law; and the observance of laws and the sanctity that attaches to law as such are sociological and behavioural facts of profound and indeed central political importance. For this respect for law, or at any rate an equal respect for law, is not found in all societies, and it is precisely this that explains the difference between the realistic constitutions and the part-fictive ones. For some societies – notably those of the western world – are profoundly law-bound. There the laws are felt *in foro interno* and not just by reason of their sanctions. In societies such as these the provisions of a constitution, in so far as they are self-consistent and unambiguous, do effectually constrain both the authorities and the public. Even the Soviet Constitution is arguably less fictive than usually alleged, while the recent efforts at revising the Civil and Criminal Codes, culminating in the new Brezhnev Constitution itself, are attempts to give the fundamentally illiberal and despotic behaviour of that state's authorities the veneer of 'socialist legality'. In practice such 'socialist legality' is often a sophisticated and perverse legalism, but it vindicates the view I have put about the behavioural foundation of public law. If, as alleged, Soviet legislative legalism is hypocritical it is as well to remember the aphorism that 'hypocrisy is the tribute that vice pays to virtue'.

In brief: in neither the USA, France, Germany nor the Soviet Union does a knowledge of the constitution alone even nearly equate to a knowledge of political reality; but it is a necessary condition of that knowledge. Whence it follows that there is no substitute for the texts themselves.

3. ON THE VARIETY AMONG
CONSTITUTIONS

ALL the classical commentators on constitutions have drawn attention to the wide difference between the contents of one constitution and another but I am not sure that their explanations as to why such differences exist are exhaustive. Sir Kenneth Wheare, for instance, rightly distinguishes between the sort of draftsmen who believe that a constitution ought to contain manifesto-like elements, such as are very apparent in the two constitutions of the USSR printed in this volume, and others who restrict themselves to drawing up a set of justifiable rules of law; between those, again, who have to cater for a federal division of powers and those who do not; between those who believe in incorporating a Bill of Rights and those who, like the framers of the Australian and Canadian constitutions, do not.[1]

These distinctions are valuable and, indeed, indispensable, but it will be seen at once that the motivations which actuate them fall into two quite different categories. That a federal document should contain material which is absent in a unitary one reflects a mechanical consideration, whereas whether the constitution should contain manifesto-like materials or a Bill of Rights reflects value preferences. And as soon as we even begin to ask what has influenced these preferences we stumble on an additional reason for the wide variegation in the content of constitutions. It is a very simple and obvious reason, but that does not make it any the less significant. It is, quite simply, that the constitution-makers in different countries, or for that matter at different historical stages in the history of any one country, have quite different preoccupations. The reason they are drafting a new instrument of government at all can only be that they are reacting to what is perceived to be a new set of circumstances. If this were not so the old constitution would go on serving perfectly well. So, all constitutions contain elements that are autobiographical and correspondingly idiosyncratic. Such features are explicit and very obvious in

21

preambles, and often in transitional provisions. They are less evident in the main text until and unless we adopt the comparative method. Then they stand out. Different historical contexts have generated different preoccupations: different preoccupations have generated different emphases.

The USA

The Constitution of the USA, for instance, which is the oldest in this collection, reflected two urgent preoccupations. The first was to replace the integrative functions (and organs) especially in matters of commerce and defence which had previously been supplied by the British Crown, by something more forceful than the arrangements under the Articles of Confederation. The second was to guarantee to citizens the limitation of government and the common-law freedoms for which the colonists had rebelled. As far as the first is concerned the problem was seen as one of grafting a federal government on to thirteen flourishing and well-established states, each with its own constitution, legal system and political institutions. This is why the Constitution devotes itself almost exclusively to the new, federal machinery and its powers and says almost nothing about the form of the state governments except that this shall be 'republican', and nothing about their revenue-raising powers or local government. Compare this with the German Constitution, which minutely records a long list of 'concurrent powers' and devotes an entire chapter to the division of finance between the federal government and the *Länder*. Or compare it in this respect with the Soviet Constitution, which closely defines the form and structure of the Union Republics as well as their relationship with their local authorities.

The second preoccupation – the limitation of governmental powers, both in range and procedure – determines the design of the US Constitution in so far as it explicitly establishes three separated 'branches' with intricate interlocking devices designed to check and balance the operation of each. None of the other constitutions printed here does this and the Soviet constitutions, based as they are on the principle of the concentration or fusion of powers (and not their separation),[2] make all authority emanate from and depend upon one organ, the Supreme Soviet. Additionally, the US Constitution contains in its main text and its first ten amendments (passed in 1790 and as a pre-condition of ratification) a Bill of specific rights, justiciable in the ordinary courts of law. It may be said that this is hardly a novel feature since most written constitutions nowadays contain similar and even more extensive Bills of Rights. But of the texts printed here the only one that clearly resembles the American is the German Constitution. In the French Constitution the rights are mentioned *en passant*, by a reference, in its Preamble, to the Preamble of the former Constitution and to the famous Declaration of the Rights of Man of 1789. As to the rights of the Soviet citizen, these have never in the past, in either the Stalin or the Brezhnev constitutions, been justiciable in the courts of law. Furthermore, the *kind* of rights laid down in the American Constitution contrasts with those found in the Soviet and French texts and even to some extent with those in the German one in two respects which, again, reflect their historical context. To begin with, the American text does not list any concomitant duties whereas the Soviet document lists a great many. Second, the rights relate only to liberties, equalities and fair-trial procedures – there are no substantive rights as in the Preamble to the French 1946 Constitution, or the German and Soviet texts. Moreover, the 'fair trial' rights are more specific than in any of the other four constitutions: they specify and stress the procedural defences of the accused under the English common law. In short the rights in the American Constitution are 'liberal' or 'Lockean' rights, drawing a ring-fence around the individual against invasion by the public authorities.

Germany

If one turns to the German Constitution of 1949, one is struck by its provisional character; by its emphasis on individual liberties which equals if it does not exceed that of the American Constitution; by the sheer number of the clauses that define the federal – state relationship; by the downgrading of the presidency

and corresponding strengthening of the chancellorship; and by
the very tight restrictions placed upon emergency powers and
defence arrangements. Each of these features reflects a reaction to
the special circumstances in which the Constitution was elaborated and to the régime from which the German people had just
escaped.

In 1949 Germany was still occupied by the Allied forces. Step
by reluctant step the three western powers (the USA, Britain and
France) had united their zones of occupation for economic
purposes, had licensed political parties, inaugurated municipal
elections, recarved the country into provinces (*Länder*) and
established *Land* governments in them. The Cold War was in full
swing. The Soviet Union was bolshevizing the Eastern Zone. In
March 1948, it walked out of the four-power Control Council,
and in April initiated the Berlin blockade. Therefore on 1 July,
the three western Allies, acting independently of the Soviet
Union, asked the heads of the eleven *Land* governments (the
Landtage) to convene a constituent assembly and draft a constitution for Germany that would be both democratic and federal.
But the principal concern of these *Land* presidents, prior to considering any text, was to do nothing that would perpetuate, let
alone legitimate, the *de facto* division of Germany. Also they
found themselves forced to steer a course between the loose
federalism pressed on them by the French and the Americans –
and which some of the German Christian Democrats favoured –
and the tight centralization on which the German Social Democratic party insisted, even to the point of quitting the discussions
at one stage.

The first of these two concerns finds expression in the Preamble,
the Transitional Provisions and Article 146. The Preamble speaks
of 'a new order to political life for a transitional period', qualifies
this by making it 'on behalf of those Germans to whom participation was denied' and states further that 'the entire German
people are called upon to achieve in free self-determination the
unity and freedom of Germany'. The Transitional Provisions
draw our attention to the *Land* boundaries, refugees, expellees, to
occupation costs and the like. And the final Article, number 146,
states: 'This Basic Law shall cease to be in force on the day on

which a constitution adopted by a free decision of the German people comes into force.'

The second concern is reflected in the sheer complication of the Articles concerning the federation. The first draft constitution, which was completed on 23 August 1948 and submitted to the occupation authorities on 2 March 1949, was so federal that the Social Democrats walked out of the Constituent Council. They insisted that German judicial and economic unity had to be guaranteed, that the federal government must have finances adequate to its tasks and that there must be a uniform social policy. The Allies responded on 22 April, markedly softening their support for the *Länder vis-à-vis* the federal government, and it was on this basis that the draft was approved, by 53 votes to 12. Half the minority consisted of Christian Democrat delegates who thought that the document was now too centralist. The long list of powers translated as 'concurrent' (a better translation would be 'alternative') and the elaborate financial provisions in Chapter X, as well as the provision for the *Land* execution of federal laws, all of which make German federalism far removed from the American prototype, stand as a monument to this struggle. But so, too, does Article 79(3): there is no legal way to abandon the 'division of the Federation into *Länder*' nor to terminate their 'participation on principle . . . in legislation'. These provisions are not amendable.

In the rest of the document the most striking idiosyncratic features represent the attempt to revert to the *Rechtsstaat* tradition after the Nazi absolutism, and to correct the faults in the Weimar Constitution which had contributed to its rise. Thus not only does the 'Bill of Rights' move from its place in the middle of the Weimar Constitution to become Chapter I of the new, Bonn Constitution, but there is no corresponding list of duties as there was in the Weimar text. Furthermore, whereas the Weimar Constitution sanctioned judicial review only by implication, here it is positively and explicitly affirmed and the individual himself is given licence to appeal to the courts. Three features go beyond the American Constitution. First, the rights are not amendable. They stand over and above the Constitution itself. Second, they are to be interpreted so as to sustain and maintain what is described as 'the free democratic order'. An individual who uses (the text says 'abuses') his basic rights 'in order to combat the free democratic basic order' forfeits them (Article 18). Third – and unique in all written constitutions – 'All Germans shall have the right to resist any person or persons seeking to abolish [the] constitutional order, should no other remedy be possible' (Article 20(4)).

Just as these provisions clearly derive from the experiences of the Third Reich, so the institutional arrangements derive from awareness of the loopholes in the Weimar Constitution which the Nazis had exploited to seize power. The presidency, abused by von Hindenburg to bring von Papen and then Hitler to office, is shorn of power and authority. Instead, the Chancellor, elected by the Bundestag, is given plenary authority over his Cabinet and can be brought down only if a majority succeeds in agreeing on his successor: thus avoiding the factitious majorities of extreme right and extreme left which had strangled parliamentary government in the Weimar Republic. Again, President Hindenburg and various Chancellors had abused the emergency-powers article (Article 48) of the Weimar Constitution to suspend the constitution and then to install Hitler as Chancellor. In the 1949 Constitution (Articles 80 and 115a) a two thirds majority is needed to authorize an emergency situation, and even when this has come into effect the legislature cannot be dissolved, the Constitutional Court must continue to sit and the basic rights contained in Articles 1–20 (except as specifically modified in the text) remain in force.

Extreme cautiousness was displayed in the Articles relating to defence. The Bonn Republic was disarmed and its disarmament supervised by the Allied powers until the Paris Agreements of 1955. When the Bundeswehr was created at this point and the Constitution duly amended to provide for it, emphasis was placed on bringing the newly instituted armed forces under constitutional civilian control. A final point will emphasize the thrust of our argument concerning the 'autobiographical' element in constitutions: in this constitution the only uses of the word 'war' (*Krieg*) relate to what are translated as 'military service', war graves, war-disabled persons, war damage, war victims – except for Article 26. This states that 'Acts . . . to prepare for aggressive war, shall be unconstitutional'. The expression which is so common in other constitutions, namely a 'state of war', does not appear at all. Instead the text uses the expression: *Verteidigungsfall* – a state of *defence*.

France

It is a far cry from the German text to the French Constitution of 4 October 1958. In the German text, only forty-five Articles out of 146 relate specifically to the executive, the legislature and the relationships between them. Out of the ninety-two Articles in the French Constitution forty-six do so. We come pretty near the whole truth when we say that apart from eleven Articles concerned with the French Community (and drafted in view of the imminent dissolution of the French Empire), and three transitional Articles to bring the new instrument into effect, the Constitution is concerned with one matter alone: to redefine the powers of the executive and the legislature to the immense advantage of the former. In this document there is no detailed and specific Bill of Rights, only a Preamble which speaks of the French people's 'solemn attachment' to the rights laid down in the 1789 Declaration of the Rights of Man and the Citizen, and to the Preamble to the 1946 Constitution. These rights, such as they are, are all but silent on 'fair trial' procedures, and the matter relating to the structure and powers of the judiciary and of local authorities is cursory; evidently the document assumes that these will continue as before. But the President and his surrogate and/or colleague the Prime Minister (according to how one interprets the text) receive massive new powers. The President has an arbitral power under Article 5, emergency power under Article 16, and in association with the Prime Minister has the power to dissolve the legislature. Correspondingly, this legislature is now trammelled. Much of its internal procedure such as the number and the role of its commissions is now defined in the constitution and this in its turn gives the Prime Minister and his Cabinet immense procedural advantages over the Opposition (cf. for example the 'block vote' provision of Article 44). Far from being omnicompetent, the legislature is confined to the passage of 'laws' only and what topics constitute the subject-matter of a 'law' is laid down in detail. Any matter not included in the list is reserved to the executive branch (Articles 34 and 37). This power to make regulations is conceived as the general rule; the passage of legislation as the exception.[3]

Again, it is the different preoccupations of the constitution-makers that explain the signal difference between this constitution and the German one. The 1958 Constitution marks the triumph of an eighty-year-old effort by the French right, unsuccessful save for the puppet years of the Vichy régime (1940–44), to replace by a powerful executive supremacy the legislative prepotence – the so-called *gouvernement d'assemblée* – which, from the resignation of President MacMahon in 1879, had condemned successive Cabinets to instability and impotence during the Third Republic and, subsequently, the Fourth. In the face of the Algerian crisis, French Cabinets found themselves unable to find a broad consensus of public opinion on which to base their actions. The Algiers revolt of 1958 and the subsequent threat of a military *coup* proved the fragility of the Fourth Republic. Over its moribund body strode the Gaullists, who seized the occasion to elevate their candidate to the premiership to draft a constitution to fit his imperious nature and express his elevated conception of the presidency and his contempt for political parties and for parliamentarism.

The USSR

Now, in contrast to all three constitutions so far discussed, the new Brezhnev Constitution of the USSR (1977) was *not* drafted in reaction to the past. On the contrary. As its Preamble is at pains to state, it is drafted in continuity with the previous constitutions of the country. There was no urgent necessity to adopt a new constitution in 1977. Discussion about replacing the 1936 Stalin Constitution by a new text had begun as far back as 1960 but that document continued to serve for the next seventeen years and could equally well have served for the next seventeen. Why, then, a new constitutional text?

On the Variety Among Constitutions

In so far as legal and institutional evolution takes place in the
USSR, and quite a lot has occurred since Stalin died in 1953,
it takes the form of individual statutes and ukazes, and glosses
on the constitutional text which the jurists enunciate in the textbooks on public law. These glosses are not simply juridical. Often
they incorporate the working practice, and the theory behind
this, of political institutions and processes. Instead of amending
the Constitution piecemeal over time to incorporate these
changes, the Soviet authorities have – first in 1936 and now again
in 1977 – swept them all up together into a new coherent document. In so far as a programmatic element is concerned, this is
enlarged and updated: the Preamble to the Brezhnev Constitution
provides an excellent example. The rights and duties are similarly
updated. The institutional changes that took place over the past
forty years are elevated from the status of the statute or ukaze to
that of 'Fundamental Law', by being incorporated into this new
Constitution. Yet the central preoccupation of the Soviet authorities remains identical with what it was sixty years ago. The Soviet
constitutions, all four of them, have existed to maximize the legal
authority of a revolutionary government and the unbounded
exercise thereof. To this end all Soviet constitutions have concentrated the 'three powers' of government, not separated them; and
they have likewise operated on the principle of the 'subordination
of lower bodies to higher ones', i.e. the principle of hierarchy.
Thus whoever controls the Supreme Soviet legislates, executes
and adjudicates without any institutional check or balance on its
authority and controls every inferior echelon of government
throughout the Union. That which controls the Supreme Soviet
is the Communist Party of the Soviet Union. This was stated implicitly in Article 126 of the Stalin Constitution. But in the
Brezhnev Constitution it is stated openly and grandly in Article 6,
along with the two operational principles: the concentration of
powers (Article 108) and 'democratic centralism' (Article 3).
These three elements – party, concentration of powers and democratic centralism – comprise the mainsprings of the Soviet polity.
All the rest of the Constitution is machinery or decoration.

Order and Importance

The *order* in which matters are laid out also tends to differ from one constitution to another. Generally speaking, constitutional draftsmen seem to place items in order of importance. This order may be the *logical* order of importance in that certain items are logically prior to others, e.g. one should stipulate the existence of a legislature before enumerating its powers, and so forth. Troublesomely, however, many items are of equal importance and, logically, might appear in any order. However, it is not always the logical order that determines the sequence of topics: this sequence may also reflect a rank order of moral or symbolic importance. For instance, in the Weimar Constitution, rights and duties appear at Article 109; in the Bonn Constitution they appear as Articles 1 to 20. Similarly, whereas the Stalin Constitution deals with rights and duties in Chapter X (Articles 118 to 133), the Brezhnev Constitution places them at Chapters 6 and 7 (Articles 33 to 69). That this was deliberately intended as a 'promotion' seems evident from the seminal article of P. S. Romashkin in 1960 which first elaborated the changes that ought to be made in a new constitutional text: Romashkin explicitly wanted the rights and duties of citizens to appear immediately after the part on social structure (which is where it now appears) because, he wrote, 'this would emphasize in constitutional terms the high position of the individual in the USSR'.[4]

One must not push this interpretation too far, however. It by no means always follows that 'earlier' signifies 'more important'; thus the French Constitution stipulates the flag, anthem and motto of the Republic immediately after the Preamble, at Article 2, while the Brezhnev Constitution places such matters at the end of the text (Articles 169 to 171), and the American Constitution does not mention them at all.

Consequently one must be cautious in inferring order of 'importance' from the order in which items appear or the different ways in which they are grouped. There are, however, a number of striking differences in the ways in which some of these constitutions are constructed, and these repay attention. The most noteworthy distinction is between the American Constitution and the rest. The point becomes the more salient if the contrast is made simply with the other two federal constitutions here, and not with unitary France. It will then be noticed that in the Soviet and the German constitutions the text opens by reciting the respective powers of the federation and the states and then goes on to lay down the federal organs of government. The American Constitution does not follow this pattern at all. Article I lays down the composition and powers of the (federal) Congress, Article II of the (federal) presidency, and Article III of the (federal) judiciary. All these are federal organs, so, if one wants to know what the powers of the federal government are, information must be collected from each of these three Articles. Article IV recites the mutual obligations of states to states and to the federation. But this is not all. Various Articles but notably Article I also recite a number of things that the states must *not* do; also a number of clauses in the text as well as in the Amendments recite things that neither the states nor the federal government may do. The 10th Amendment (Article [X]) states that 'The powers not delegated to the United States ... nor prohibited ... to the States, are reserved to the States respectively, or to the people'. But this, so it has been held, does not mean what it says. A distinction has been drawn between powers delegated to the US 'exclusively' (e.g. the war power) and others, like taxation or the control of commerce, which are held to be 'not exclusive' (*Houston* v. *Moore*, US 1820). In the latter event the power is held concurrently by the federal government and the states.

Apart from this somewhat radical distinction between the way the American Constitution has been drafted as compared with all the others, little, then, can be authoritatively gleaned from the sequence in which matters appear or the way they are grouped. Some items indeed, like Part IV in the Brezhnev Constitution, or Title 6 (Treaties and International Agreements) in the French Constitution, seem to have been spatchcocked in. In the Bonn Constitution, Chapter X, which deals with finance, ought logically to have come earlier than Chapter IX on the judiciary, and Chapter Xa, on defence, which is a late addition of 1968, owes its awkward position precisely to that fact.

These constitutions consequently offer no clear guidance as to the order in which one ought to set out the salient features of the British Constitution, which is the object of the remainder of this Introduction. These are therefore set out in the order established in the Analytical Index. Briefly, they seek to answer the following questions. First, what the status of the constitution is, and second, how powers are divided among the territorial units of the state. Third, what the respective powers of the executive, the legislative and the judicial branches of government are. Fourth, how and why normal constitutional arrangements are suspended in circumstances of emergency. Fifth, what the rules are that regulate the conduct of the state towards other states. And finally, what the rules are that regulate the respective rights of the state and its citizens.

4. ON THE CONSTITUTION OF BRITAIN

WE have seen that the five constitutions contain, among programmatic matters and the like, a self-consistent set of laws which control the conduct of government. We have also seen that these laws are merely a selection: for instance, while the Soviet Constitution contains clauses relating to political parties, the American Constitution does not even mention these. A second characteristic of these constitutions is that these laws have a special, indeed a superior, status *vis-à-vis* all other laws. Indeed the very words for the document as found in the USSR or Germany or the USA underline this point. The Soviet Constitution is called *Osnovnoi zakon*, i.e. fundamental law; that of Germany is called the *Grundgesetz*, or basic law; that of the USA contains the phrase 'This Constitution . . . shall be the supreme Law of the Land' (Article VI, Clause 2).

Each one of these constitutions contains three elements to secure this higher or special status to the constitution relative to any other laws. They are: (1) an arrangement for signalling repugnancy of the ordinary law to the constitution – in the USA and Germany this is a court of law, in France it is the Constitutional Council, in the USSR it is the Presidium of the Supreme Soviet (Article 121(5)); (2) nullification of the said law in the case of repugnancy to the constitution; and (3), where it is desired to change the constitution rather than the law which is repugnant to it, a more arduous procedure for the abrogation or alteration of a constitutional provision than that established for ordinary laws. So, the Soviet Constitution requires a two-thirds majority of the total number of the Deputies in each of the Supreme Soviet's two Houses (Article 174), and not a simple majority as with any other law. And indeed, in two of these constitutions there exist clauses which cannot be changed at all: Articles 1 and 20 of the Bonn Constitution, and Article 89 (fifth paragraph) of the French Constitution.

33

None of these characteristics applies to the Constitution of Britain. In the first place, there is no authoritative selection of statutes, conventions, common-law rules and the like which together comprise 'the Constitution'; every author is free to make his own selection and to affirm that this is the one, even the only one, that embraces all the most important rules and excludes all the unimportant ones – though nobody has ever been so foolish as to assert this. What is or is not 'the Constitution' is a matter for the scholars' individual judgements. As Dicey put it:[5] 'English writers on the Constitution have good reason to envy Professors who belong to countries such as . . . the United States, endowed with Constitutions of which the terms are to be found in printed documents, known to all citizens and accessible to every man who is able to read . . .' Second (and third) there is no special device to signal the repugnancy of 'ordinary' laws to those we choose to regard as laws forming part of the Constitution. The Constitution is a rag-bag of statutes and judicial interpretations thereof, of conventions, of the Law and Custom of Parliament, of common-law principle and jurisprudence. Inside this miscellany all that we can assert with certainty is that statutes override non-statutory provisions, and that among statutes the later overrides the earlier one. So, if it be a statute relating to political practices that is being broken, this will be cognizable and dealt with by the ordinary courts and not by any specially constituted tribunal. And an infraction will be handled just like an infraction of, let us say, the Lotteries Act. If, on the other hand, the rule that is being broken is not a law but a convention, the only way in which this is signalled is by private persons like the author writing or making speeches on the subject, supported by some and opposed by others. And finally: statutes relating to political practices, i.e. 'constitutional law', are changed or repealed in exactly the same way as any other statute.

Now statutes are made, and made exclusively, by one organ. This is the Queen-in-Parliament. Often in this particular context this is simply called Parliament. The Queen-in-Parliament therefore becomes the starting-point for the exposition of the Constitution of Britain.

The Supremacy (or Sovereignty) of Parliament

For present purposes Parliament is the Queen, the House of Lords and the House of Commons combined. Except as when otherwise laid down by a statute, a statute is made by the Queen assenting to a Bill which has been passed by each of the two Houses. The Parliament Acts of 1911 and 1949 lay down the circumstances and the procedures by which a Bill can become law without the consent of the House of Lords, i.e. by being passed only by the Commons and thereafter receiving the Royal Assent.

The law assumes that Parliament is omnicompetent and paramount. It can, that is to say, make or unmake law on any matter whatsoever, and indeed, it can do so with retrospective effect. No court in the kingdom is competent to question the legal validity of any Act of Parliament, i.e. of a statute. Every lawmaking body in the country is subordinate to it, since even if it does not derive its original authority from Parliament, it exerts this authority only as long as Parliament cares to suffer it.

This attribute is sometimes called the *sovereignty*, sometimes the *supremacy* of Parliament. There are many devious questions arising from this concept[6] and both lawyers and politicians have debated them widely. But on the basic proposition stated in the preceding paragraph there is no doubt at all and if we were codifying the Constitution of Britain we should be safe in leaving it at that, allowing lawyers and other commentators to argue the niceties, just as they do about the clauses of the constitutions in Bonn, Washington and Paris (but not the USSR). In Blackstone's famous lines:[7]

The power and jurisdiction of parliament, says Sir Edward Coke, is so transcendent and absolute, that it cannot be confined, either for causes or persons, within any bounds. And of this high court he adds, it may be truly said '*si antiquitatem spectes, est vetustissima; si dignitatem, est honoratissima; si jurisdictionem, est capacissima.*' It hath sovereign and uncontrolable authority in making, confirming, enlarging, restraining, abrogating, repealing, reviving, and expounding of laws, concerning matters of all possible denominations, ecclesiastical, or temporal, civil, military, maritime, or criminal: this being the place where that absolute despotic power, which must in all governments reside somewhere, is entrusted by the constitution of these kingdoms. All mischiefs and grievances, operations and remedies, that transcend the ordinary course of the laws, are within the reach of this extraordinary tribunal. It can regulate or new model the succession to the crown; as was done in the reign of Henry VIII and William III. It can alter the established religion of the land; as was done in a variety of instances, in the reigns of king Henry VIII and his three children. It can change and create afresh even the constitution of the kingdom and of parliaments themselves; as was done by the act of union, and the several statutes for triennial and septennial elections. It can, in short, do every thing that is not naturally impossible; and therefore some have not scrupled to call it's power, by a figure rather too bold, the omnipotence of parliament.

Territorial Provisions

From what has been said it logically follows that the United Kingdom is, like France, a unitary state, unlike the USA, the USSR and Germany, all of which are federal. In the United Kingdom there exist many territorial bodies with rule-making powers: none of these, whether they be the local councils or the former Parliament of Northern Ireland at Stormont, are co-ordinate with the British Parliament at Westminster. All are subordinate.

But although the United Kingdom is a unitary state whose seat of government is at Westminster and whose unique sovereign organ is the Queen-in-Parliament, this does not signify that the form of administration and the provisions of law are identical throughout the United Kingdom. For special provisions apply in Northern Ireland, in Scotland and, to a lesser extent, in Wales.

It is important, from the very beginning, to be clear about nomenclature. *The United Kingdom* signifies, in law, Great Britain and Northern Ireland, exclusive of the Channel Islands and the Isle of Man. *Great Britain* means England, Wales and Scotland. *Northern Ireland* is part of the Crown's Dominions, and an integral part of the United Kingdom.

The Channel Islands and the Isle of Man are known as *the British Islands*. Their defence and international relations are undertaken by the government of the United Kingdom: but these islands all have their own legislatures, local-government arrangements and fiscal and legal systems as well as their own law courts. For the most part, this legislation only becomes valid on the passage of an Order in Council, made by the Privy Council (to wit, the Crown). In practice, the Order is made by the Home Secretary acting on behalf of the Crown. Appeal lies from the islands' courts to the Judicial Committee of the Privy Council (see below).*

Northern Ireland, which comprises six counties, possessed its own Parliament from 1922 (The Government of Ireland Act, 1920) to 1972. The authority of this Parliament was, however, restricted; first, by the 'excepted matters', which include matters relating to the Crown, to defence and international relations, naturalization and control of aliens, foreign trade, currency, radio communication, patents and copyrights; and also by 'reserved matters', which are those to be dealt with by the United Kingdom Parliament and which include the postal services and such taxation as the United Kingdom Parliament continues to levy, e.g. income tax. In the United Kingdom Parliament, Northern Ireland is represented by twelve Members of Parliament (M.P.s). Northern Ireland thus represented a *devolution* of power by the United Kingdom Parliament, which remained sovereign. The subordinate nature of the Northern Ireland Parliament was clearly demonstrated by the Northern Ireland (Temporary Provisions) Act, 1972, which transferred all legislative and executive powers concerning Northern Ireland to the United Kingdom Parliament and to the Secretary of State for Northern Ireland.

Wales, by contrast, was fully incorporated into the English political and administrative system by the statutes of 1536 and 1542, while the judicial system of the two countries was fully amalgamated in 1830. The country is governed directly by the United Kingdom Parliament, to which the Welsh people return thirty-six M.P.s. The only significant concession to its local peculiarities is the establishment in the House of Commons of a Welsh Grand Committee to consider matters which relate exclu-

---

*The status of these islands is considered as one category, and the detail concerning individual islands is immensely more complicated than the summary suggests.[8]

sively to Wales; and a considerable decentralization of administration via the Welsh Office, most of whose personnel are located in Cardiff, the capital city of Wales.

There remains *Scotland*, containing 9·4 per cent of the population of the United Kingdom. Following the Act of Union, 1707, the formerly distinct Parliaments of Scotland on the one hand and of England and Wales on the other were extinguished and replaced by a new common Parliament of Great Britain; in this Scotland is represented by (at the moment of writing) seventy-one M.P.s. In agreeing to the Act of Union, the Scots also accepted the English Act of Succession (1700) and, in this way, it was ensured that the union of the two Crowns which had come about in 1603 would be preserved. Thus the independent Kingdom of Scotland became incorporated into the new political entity entitled Great Britain and subject to the authority of its Parliament.

However, the Act of Union reserved to Scotland a number of existent rights and privileges. Consequently, to this day it has its own legal system and its own system of law, its own established church (the Church of Scotland is Presbyterian) and its own local-government and educational systems. Since 1892 a Secretary of State for Scotland has sat in the Cabinet; the Secretary heads the Scottish Office, whose staff are almost entirely located in Edinburgh, the capital city of Scotland. To this office very substantial areas of administration have been transferred. In addition the main central-government departments have regional offices for Scotland, most of them with Scottish directors. There exist also numerous boards and commissions catering to various aspects of Scottish life such as, for instance, the Highland Development Board or the Crofters' Commission.

[Following referendums in Wales and Scotland and subsequent parliamentary proceedings in 1979, the provisions of the Wales Act, 1978 (see below), do not apply, and the state of affairs outlined above continues. Likewise, the provisions of the Scotland Act, 1978, also outlined below do not apply and the state of affairs outlined above continues.

The Wales Act, 1978. This sets up an elected Assembly of some eighty members. It works through a system of specialized committees, its executive committee (headed by the chairman) consisting of all the committee chairmen. It has no independent sources of finance, being funded by a block grant from the central government. Nor does it have power to pass primary legislation. Its function is to carry out the provisions (subject to certain exceptions set out in the Act) of a number of United Kingdom statutes relating chiefly to: local government; local matters such as markets, burials, food and drugs administration; education; landlord-and-tenant relationships and housing; health and the social services; pollution, land use and development, town and country planning; and water and land drainage. The Secretary of State for Wales, on behalf of the United Kingdom Cabinet, has certain powers to intervene. He can issue guidelines on economic and industrial matters. Also, if satisfied that action by the Assembly may directly or indirectly affect an issue reserved to the United Kingdom Parliament he can veto it; and he can do likewise for actions on its part which appear to him to conflict with the international and EEC obligations of the United Kingdom. Furthermore, he can on a similar set of considerations revoke subordinate legislation made by the Assembly.

The Scotland Act, 1978. In contrast, the Scottish Assembly, to consist of some 150 members, is empowered to pass primary legislation in its own right as well as to administer and make subordinate instruments under it. The 'devolved' matters include the areas of: health; social welfare; education; housing; local government and finance; land use and development; environmental control; roads; agricultural laws and laws relating to fisheries; water supplies; crime; tourism; and main roads. (Some items in these areas have been specifically excluded, e.g. the universities, social security and the operations of British Rail.)

The Scottish Assembly, like the Welsh, has no independent sources of finance, receiving its funds from a central-government block grant. It is steered by an executive whose head, the First Secretary, is nominated by the Assembly and appointed by the Secretary of State for Scotland (the representative of the British

Cabinet). The First Secretary in turn appoints the other Secretaries, i.e. the members of his executive.

Since the legislative powers of the Assembly are extensive, the probability of demarcation disputes is correspondingly wide. The Secretary of State for Scotland can, in the first place, issue guidelines to the Assembly for the administration of certain Scottish economic agencies like the Scottish Development Agency and the Highland Development Board. Again, if he believes that an Assembly Bill is *ultra vires*, he is empowered to refer this to the Judicial Committee of the Privy Council, and if this finds it to be *ultra vires*, the Secretary of State does not submit it for Royal Assent, i.e. it fails. Additionally, he can intervene when Bills, actions or subordinate legislation seem to him to affect, directly or indirectly, a 'reserved' matter *and* to be 'not in the public interest'. If it be a Bill that is in question, he is empowered to lay it before Parliament with a reasoned statement as to why it should not be submitted for Royal Assent, for a decision by Parliament within twenty-eight days. If it be an action by a member of the Scottish Executive that is objectionable on the above grounds (and likewise, actions in conflict with British international or EEC obligations) the Secretary of State can veto it. And if, on similar grounds, he finds a subordinate instrument objectionable, he has power to revoke it.]

The Sovereign Authority

The supreme legal authority in the United Kingdom, then, is the Queen-in-Parliament. In law, the Queen is the executive branch of government, so that the very expression, Queen-in-Parliament, suggests the fusion in one organ of the two traditional branches of government, namely the executive and the legislature. But the Queen-in-Parliament is also regarded, in law, as the High Court of Parliament; a court of record, whose record, i.e. the Parliament Roll, must be accepted as valid by all other courts in the kingdom which, *ex hypothesi*, are inferior to it.[9] 'Parliament' therefore is the supreme executive, legislative and judicial authority all rolled into one, and this state of affairs, sometimes called the *fusion* of powers, stands in contrast to the arrangements in the USA, which is a system of separated powers.

However, the concept of the 'separation of powers' has been shown to be imprecise, confused and confusing when closely examined. For our present purpose, it is more useful to use the related concept of 'checks and balances', since this can be defined and evaluated by asking whether, how far and in what respect any one of the three branches of government can either impose its will on the others, or alternatively, prevent them from acting. The American Constitution goes furthest in this respect. A statute requires the concurrence of President and Congress, and if challenged in proceedings involving its constitutionality, may be declared invalid by the Supreme Court. The Congress and the President are each independently elected, and for different terms, the latter being unable to dissolve the former, while the former is able to remove the President only by the difficult and highly circumscribed process of impeachment. The Supreme Court is admittedly appointed by the President and the Senate, but once the judges are appointed they can only be removed by impeachment. In practice it is very hard or even impossible for the incumbents of one branch to remove the incumbents of the others or to pressure them by threat of removal; yet each branch can seriously obstruct, even where it is not permitted to veto, the plans of the others. To speak very broadly, these three branches have coordinate status and in certain circumstances each can veto the others. In Britain, however, these three branches do not have coordinate status since the Crown, whose origin is certainly independent of Parliament, must by law exercise most of its functions via Ministers whose authority depends on Parliament. As to the judges, the effect of their judgments can be (and have been) altered retrospectively by Act of Parliament. The authority to veto a parliamentary Bill still vests in the Crown, it is true, but it has not been used since 1707.

Thus authority ultimately rests in the legislature, on whose confidence the Ministers of the Crown depend, and although a Prime Minister may get the Crown to dissolve Parliament and call a general election in the hope of securing such confidence, his Cabinet could not continue to govern if the election returned a

41

hostile majority. A new Prime Minister and Cabinet would have to be installed, such as to command the confidence of the new parliamentary majority.

These remarks are intended to do no more than point to the contrast between, on the one hand, a system of effective checks and balances among the three branches of government, as in the USA, and, on the other, one where this hardly exists, as in Britain.

However, all five constitutions printed in this volume do acknowledge the existence of the 'branches' of government – executive, legislative and judicial – and much (in some constitutions the greater part) of their text is devoted to detailed explanation of the precise relationships between them. This detail is the 'fine print' and it is precisely because it qualifies in so many ways the simplistic generalizations of the kind that have just been made that this collection of the constitutions is desirable and an elaborate cross-index to them necessary, for the student of government. As Figgis once observed: 'Liberty will be found secreted in the interstices of constitutional procedure.' Hence the foregoing remarks should be read as a general orientation in whose light we can proceed to examine the details of the respective powers and duties of the executive, legislative and judicial branches.

The Executive Branch

Nowadays the executive branch of a government is organized into various strata of authority, from high to low. The relationship between these strata may be as important as the relationship of the branch as a whole to the legislature and the judiciary.

A comparison of the five constitutions shows that with the exception of the USSR the branch is headed by a single individual who in some sense personifies the state, and who may be styled generically, therefore, the *head of state*. In every case this individual is styled the *President*. In Britain, however, the head of state is the Queen.

Further comparison reveals also that we may have to distinguish between constitutions where the head of state is the effective chief executive officer – and this is the case in the USA – and those constitutions where the role of the head of state is very largely titular and honorific, the effective headship of the executive branch being vested in an officer who is nominally inferior. Such is the situation in Germany, where this officer is the Chancellor, and so also in Britain where he is styled the Prime Minister. (The French Constitution stands midway between these two types of constitution with its so-called 'bicephalous executive'. Here the President has more than mere titular power, but the Prime Minister enjoys significant authority also.)

In those constitutions which vest effective headship of the executive in a Prime Minister or Chancellor, however, it is necessary to inquire further and ask: in what sense is such an officer a *chief* executive? For in all these constitutions, and this applies equally to Britain, the executive branch is divided laterally as well as vertically between a number of individuals who head up government departments, i.e. between *Ministers*. And questions about three distinctions immediately suggest themselves here. First, does the constitution prescribe that these Ministers shall act collegiately, i.e. as a body? Second, what is the relationship between this body and the chief executive where such an office exists? And third, in what relationships do these Ministers stand towards the chief executive in their individual – as opposed to their collective – capacities? With the exception of the American Constitution, all of them envisage colleges of Ministers variously styled the Council of Ministers (France), the Government (*Regierung*) in Germany, and the Council of Ministers in the USSR. In Britain this body is the Cabinet. Certain duties have to be performed by such bodies collectively. Next: the relationship between these bodies and the chief executive varies from *primus inter pares* in the Soviet Constitution, whose Council of Ministers is headed by a Chairman, to primacy, as in Germany where the Chancellor is responsible for general policy. Finally, as in the French Constitution, it may be laid down that individual Ministers have certain rights and duties in respect to the departments they lead, and that likewise they may stand in a relationship of equality with the chief executive in certain matters and subordination in respect to others. In this connection, it may be noticed, whether the chief executive has the authority to dismiss a Minister is of major importance.

But even this catalogue does not exhaust the constitutional concept of the executive branch. Heads of state, chief executives and ministers, who are usually both temporary and politically partisan, are the directing heads of the very numerous body of subordinate officials known as the 'civil service' or 'the bureaucracy', who are, on the whole, permanent, paid, full-time professional career officers. A constitution like the German one may devote a fair amount of space to the nature, rights and responsibilities of such officers, or say relatively little except in connection with the highest posts, as in the French and American constitutions. Or, indeed, it may say nothing at all, as in the Soviet Constitution.

Using these distinctions as signposts it is possible to outline the main features of the British constitution.

The Head of State: the Queen. Unlike the American Constitution (and to a lesser extent the French) the *convention* of the British Constitution (totally contrary to its strict *law*) distinguishes sharply between the head of state and the chief executive. Again, unlike these two constitutions – and the German as well – the head of state in Britain is neither appointed nor elected for a fixed term but is the holder for life of a hereditary office, namely the Crown. A third distinction is this: whereas all these other constitutions have created an office (the presidency) and invested it with certain powers, in Britain the converse obtains. The office is primeval, and the historical role of the constitution has been to whittle away its powers and transfer them to other offices.

The head of state, then, is a hereditary queen (or king) and the form of government is not a republic but a monarchy. However, it is a *constitutional* monarchy, in the following sense: virtually all the executive powers which legally inhere in the monarch must – by virtue either of statute or of convention – be exercised by her officers. Yet, for all that, the monarch is still invested with a range of powers some of which have been and others of which conceivably might be exercised in circumstances where the existing laws or conventions or precedents give no clear guidance. These reserve powers of the Crown could be exercised only in grave crises and only with the utmost circumspection – such is the political tradition. But in so far as this tradition persists, its rationale has best been expressed by the Frenchman, Benjamin Constant, who wrote, in 1815,

> The royal authority (by which I mean that of a head of state irres-pective of the precise title he may bear) is a neutral authority. The authority of Ministers is an active one ... Constitutional monarchy established the neutral authority in the person of the head of state. The true interest of this head is noway that one or other of the (three) branches of government should impede the other, but that all of them should sustain and understand one another and act in concert.[10]

A trace of this view of the function of the head of state is to be found in Article 5 of the French Constitution, which states that the President of the Republic shall 'watch to see that the Con-stitution is respected ... [and] ensure, by his arbitrament (*arbitrage*), the regular functioning of the public authorities, as well as the continuity of the state'. (However, this notion of an arbiter or umpire was soon interpreted by the imperious President de Gaulle to be that of the '*Guide de la Nation*', and far from being used neutrally was utilized to permit the presidency to dominate the other organs of the government.)

Succession to the Throne. The descent of the Crown is prin-cipally regulated by the Bill of Rights (1689) and the Act of Settlement (1701). The Crown vests in the heirs of the Princess Sophia of Hanover subject to these conditions: (a) an heir who is a Catholic or is married to a Catholic is excluded from the suc-cession, and the Crown then descends to such an heir, being Protestant, as would have inherited in the case of the excluded heir's being dead; (b) any person coming into possession of the Crown must join in communion with the Church of England; (c) such a person must, under the Act of Union, 1707, take oaths to preserve the Church of England and the Presbyterian Church of Scotland.

The King never dies. There is no interregnum. On the death of the reigning monarch the Crown vests immediately in the person entitled to succeed, and such a person, being King or Queen, is entitled to exercise his or her full regalia without further ado.

The powers of the Crown. (1) The Queen (or King) is the supreme executive officer in the state. She is head of the Established Church, the head of the army, navy and air force; she is the source of justice and all courts in the country are her courts. It is in her name that foreign affairs are conducted, treaties made or dissolved, and laws administered. She appoints and dismisses Ministers, dissolves, prorogues or convenes Parliament, creates peers and distributes titles and dignities. She assents to legislation.

(2) But by convention she must – subject to certain exceptions explained below – act only on the advice of her Ministers and through the recognized departments and officers. In particular she must, by *convention*, appoint as her Prime Minister a person who can acquire or has the confidence of the House of Commons; must, too, appoint as Ministers and to the Cabinet (see below) those persons her Prime Minister recommends to her; must also, in the ordinary way, accede to her Prime Minister's request to dissolve Parliament; and must, finally, assent to every Bill that has been passed by the two Houses or, if the Parliament Acts of 1911 and 1949 are being applied, that has been passed by the House of Commons in due form.

(3) In certain exceptional circumstances, however, the Queen may or must act without the advice of Ministers: (a) The most obvious case is the appointment of a Prime Minister in circumstances where no single party with a duly recognized leader commands a majority in the House of Commons.

(b) The Queen has the right to dismiss a Prime Minister. It was last exercised in 1834, to be sure, but it is possible to imagine circumstances in which she might legitimately still use it.

(c) She retains the right to refuse her Prime Minister's request for a dissolution of Parliament. Again, this power has not been used in this century but, as in the previous case, it is possible to dream up scenarios in which she might legitimately refuse a dissolution. The very passion with which the contrary has been argued in cases (b) and (c) above suggests that the view that these prerogative powers of the Crown are in desuetude (a concept which is unknown to English law, in any case) is, to put it at its lowest, contestable.

(d) She retains the right to refuse to create new peers in order to secure a majority in the House of Lords favourable to the government of the day. Circumstances might arise to make such an action on her part useful, or desirable. At the moment, the Parliament Act of 1949 permits the House of Lords to delay non-money bills of the Commons for a period of just over one year. A Prime Minister might desire that a particular measure pass immediately, only to find a majority of peers refusing to pass his Bill. It is in a circumstance of this kind that he might request the Queen to create new peers in sufficient numbers to create a majority for the measure. Perhaps the best judgement one can make in a case like this is that the Crown's power to refuse is extant, but, depending on the precise circumstances which generated the Prime Minister's request for its exercise, it might be very impolitic for the Crown to refuse.

(e) The Crown possesses the right to refuse assent to bills passed by the two Houses of her Parliament. But this power, last exercised in 1707, by convention is never used.

(4) Some powers of the Crown must be exercised by the sovereign in person or, in her absence or indisposition, by Counsellors of State under the Regency Act, 1937. Among such actions are comprised assent to such subordinate legal instruments, known as Orders, as have to be made in her Privy Council (hence their full title, Orders in Council). Other such actions include the appointments or actions that are required by law to be made under the sign manual, for instance, a Royal Pardon. This distinction between actions that must be performed personally and those that need not is clearly not of major constitutional importance. What matters is that, except for the instances noted above, the Queen is only the titular head of the executive. In modern terminology she is the head of state but not the chief executive. In Britain this position is occupied by the Prime Minister and his Cabinet. For purposes of comparative analysis it is desirable to discuss these separately.

The Chief Executive: the Prime Minister. In the United States the head of state is also the chief executive; in the USSR the Constitution vests supreme executive power in a college, not an individual; so only France and Germany have an office even comparable to that in Britain.

Yet in Germany the Chancellor (who is the chief executive) and in France the Prime Minister, are both clearly recognized and their roles defined in the respective constitutional texts. In contrast, even the existence of a British Prime Minister is but marginally recognized by statute, while his powers and duties are not laid down by law at all. A future historian who had nothing but the statute book to consult could certainly infer that there had once been an office of Prime Minister: he would do so by consulting the Chequers Estate Act, 1917, which bequeathed the country house called Chequers as an official residence for somebody called the Prime Minister, and a similar bequest under the Chevening Estate Act, 1959. He would learn of the existence of the office, too, by way of the Ministers of the Crown Act, 1937, and the Ministerial Salaries Consolidation Act, 1965, which lay down how much the Prime Minister is to be paid. The rest is silence. The office, its powers and duties, are determined wholly by convention and usage.

Appointment and dismissal. A Prime Minister is appointed by the Queen, who is governed by the following consideration: can the person she commissions command a majority of votes in the House of Commons? Where one political party has an absolute majority, and where too it possesses a recognized leader or has procedures for acquiring one (and this is true of all three national parties in Britain today), the Queen's choice would be confined to the leader of the majority party of the Commons. Her discretion becomes personal only where no single party commands an absolute majority of the Commons. In a situation like this she would, normally, send for the leader of the largest party in the Commons, but not necessarily: King George V did not do so in 1923, when he sent for the leader of the second largest party, the Labour Party, instead of the Conservatives, who had been returned as the largest party but with a reduced number of seats. Nor did he send for Baldwin in 1935, though the Conservative Party, of which he was the leader, was the largest in the House; instead he sent for Ramsay MacDonald, leader of a small rump of the Labour Party, because he was so placed as to lead a coalition government. But there were exceptional reasons for both decisions, and, in general, the rule is that the Queen would invite the leader of the largest party.

The French Constitution, by way of comparison, vests unfettered discretion in the President; and the likelihood of his appointing to the Prime Ministership a member of a minority party, or even of no party at all, is very high in the Fifth Republic. In contrast to both France and Britain, the German Constitution allows the President no discretion at all, except in one case: normally he must appoint the person elected by the Bundestag, but if this body fails to elect any person by an absolute majority, the President has the choice of either appointing a minority Chancellor or dissolving the Bundestag and calling a new general election.

Dismissal. The German President has no personal discretion to dismiss a Chancellor whatsoever; he must do so only at the request of the Bundestag (Article 67). The French Constitution states that the President shall dismiss the Prime Minister on the latter tendering the resignation of his government, but is silent as to the motives for such a resignation. Clearly this motive might well be the Prime Minister's defeat in the legislature on a confidence vote, but the practice of the French Constitution shows that it is more likely to have been the request, or even the demand, of the President that the Prime Minister shall resign, since each one of the Fifth Republic's three Presidents has in fact dismissed his Prime Minister(s) at will. Such a discretionary power continues to reside in the British Crown but, as already explained, would be exercisable – if at all – only in bizarre, one might almost say revolutionary, circumstances. For everyday purposes the dismissal comes about either because the Prime Minister has already tendered his resignation for personal reasons, like Sir Harold Wilson in 1976, or because he has been defeated in the House of Commons or at a general election.

The German Chancellor, however, is better protected than a British Prime Minister against a 'no confidence' defeat in the legislature. It is not enough for the Bundestag to outvote him: the majority must also agree on the name of the alternative Chancellor. Thus 'unnatural' combinations of right and left can defeat a

Chancellor but not force him to resign. In Britain, the conventions of the Constitution make no such requirement.

Eligibility. The French Constitution makes only one condition respecting the eligibility or otherwise of a candidate for the Prime Ministership, namely, that he must not be a Deputy. The German Constitution merely debars a candidate from following a number of secondary occupations. In Britain there is apparently no restriction at all on the class of person the Crown may invite to become Prime Minister. In law, a Prime Minister could be of half-Persian half-Mongolian descent, of indeterminate nationality, perhaps born in an aircraft as it passed over the International Date Line: but provided that he (or she) could command the majority support of the Commons, and the confidence of the Queen, it would appear that such an exotic individual would be eligible.

In practice, however, the questions of eligibility reduce themselves to two. Must the person selected by the Crown be a member of one of the Houses of Parliament, and if the answer is a 'Yes', must he or she be a Member of the House of Commons? The practical imperatives of commanding the confidence of a majority of the Commons suggest that the answer to both questions is 'Yes'; but this is a matter of usage based on utility and nothing more – or (to be more precise) nothing less.

Powers. The British Prime Minister is always, by convention, the First Lord of the Treasury (the Second Lord is always the Chancellor of the Exchequer), and he draws his salary and collects his pension by virtue of his holding that post. As First Lord he used to be generally responsible for civil-service matters, his approval being required in the appointment of Permanent Heads of the departments. Since the Civil Service Department was set up in 1968, he continues to retain this responsibility, but in the capacity of the Minister in charge of this department.

For the rest, his powers depend wholly on convention and usage. He recommends to the Queen, who must give her assent, the persons he wishes her to appoint as principal Ministers, and from those he selects his Cabinet (q.v. below). He appoints the junior Ministers without further reference to the Crown. He can require a Minister to resign at any time and for any reason and if that Minister chooses not to do so, he can advise the Queen to dismiss him. He enjoys great patronage – to the Church hierarchy, to the upper ranks of the civil service, to government corporations and commissions of inquiry, as well as to titles and honours. It is he who presides over the Cabinet, draws up its agenda, establishes its committees and appoints their membership, presiding personally over the most important of them, notably over the Defence and Overseas Committee. And he is the channel of communication between the Cabinet and the Queen.

Finally, if the Prime Minister resigns then the entire government must resign with him.

So influential is the Prime Minister today that the late Richard Crossman, in a characteristic hyperbole, described the British polity as 'Prime Ministerial Government'. This it certainly is not, but neither is the Prime Minister only a 'first among equals'. He is unquestionably the keystone of the Cabinet arch and the leader of the entire governmental team. His conventional powers are far greater than those of his French counterpart who, under the usage of the Fifth Republic, enjoys no more than that residue of powers which the President chooses to leave to him and is, at the lowest, no more than the President's parliamentary manager, dispensable as soon as he loses either the confidence of the legislature or that of the President: indeed his situation is not dissimilar from that of Lord North under George III. At the same time the powers of the British Prime Minister are more circumscribed than those of the German Chancellor. For the German Constitution specifically lays down not only that the Chancellor shall appoint and dismiss his governmental colleagues (the *Regierung*) but that he and only he 'shall determine, and be responsible for, the general policy guidelines' (Article 65).

The Cabinet and the Government. Ministers collectively are sometimes known as 'the Government', sometimes as 'the Ministry' and sometimes (though this is rather old-fashioned nowadays) as 'the Administration'. However, from all of these Ministers, the Prime Minister makes a personal choice of a small number, ranging in recent years from seventeen to twenty-three, to comprise the *Cabinet*.

Like the office of Prime Minister the composition, power and status of this body is almost unrecognized in statute law. Only the Ministerial Salaries Act, 1965, which distinguishes between the salaries of Cabinet and non-Cabinet Ministers, and the Parliamentary Commissioner Act, 1967, which states that Cabinet records must not be divulged to the Parliamentary Commissioner, even mention the Cabinet.

Ministers. The law does not say that Ministers must be members of one of the Houses of Parliament but does specify that no more than ninety-five Ministers may sit and vote in the Commons at any one time (House of Commons Disqualification Act, 1975). Furthermore under the Ministerial Salaries Act, 1972, a limit is set to the number of Ministers who may receive a salary. These salaries can be altered by executive action – not requiring parliamentary approval – by an Order in Council.

In practice, however, and in complete contrast to the French constitutional provisions, which make ministerial office incompatible with membership of either House of the French legislature, and similarly, to the American Constitution's provisions which go further and do not permit any executive officers except in limited cases the Vice-President to conduct any government business in the legislature, the British Cabinet in the normal way is composed exclusively of peers and M.P.s. It is certainly possible for a Minister to head a department although he is not an M.P., but this situation is remedied either by making a peer of him or by trying to arrange his election as M.P. for some conveniently vacated constituency.

The Cabinet. The Cabinet, as a collective body, is responsible for formulating the policy to be placed before Parliament, and is also the supreme controlling and directing body of the entire executive branch. Its decisions bind all Ministers and their officers in the conduct of their departmental business.

The Cabinet meets in plenary session once or twice a week, at the P.M.'s summons. Most of its work is prepared in advance in its committees and subcommittees, whose number at any one time may well total one hundred. These committees are serviced, like the Cabinet itself, by the Cabinet secretariat, whose head also serves the Prime Minister as his Permanent Secretary and adviser. Voting in Cabinet is unusual: in contentious matters it is more common for the Prime Minister to 'collect the voices'.

The executive powers of the Cabinet derive from the legal status of its members: these are Ministers of the Crown and as such have defined responsibilities to discharge, and what these are can be ascertained from the law relating to the Royal Prerogative and to statute. Its supreme policy-making power, however, is a political matter and it can only exercise it to the extent that the House of Commons permits. For it is in Parliament that, by law, the power to legislate and to tax resides. The Cabinet is generally able to exercise its power freely because in the usual way it consists of the leaders of the majority party in the House of Commons and the support it is likely to receive is the more predictable and stable because of the convention that the Cabinet shall be *collectively* responsible to the Commons for matters of policy. In consequence it presents a united view, so that its supporters are confronted with the brutal alternatives of either supporting it or turning it out. This convention, or rather, this usage, can be dated to the years 1827 to 1834. The usage was assisted by the increasing ideological solidarity of political parties after 1874 and this, in its turn, was reinforced by the usage. One consequence is that, to quote Lord Salisbury, speaking in 1878, 'for all that passes in a Cabinet, each Member of it who does not resign is absolutely and irretrievably responsible . . .'; and its corollary is that if such a Minister is not willing to accept this responsibility, then he must resign.

The consequences of a situation in which there were no usage of collective Cabinet responsibility for policy would be that the Cabinet could be supported for one measure and defeated on another, so that legislative initiative and not executive leadership would prevail. For over a century the latter has prevailed and the style of British government is therefore not 'Parliamentary government' but 'Cabinet government'.

There has grown up a belief that 'the collective responsibility of the Cabinet' is a 'convention of the Constitution', meaning that it is a normative rule which it is improper ever to break. This is not true. 'Collective responsibility' has been, simply, the working practice of Cabinets since at least 1832 and, until 1975, had been breached only once, in the famous – or notorious – 'agreement to differ' of 1931. Even that breach was condoned on the grounds that the then government was a coalition. But the principle was waived by Sir Harold Wilson in 1975, again, as a 'unique' situation (the European Economic Community Referendum issue), although his party had a majority in the House of Commons. It was breached, again, over the European Elections Bill in June 1977. It was on this occasion that it was argued that 'collective responsibility' was a binding rule and that the then Prime Minister, Mr Callaghan, ought to have followed it although this would have meant his defeat in the Commons and a general election. But this is not my view of this matter. 'The collective responsibility of the Cabinet for a programme decided at the polls depends on its solid party support.'[11] But in the 1975 case and in 1977 alike, the majority party was split in two, and so was the Cabinet. If a Prime Minister is prepared to allow his Cabinet and his party to accept the shame of indecisiveness and the ignominy of disarray in order to cling to office, I know of no historically binding precedent that would compel him to insist on solidarity at the certain risk of resignation and a devastating defeat at the polls; while there exists a fair number of (admittedly somewhat weak) precedents to support the line that Mr Callaghan took.[12] In short the collective responsibility of the Cabinet for policy has been central to the working of the constitution, but it is a central *usage*, not a convention.

In this connection it is interesting to see if the constitutions of Germany or France offer more specific guidelines. In both, it is clear that the legislature can dismiss the chief executive and his team of Ministers. The French Constitution (Article 20, third paragraph) states that the government is 'responsible to Parliament'. This implies that the government is a collective unity that stands or falls together. The German Constitution merely makes reference to the Chancellor being responsible to the Bundestag (Article 67), but as under Article 65 he is the sole author of general policy we have to infer that if he resigns his entire team or *Regierung* must resign with him.

It remains only to distinguish the British, French and German models from the American on the one hand and the Soviet on the other. Generically the three former polities may be styled 'parliamentary' or, in the British case, specifically, the 'Cabinet' type of government. Their essential feature is that a corporate executive team is responsible to and dismissable by the elected legislature. This type contrasts with the American, which is the 'presidential' type: here the Congress can frustrate the President's policies but cannot remove him short of treason, bribery 'or other high Crimes and Misdemeanors' (Article II, Section 4) and even then only by the clumsy and arduous process of judicial impeachment. The parliamentary or Cabinet styles of government contrast equally with the Soviet model. Here, many important executive powers which in the former type of government vest in the executive branch are vested in the Presidium of the Supreme Soviet, i.e. in what is, in effect, a grand Standing Committee of the legislature. The remainder of the executive powers vest in a Council of Ministers, which is conceived as collectively responsible to the Presidium in the first instance and to the plenum of the Supreme Soviet in the last resort.

The discussion now points to a further and formidable aspect of the responsibility of the collective Cabinet to the legislature: whether or not it has the power to dissolve this, and to invoke a new general election.

No such power exists in the executive branch in the American or USSR constitutions. But both the French and the German constitutions do make provision for the Prime Minister or the Chancellor, respectively, to require the President, i.e. the head of state, to dissolve the legislature and call new elections. Indeed, there is a unique circumstance in which the German President can himself dissolve the Bundestag and call new elections (Article 63(4)). In Britain it is the Prime Minister himself – not the Cabinet collectively – who has the right (by convention) to require the Queen to dissolve Parliament and issue the writs for a new general election.

The dissolution power serves the same purpose in all these constitutions: it provides the means whereby a deadlock deriving from a legislative majority hostile to the executive, i.e. the Cabinet, can be broken. It is broken by a fresh appeal to the electorate. Such an appeal brings about the only circumstances in which the parliamentary or Cabinet style of government can work: namely, where the legislative majority and the executive branches are of the same mind.

The dissolution power of the chief executives in these parliamentary-style governments has a latent function, as well as the manifest one stated above. It offers the formally dependent executive a weapon to warn or to threaten a hostile legislature.

Ministers Individually. In their private capacities Ministers are responsible to the ordinary courts of law for their personal acts, but the constitutional texts do not always state this specifically. Here we are concerned with the *political* responsibility of Ministers. Whereas the French Constitution does not clearly distinguish the collective responsibilities of the Ministers from their individual political responsibilities, the German text does when it states (Article 65) that, within the guidelines laid down by the Chancellor, 'each . . . Minister shall conduct the affairs of his department autonomously and on his own responsibility'. In practice the French tradition approximates to this, and both cases resemble British practice, supposedly governed by a convention, namely, the convention of 'the individual responsibility of Ministers for their departments'. Supposedly, each Minister is vicariously accountable to Parliament for all acts of omission or commission by the officials in his department, and a distinction is drawn between a Minister's faithful (even if politically objectionable) execution of the policy of the Cabinet, and his defective management of the administrative detail under his control. This is the purported distinction between 'policy' and 'administration'. For the first, the entire Cabinet must assume responsibility, as we have seen above. For the supposedly purely departmental aspect, the Minister alone is held to be accountable and must speak to and answer challenges in the Commons. The supposed convention stipulates that he must assume responsibility for all his officials' acts and omissions and, if censured by the Commons on this account, is bound to resign. In fact the convention, such as it is, falls far short of this. For one thing it has been regarded as a sufficient defence for the Minister to demonstrate that the acts complained of either took place in such a manner that he was physically or materially incapable of knowing them, or alternatively were carried out against his explicit instructions. For another, the line between what is collective 'policy' and departmental 'administration' has proved a fluid one. Again, even on occasions when the action is clearly of the latter departmental type, Prime Minister and Cabinet have most often extended the span of 'collective responsibility' to shelter the delinquent colleague from individual censure. In the end the 'convention' turns out to be the truism that if a Minister is not supported by his Cabinet colleagues and/or members of his parliamentary party in the course of debate censuring his conduct, it is highly possible that he will face a majority of M.P.s demanding his resignation, and in those circumstances would have little option but to comply.[13]

Government Departments. In all modern states the executive powers are parcelled out into bundles of duties which are thereupon assigned severally to individual Ministers. The office which attends to these duties and of which he is the head is, generically, a 'department'. Of the five constitutions none specifies the names or even the number of such departments except the old (Stalin) Constitution of the USSR (Articles 70, 77 and 78, and also Article 134). Consequently this constitution had to be formally amended every time these departmental arrangements altered – a frequent occurrence.

Clearly then, none of the four states concerned nowadays regards the number and names of the government departments as matters of 'constitutional importance', and therefore we may similarly disregard them here.

The Civil Service. In each of the four countries concerned, as in Britain, the day-to-day work of governing is carried out by corps of permanent, professional officials, in Britain the civil service. In each country, again, these officials are immediately responsible to their respective Ministers, who are officially the policy-makers and as such are responsible for the officials' conduct, either to the elected chief executive (as in the USA) or to the legislature (as

elsewhere, including Britain). In short in none of these countries
is the civil service directly responsible to the electorate. This point
is not stated explicitly in any of the five constitutional texts, however, and, indeed, their references to the civil service are scattered
and perfunctory.

For the purpose of the present exercise, i.e. for an explication
of the British Constitution against the background of our five
constitutional texts, all that seems necessary is to outline the
barest essentials.

In Britain there exists a Civil Service Department, headed by
the Prime Minister, which is responsible for the conduct, the remuneration and working of the Home Civil Service; while the
Secretary of State for Foreign and Commonwealth Affairs plays
the same role as the Prime Minister as far as the Foreign Service
is concerned. With a few exceptions, nobody may be appointed to
a permanent post until his qualifications have been approved by
the Civil Service Commission which, in respect to the selection of
personnel, is independent of Ministers. It is the commission that
formulates the regulations concerning recruitment, which provide
for open competition. There are an increasing number of regret-
table exceptions, however, especially in quasi-autonomous
governmental and non-governmental organizations which are
outside the civil service proper. The civil servant holds office 'at
the pleasure of the Crown'; this means that he cannot be dismissed without cause being assigned. In practice tenure is
permanent, except for personal misconduct, ill health and – but
this is in very exceptional cases – gross inefficiency. Under recent
legislation, moreover, a dismissed civil servant may sue for
wrongful dismissal and if successful can recover damages.

Furthermore the civil servant is politically neutral. No civil
servant may sit, as such, in the House of Commons. Apart from
the grades that are excepted by law (arrangements which are
under review at the time of writing), none may even stand as a
parliamentary candidate without first resigning from the civil
service. Certainly, this is true of all members of the highest grade.
For the intermediate grades, special arrangements apply, and it is
only members of the industrial, minor and manipulative grades of
the service who are free to stand as candidates. Finally, all, except

the latter grades, are required to act discreetly in discussing any matters relating to public policy.

The civil servant answers to the House of Commons only via his Minister. Civil servants can be and often are summoned to witness before the major scrutiny committees of the Commons, notably the Public Accounts Committee, the Expenditure Committee, and the various Select Committees that have been established to scrutinize major areas of policy (and which alter from time to time). However, what they are to witness to is held to be 'administration': when matters of 'policy' come up, they explain that these are for Ministers to speak to. With the exception of this particular kind of communication, it remains true that the sole constitutional channel between the Commons and the civil service is the Minister of the appropriate department.

The Legislative Branch

In each of the five constitutional texts the legislature is described as consisting of two assemblies: an upper and a lower House or Chamber. Nowhere does a text give a rationale for this arrangement and, indeed, this varies from one country to another. In federal states – the USA, the USSR and Germany – the obvious rationale is that the component units of the federation shall be represented as such, in contradistinction to the population at large.

No such justification can be urged for the upper Chambers of France or of Britain. It is arguable that the widespread adoption of an upper House throughout most of Europe and, then, through the wider world springs from the historical accident that Britain had a bicameral legislature in 1815, when her institutions were regarded as a model for western Europe. However, the arrangement was subsequently justified on supposedly rational grounds: a century and a half ago, one of the supposed advantages of having an upper House was to check the pretensions of the democracy that was expressing itself in the popularly elected lower House. It is unfashionable nowadays to see this as anything but a drawback, so that quite other advantages of a second Chamber are the ones that are stressed today: notably its value as a body for revising the texts produced in the lower House, together with the assumed advantages of more, and slower, deliberations.

Apart from this similarity, the British Parliament differs notably from the legislatures of the USA and of France in two different ways. It differs from the former in that the executive authority resides in and is dependent upon the confidence of this legislature, instead of being independently elected, all but irremovable and constitutionally endowed with a great number of powers in its own right. It differs from the French Parliament in a different way: the British Parliament is omnicompetent, whereas the powers of its French equivalent are restricted to what the constitution stipulates, with the unspecified remainder of governmental authority inhering as of right in an autonomous executive power, that is to say, in the presidency, the prime ministership and the Ministers themselves. As Cadart comments, 'The domain of Legislation is exceptional . . . The domain of Regulations thus constitutes, juridically, the common rule . . .'[14]

The House of Lords: Composition and Procedure. The House of Lords is perpetual and it is non-elective. Its members, who are styled 'Lords of Parliament', sit there by virtue of one of three possible characteristics. First, they may be hereditary peers. Such peers are created by the Crown under its prerogative powers (though, effectively, via the nomination of the Prime Minister). A hereditary peer is by law entitled to receive a writ of summons to sit and vote in the House of Lords: but he must be twenty-one years of age and is disqualified if he is an alien (The Act of Settlement, 1701) or a bankrupt, or has been convicted of treason or felony or sentenced to a term of imprisonment, such disqualification lasting until he has discharged his term of punishment or has been pardoned, or (where relevant) has discharged his bankruptcy. Any male who succeeds to the peerage and can prove his right to the Lord Chancellor is entitled to a writ of summons. Thus, the vast bulk of the membership of the House still sits by virtue of hereditary descent. No new hereditary peers have been created since 1965. In the year 1976 there were 822 hereditary peers of whom 105 were, for various reasons, without a writ of summons and, accordingly, not members of the House.

The second category of membership consists of the life peers, created under the Life Peerages Act, 1958. These are created by the Crown on the recommendation of the Prime Minister and in 1976 numbered 254. Third, and finally, a number of persons are peers *ex officio*: the two archbishops and the twenty-four diocesan bishops of the Church of England, and the Lords of Appeal (active and retired) who are known as the Law Lords. Altogether, in 1976, the total membership of the House was some 1,118, although the average attendance was only 150.

The presiding officer is the Lord Chancellor. The House is the sole judge of its own procedure, as laid down in its standing orders or as sanctioned by custom. Unless it otherwise resolves, its meetings are public. Its sessions tend to coincide with those of the Commons but the Lords can adjourn at discretion and resume their sittings at a different date from the Commons. Proceedings on pending legislation lapse immediately the Queen prorogues Parliament. The Lords then cease to sit and reconvene on receipt of a writ of summons to the next Parliament at the date therein stated.

Like the Commons, the Lords is the guardian of its own privileges and the sole judge of anything that appears to them to infringe them. Again, like the Commons, it has the right to punish breaches of such privileges. Some are similar to those of the Commons, notably freedom from arrest except on a criminal charge or bankruptcy; exemption from jury service; and the famous freedoms of 'speech, debate and proceedings in Parliament'.

The House of Commons. The House of Commons is elected for a period not exceeding five calendar years (Parliament Act, 1911). The Bill of Rights (1689) stipulates that Parliaments ought to be held 'frequently'. By convention it must meet at least once a year because certain legislation, like the Finance Acts, requires the assent of the House and is introduced on an annual basis.

For electoral purposes the country is divided into a number of single-member constituencies (currently 635). In each of these the candidate who secures the highest number of votes is elected. The electorate (see below) comprises all citizens of the United

Kingdom and (anomalously) of the Irish Republic above the age of eighteen who have satisfied the residence requirements in a constituency – with the exception of peers and the mentally ill. The distribution of seats by constituencies is kept under review by four boundary commissions for England, Wales, Scotland and Northern Ireland respectively. These commissions are politically neutral. They have the right and in certain circumstances the duty to report to the Home Secretary. Their report is laid before Parliament. If the commission has recommended a boundary change the Home Secretary lays a draft Order before Parliament to give effect – with or without modifications – to the recommendations.

To be validly elected, candidates must be at least twenty-one years old. Certain categories of citizens are precluded from sitting in the House. They are: clergymen of the Church of England, the Church of Scotland and the Roman Catholic Church; civil servants and members of the regular armed forces; and most judicial officers. Although Irish peers may sit, English and Scottish peers are debarred unless they have disclaimed their titles under the Peerage Act, 1963.

M.P.s receive an annual stipend plus a tax-free secretarial allowance. Although the maximum legal term of a Parliament is, under the Parliament Act, 1911, five years, Parliament may – and in this case the assent of both Houses is necessary – prolong its life by passing an appropriate Act. Correspondingly, the Prime Minister may advise the Queen to dissolve the Parliament before its five-year term is complete: in fact, Prime Ministers have always done this.

The chief officer of the House is its Speaker. He is elected by the M.P.s at the beginning of each session but by custom is re-elected annually until retirement or death. The first of his two principal functions is to regulate debate and enforce the rules of the House. The second is to guard the privileges of the House *vis-à-vis* all external bodies – Crown, courts or the public. In presiding over debates and interpreting the standing orders the Speaker is bound to the strictest impartiality. He votes only when members' votes are tied, and in such cases must by convention support the *status quo*, not the innovation that has been proposed.

The House is complete master of its own procedure. Like the Lords, it too lays claim to privileges. The chief of these are freedom from arrest save for certain criminal and bankruptcy charges, the exemption from jury service, and above all the freedom of speech, debate and proceedings in the House. This body of privileges is subsumed in the Law and Custom of Parliament, which is a body of true law independent of the common law, so that on certain occasions collisions have occurred between the House and the courts of law. For contempt of the House or a breach of its privileges, the House can punish and commit. Its own members as well as the public are subject to these enforcement powers. The House can also expel one or more of its own members, as it is the sole judge of its own composition.

Immunities for the elected members of legislatures, somewhat similar to the ones just related, are to be found in all five of the constitutions printed here. Such immunities are essential to the authority of an elected assembly. But two are sufficiently idiosyncratic to Britain to warrant special attention. If ever the British Constitution were to be codified in a single document, then certainly these two immunities would have to be specified.

They are on the one hand the protection of the dignity and freedom of the Commons as a corporate body, and on the other the freedom and dignity of the individual M.P. Disrespects to the House as such are styled 'contempts'; for instance, libels on the House, the Speaker or the Select Committees. Statements that M.P.s are, generally speaking, drunkards or parasites, would come under this heading of 'contempts'. At the same time, threats and intimidation of individual M.P.s are 'breaches of privilege', and come under the general heading of 'molestation'. A former Clerk to the House (Lord Campion) advising the Select Committee on Privileges in 1947 stated the matter thus: [15] 'Any punitive or discriminatory action by an outside body or persons against a Member for speeches or votes in Parliament, or the threat of such action, is a breach of the privilege of freedom of speech . . .' This threat has become very salient in the last half-century, since large numbers of M.P.s have begun to receive financial assistance, and/or have entered into certain contractual arrangements with outside bodies, notably with trade unions.

When these or other outside bodies are disappointed at the way such M.P.s speak or vote in the House there arises the possibility that they might withdraw or threaten to withdraw the assistance they are affording. There has been a number of such threats: in each case the warning that the House might consider this a breach of its privileges has been enough to cause the threat to be withdrawn. Now, in France and Germany this kind of threat is not countered by the law and custom of the legislatures, as it is in England, but by specific clauses in the Constitution. The French text says (Article 27, first paragraph): '*Tout mandat impératif est nul.*' The German Constitution states (Article 38(1)) that the Deputies to the Bundestag 'shall be representatives of the whole people, not bound by orders and instructions, and shall be subject only to their conscience'.

Lords versus Commons. In the USA and the USSR neither of the two Houses of the legislature can overrule the other, which means that the upper House has a full veto over the bills passed in the lower House. In Germany the same is true for a range of items duly specified in the text as requiring the consent of the upper House, which in that country is the Bundesrat, the Council of States, i.e. the House specifically charged with the protection of the interests of the *Länder* into which this federal republic is divided. On all other matters, however, the lower House can override the upper House provided it does so by a majority vote which is not less than that by which the upper House made its decision.

The French Constitution, however, contains a rare if not unique provision relating to this matter (Article 45). When the Senate (i.e. the upper House) rejects the text of the National Assembly (the lower House), the outcome depends on the government of the day, i.e. on the executive. It may decide to do nothing, which is tantamount to upholding the veto of the upper House, since the Constitution requires that both Houses pass an identical text. Alternatively, however, it can override the veto of the Senate by asking 'the National Assembly to make a final decision'.

It should be noted in conclusion that in every one of these constitutions a Bill may originate in either of the two Houses, with the exception of money Bills which – with the solitary exception of the USSR – must originate in the lower House.

The relationship between the two Houses in Britain is regulated by the Parliament Acts, 1911 and 1949. Money Bills, duly certified as such by the Speaker of the House of Commons, can become law without the assent of the Lords provided they are sent to this House for consideration at least one month before the end of the parliamentary session. With certain important exceptions, notably with the exception of a Bill to prolong the life of a Parliament beyond the statutory five years, all other public Bills (see below) do not require the assent of the Lords provided that (1) the Bill has been passed by the Commons in two successive sessions, whether of the same Parliament or not; and (2) one year has elapsed between the date of second reading of the Bill in the first of these two sessions and the final passing of the Bill in the second of these two sessions.

Among the exceptions to this procedure, apart from the prolongation case mentioned above, are Bills to confirm provisional orders, finance Bills not certified as money Bills by the Speaker, private Bills (see below) and, finally, such Bills as are initiated in the House of Lords itself.

Legislation. The sole constitution among the five texts here that devotes considerable attention to parliamentary procedure is the French. The main object of the constitution of the Fifth Republic was, precisely, to exalt the executive and to constrain the legislature. So, it includes much material prescribing procedure, and makes any alteration of this subject to the decision of the Constitutional Council. Because this is exceptional – other constitutions devote little attention to the matter – what follows will be the most summary outline of the British Parliament's legislative procedure.

Private Bills. Private Bills confer special powers or advantages on any persons or body of persons (e.g. corporations, local authorities), as distinguished from public Bills, which apply to the community or categories of the community, generally. The procedure for deliberating on private Bills is, apart from the requirement that such Bills must be read three times in each House, substantially different from that on public Bills; it resembles a judicial hearing more than an act of legislation.

Public Bills. When these are introduced (in either House) by individual members, as they may be, they are known as Private Members' Bills as distinct from Government Bills, although the procedure is identical for both categories. Since the Cabinet controls the parliamentary timetable the passage of Private Members' Bills is highly dependent on its benevolence.

The first reading is a formality. Debate on the text begins with the second reading. In the Commons, after receiving its second reading, the Bill goes to a committee: either a standing committee, which is a microcosm of the entire House, or to the entire House itself, operating under more relaxed rules and known as a Committee of the Whole House. The text as amended is then brought back to the House for a report stage, and then proceeds to the third-reading debate. After this it goes to the Lords, where the procedure is similar, though not identical.

Subordinate Legislation. Ministers may make subordinate legislation either by virtue of the Crown's prerogative vested in them or by virtue of statutory authority. This is an untidy field, but most of it is regulated by the Statutory Instruments Act, 1946. This Act stipulates that a Statutory Instrument is an instrument made under this Act or by a subsequent Act which is exercisable either by Order in Council or by another Statutory Instrument. The Act does not require that all Statutory Instruments shall be laid before Parliament. Whether this is required or not is decided by the parent Act in question. Where a Statutory Instrument is to be laid it is usually provided that it is laid before both Houses. In financial matters, however, it is laid only before the Commons. Nor is there uniformity in the other requirements. Some Statutory Instruments take immediate effect when laid, subject to subsequent annulment by a resolution of both Houses. This is the commonest form. A rarer form is for the instrument or its draft to take no effect unless it is expressly approved by resolutions of both Houses.

Financial Legislation. The basic principles of financial legislation, as opposed to the details of the procedure itself, are these. First, only the Crown, i.e. Ministers, may propose additional expenditure or a new charge on the public revenue. Characteristically, this is not stipulated in a statute but by a standing order, to wit S.O. 89, which is the very oldest, dating to 1713. Next, proposals to raise or spend money must originate in the Commons, not the Lords. Third, by the Bill of Rights, 1689, taxation requires the consent of Parliament. Similarly, money can only be expended under the authority of an Act of Parliament. Most expenditure is authorized by annual Acts, or grants incorporated annually into an Act, and this device ensures that Parliament must meet at least once every year. Some expenditure, however, is authorized under permanent Acts; the purpose here is to insulate the recipients from parliamentary control. Not surprisingly, the Queen's civil list (annual allowance) and the salaries of judges of the higher courts, of the Speaker and of the Comptroller and Auditor-General are all paid out in this way. Fourth, the House not only votes the totals of expenditure requested by Ministers in the 'Estimates', but specifies how the money is to be spent. The 'Estimate' is broken down into 'Votes' and these into heads and subheads, and it is in this form that the money is granted in an Appropriation Act, passed annually. The Comptroller and Auditor-General, by means of his post-audit, together with the subsequent help of the Treasury and the Public Accounts Committee of the Commons, ensures that the various departments spend the money exactly as appropriated and in no other wise, unless by express permission of either the Treasury or the House itself. Fifth, the arrangements for taxation are introduced by way of another annual Act, the Finance Act. Lastly, taxation may be imposed by simple resolution of the House until 5 August of any year: this, in the case of the resolution having been passed in the previous March or April. If the resolution should be passed at some other time, it has taxable effect for four further months, provided that the Bill which will incorporate this resolution has received its second reading within twenty-five days of the passing of the resolution.

Scrutiny of Administration. The efficiency of administration is reviewed by the two Select Committees of the House which have regard to expenditures. They are the Public Accounts Committee, which reviews the reports of the Comptroller and Auditor-General on his audits of the departments' accounts; and the Expenditure Committee, whose remit is to examine the Estimates of the current year and to report to the House thereon.

The day-to-day conduct of administration is challengeable on the floor of the House in Question Hour, when Ministers appear according to a roster to answer oral questions on their departments. Question Hour occurs every day of the parliamentary week except Fridays. Further opportunities for challenge are provided by debates on the adjournment of the House; by the set debates, whose topics are nominated by the Opposition, on the Estimates; and, finally, by the rare motions of censure put down by the Opposition and, traditionally, always accepted by the government for debate.

The Cabinet's Responsibility to the Commons. We have already noticed one aspect of this when discussing what is meant by the 'collective responsibility of the Cabinet' for matters of policy. There, we picked out the notion of 'collectivity' for discussion. Here we have to ask whether there exists in the Constitution a definition of the circumstances in which a Cabinet, having suffered a defeat on the floor of the House, must resign. It seems fairly clear that if a government says in advance that it is treating a particular vote as a 'matter of confidence', this is tantamount to its stating that, if defeated, it intends to resign. Accordingly, if defeated in these circumstances, we might confidently expect it to do so. If the Opposition puts down a motion of censure and carries it, then, too, we might expect the government to resign: but one cannot be absolutely sure that it will do so since it might argue that the vote was a 'snap' vote, or freakish and unrepresentative of the government's majority in one or other of a number of ways. However, the probability that a government would resign after defeat on a censure motion is certainly very high indeed.

However, apart from these two highly formal occasions, certain traditions as to when and when not a government ought constitutionally to resign used to exist in the past. On the one hand, a defeat in committee is not a confidence matter, since in principle this could always be reversed by the House as a whole. On the other, defeats on the second reading of a Bill used to be regarded as a matter of confidence entailing the government's resignation. It is traditional also that snap votes and defeats by 'ambush' might be disregarded by a government, since, *ex hypothesi*, such defeats do not express the normal balance of votes in the House. These traditions worked well enough in the heyday of majority one-party governments but have become more and more elastic under the minority governments of Wilson and Callaghan, from 1974 onwards. Mr Callaghan's government actually lost a Bill (the Redundancy Rebate Bill, on 7 February 1977) at its second reading – the only instance this century! It ignored the defeat and simply carried on. It is increasingly clear that the usages governing the occasions on which it is requisite for a government to resign are much more flexible in the case of a minority government than where the government has an absolute majority in the House; and that such a minority government is allowed a good deal of latitude to blunder along, disregarding occasional defeats on the way. In such circumstances only a motion relating to 'Confidence', whether formulated by the Opposition or by the government itself, seems to be the appropriate mechanism for bringing such a minority government down.

The Judicial Branch

There are five major points of similarity/dissimilarity between the scope and jurisdiction of the judicial branch of government in Britain and in the five constitutions under discussion here.

First, the British courts resemble those of all the other countries save one in that they interpret the laws in force, and their interpretation *is* the law until or unless it is altered. The exception here is the USSR; both in the Stalin and the Brezhnev constitutions, the interpretation of the laws in force is vested in the Presidium of the Supreme Soviet, i.e. in the standing committee of the legislature itself.

Second, British courts resemble those of the USA in that they interpret such law as may be deemed 'constitutional', i.e. relating to the distribution and allocation of public authority, as well as all other aspects of law. Another way of putting this is to say that in these two countries, the interpretation of constitutional law vests in the 'ordinary' courts of the land. In Germany, by contrast, the court that handles these matters is a specially constituted one, the Federal Constitutional Court or Verfassungsgericht (Article 93). In France only a limited number of 'constitutional' issues are reviewable; principally, for our present purposes, the compatibility of a Bill, already duly enacted by Parliament but not yet promulgated, with the constitution. (And not all bills, at that – see Title V of the constitution.) Furthermore the body that reviews such a matter is not a court at all but a special tribunal called the Constitutional Council.

Third, unlike the appropriate court or tribunal for constitutional laws in the USA, Germany and France, the British law courts cannot set aside a duly enacted parliamentary statute.

Fourth, the British arrangement resembles the American in that both these countries have but one set of courts to deal with all cases, whether these pertain to the executive branch or otherwise. Both France and Germany have a further set of special administrative courts in parallel to the 'ordinary' courts of the country.

Fifth, Britain differs from France, but not from the other three countries concerned, in that not one legal and judicial system obtains, as in France, but one for England and Wales and another for Scotland.

The Organization of the Judiciary. For civil cases (except for a small number of such cases handled by the magistrates' courts, as described below), the lowest tier is that of the county courts. Above them stands the High Court, functionally divided into Chancery Division, Queen's Bench and the Family Division. Appeal lies to the Court of Appeal (Civil Division) and thence to the House of Lords – the supreme court of the United Kingdom. For criminal cases the inferior courts are the magistrates' courts, which also handle a limited number of civil cases. Above them stands the Crown Court, established under the Crown Courts Act, 1971, with both appellate and original jurisdiction. Appeal lies from this to the Court of Appeal (Criminal Division). On a very restricted range of issues, there is further appeal to the House of Lords. After that there would remain, in criminal matters, only the appeal to the Royal Prerogative of mercy as exercised by the Home Secretary. The death penalty, for murder, was abolished in 1965, but remains in force for treason.

Scotland. In Scotland, civil jurisdiction is exercised by the Court of Session, divided into an 'inner House' of two divisions, and an 'outer House' comprising twelve single judges. Appeal lies to the House of Lords. Criminal jurisdiction resides in district courts and the sheriff court, and appeal lies to the High Court of Justiciary. There is no appeal from this to the House of Lords.

The House of Lords as the Supreme Court. The Lords hear appeals, civil and criminal, from England. They also exercise appellate jurisdiction over civil but not criminal cases originating in Scotland, and over both civil and criminal cases from Northern Ireland and also Wales.

In law, any peer may sit, uninvited, to hear an appeal. This last happened in 1883; the intrusive lay peer's opinion was superciliously ignored by the judges. These consist of a number of Lords of Appeal in Ordinary, i.e. life peers who formerly had held high judicial office for two years or, alternatively, who had been barristers of at least fifteen years standing. To them may be added the Lord Chancellor, ex-Lord Chancellors, and other peers who hold or have held high judicial office. Normally an appeal is heard before five such Lords.

The Judicial Committee of the Privy Council. There also exists a court which in law is a committee of the historic Privy Council (whose membership exceeds three hundred), which is styled the Judicial Committee of the Privy Council. Its domestic jurisdiction is slight. It hears appeals from the tribunals which maintain the professional discipline of various organizations, such as those, for instance, of the medical profession. Also, it can be asked to give an advisory opinion on any question in law which the Crown remits to it: for instance in 1958 the Commons sought its opinions on the nature of disqualification from sitting in that

House. Its chief function, however, is to act as the Court of Appeal from the courts in the Channel Islands and Isle of Man, the remaining colonies, protectorates and associated states; and from such Commonwealth countries as have so decided. Its quorum is three. Its composition includes the Lord Chancellor and the Lords of Appeal in Ordinary (i.e. the Law Lords of the House of Lords). In addition, the Lord President of the Council and former Lords President are also members; but they never sit. Lords Justices of Appeal are also members of the committee. They have sometimes been known to sit, but seldom do so. It also includes some Privy Councillors from other Commonwealth countries, e.g. currently it includes the Chief Justices of Australia and of New Zealand, as well as a retired judge from Singapore.

Judicial Independence. The independence of the judiciary from the pressures of both the legislative and the executive branches of government is a cardinal entailment of the doctrine of the separation of powers. The Soviet Constitution, which does not subscribe to this principle, stipulates that judges shall be elected by the Supreme Soviet for five-year terms, but qualifies this by stating that 'judges . . . are independent and subject only to the law' (Article 155). Elsewhere – in Britain too – judges of the high courts, sometimes of all courts (e.g. in Britain, France and Germany) are *appointed*. In the last three countries mentioned, it is the executive branch that appoints. In the USA it is the President, but by and with the consent of the Senate. Thus, in all these instances the appointment is in the hands of a politically charged body. How then is the 'independence' of the judiciary secured?

The answer lies in the respective provisions for payment, and for removal. The principle seems to be that though a judge may be appointed by the executive, he shall not – or not easily – be removed by it. Thus the German Constitution provides (Article 97) that the judge cannot be dismissed 'except by virtue of a judicial decision', and under this is subsumed removal by the process of impeachment (Article 98). The French Constitution declares that 'Judges shall be irremovable' (Article 64) and that disciplinary proceedings must take place in the Conseil Supérieur de la Magistrature. It must be remembered, however, that in these two countries, as in all 'civil law' countries, judges are civil servants. In the USA, a common-law country like Britain, the judges are appointed during 'good behaviour', their salaries may not be tampered with, but they may be impeached before the Senate for misconduct.

In Britain judges are not, or rather do not seem to be, Crown agents. Their independence is secured by the conventional and statutory provisions for their appointment, payment and removal, and for their judicial immunities. They are appointed by the Crown, which in practice means by the Prime Minister or the Lord Chancellor, depending on the status of the court in question. The possibility of appointing for primarily political reasons is mitigated by the convention that only barristers of many years standing shall be appointed to the Bench. Once appointed, the judges' salaries are charged on the Consolidated Fund (which is not subject to annual review by the Commons) and, furthermore, if changed (which is done by Order in Council) can only be raised, and never lowered. While in office, a judge enjoys judicial immunity for all acts said or done within his jurisdiction. He is disqualified from sitting in the House of Commons as an M.P.

The judge is indeed removable by the Crown but, by convention, only under the procedures laid down in the Act of Settlement (1701) as restated by the Appellate Jurisdiction Act, 1875, and the Supreme Court Judicature (Consolidation) Act, 1925. These Acts require removal to take place only on an address to the Crown presented by both Houses of Parliament. The last occasion on which a judge was removed was in 1830. He was an Irish judge, and the reason for his removal was emphatically not political.

Escape Clauses and Discretionary Powers

Written constitutions have great difficulty in providing for emergency situations. By their nature they impose legal constraints – they prescribe complicated and dilatory procedures. Consequently, they have to provide certain escape clauses to allow the government discretionary powers to cope with emergencies.

Examination of the five constitutions suggests a double distinction. On the one hand they lay down what may be called the 'circumstances of emergency', i.e. specifications of the conditions which must prevail for the situation to be regarded as an 'emergency'. On the other, they regulate '*states* of emergency', by which is meant the new legal conditions that prevail in these 'circumstances of emergency'.

One circumstance that is always provided for is a state of war, although in the German Constitution this is referred to as a 'state of defence'. Another is what the American Constitution refers to as 'domestic violence' and 'insurrection'. The Soviet Constitution puts this positively: it stipulates (Article 131(3) and (4)) that the Council of Ministers has the positive duty to 'maintain public order', and 'state security'. The German Constitution refers mysteriously to a 'state of tension' (*Spannungsfall*) without defining this (Article 80a). The French Constitution, at Article 16, stipulates, by way of contrast, a set of highly specific circumstances which constitute the circumstances of emergency.

States of emergency may consist of the suspension of the writ of *habeas corpus* in the American Constitution; the declaration of martial law; the declaration of a state of siege; and/or other unspecified powers to take what action the circumstances demand. In every case except that of the USSR, where the authority, as we have seen, is wholly concentrated in the legislature, the constitution-framer's problem is how to permit the executive to take emergency action and yet prevent it from using this permission to subvert the rest of the constitution; as happened to the Weimar Constitution under the use of 'Article 48', and more recently, in India in 1976, where Mrs Gandhi used the emergency powers of the constitution to establish a personal dictatorship and to subvert the guarantees of civil rights contained in the rest of the document. It is in order to escape this dilemma that a constitution such as the French one provides that where its emergency Article 16 is invoked, Parliament sits of right and cannot be dissolved; while the German Constitution goes to most elaborate lengths to ensure that the legislature shall meet and above all that the Constitutional Court shall continue to sit and carry out its functions.

This dilemma does not exist under the British Constitution.

The Queen-in-Parliament is supreme and omnicompetent and in principle can do anything it likes under any circumstances it thinks fit. The problem is reduced to the technical one of providing the executive with the power to act quickly and widely without having to get separate parliamentary approval for each one of its measures: in short to confer decree-making powers on the executive.

In Britain the Crown, i.e. the government, can always call on the police and if necessary the armed forces to repress 'domestic violence' or 'insurrection'. How far it can go without express parliamentary sanction – i.e. by virtue of the prerogative power alone – is abstruse, and not at all clear in law. As far as martial law is concerned, the last time it was proclaimed in time of war was as far back as the days of Charles I. The proclamation of martial law in times of peace cannot be made simply under prerogative powers. On the contrary, were a state of martial law proclaimed, the English courts would recognize it 'in appropriate circumstances' – but this implies that it is a matter for the courts to judge. In practice, martial law was quite extensively used in Ireland in the early 1920s.

However, the usual exercise of emergency power nowadays is through the Emergency Powers Act, 1920, as amended in 1964. This is a permanent statute. It envisages the circumstances where the community or a part of it is likely to be deprived of the essentials of life by reason of interference with the supply of food, water, fuel, light and transport. If the government considers that this has occurred or is likely to, it may, under the authority of this statute, proclaim a state of emergency.

This proclamation expires within one month, but can be superseded by a new proclamation – and so on. However, Parliament must be informed immediately and if the Houses are in recess or prorogued they must meet within five days. Once the state of emergency has been proclaimed the government has the authority to make Orders for securing the essentials of life to the community; they must be laid before Parliament and, unless approved by both Houses, expire after seven days. Moreover, the substance of the emergency regulations is circumscribed: they may not impose military or industrial conscription, nor alter the rules of criminal procedure, nor make it an offence to strike or peacefully persuade others to strike.

Such states of emergency have been proclaimed quite often in peace-time to deal with situations created or threatened by strikes. In time of war, however, governments have gone to Parliament to secure the grant of much more sweeping powers to make regulations for securing public safety and prosecuting the war. The First World War witnessed the Defence of the Realm Acts, 1914, 1915. In the Second World War the Emergency Powers (Defence) Act, 1939, empowered the government to make regulations requiring 'persons . . . to place themselves, their services and their property at the disposal of His Majesty'. This Act, conferring this vast power on the executive branch, was rushed through both Houses of Parliament and received the royal assent within a few hours. Such safeguard as there was lay in the provision that every Order in Council containing defence regulations had to be laid before Parliament, subject to amendment by either House, within a period of twenty-eight days.

Defence and External Affairs

Who conducts foreign affairs? The Crown, as head of state, acts in this area as the representative of the nation, but the conduct of foreign affairs is in the hands of Ministers, as are all other matters. However, the regal power to conduct external affairs is a 'prerogative' matter so that, with certain exceptions to be noted below, what Ministers do in this field is legally binding on the nation and does not require parliamentary consent. For instance, the appointment of ambassadors does not require parliamentary approval. For all this the convention of the responsibility of Ministers to Parliament for their actions always permits the Commons to question any action by them. This was well illustrated when the Secretary of State for Foreign and Commonwealth Affairs appointed Mr Peter Jay as H.M. Ambassador to the USA in 1977. Mr Jay was a journalist; he was also the Prime Minister's son-in-law. Many M.P.s took exception to the appointment and raised the matter in Parliament. Similarly, although declarations of war or of peace and the conduct of foreign relations generally are, in law, the province of the executive, they must by convention conform to the wishes of Parliament.

Within this general framework it is the Crown, acting through its Ministers, that appoints ambassadors and all other diplomatic agents and receives the credentials of those from other states. The treaty-making power likewise is vested in the Crown, but it is wise for Ministers, if it is not perhaps necessary, to ensure parliamentary approval. Where a treaty imposes taxation or makes a money grant or affects existing law or interferes with the private rights of an individual, the consent of Parliament is *positively* required if the treaty is to be binding on the subject and enforceable at law.

The Armed Forces. The supreme command of all air, sea and land forces is vested in the Crown but, again, in all such matters the Crown has to act on the advice of Ministers. It is the Secretary of State for Defence (always a member of the Cabinet) who is specifically responsible to Parliament for giving such 'advice'.

The abuse or potential abuse of a standing army in peace-time was one of the prime issues in the struggles between Crown and Parliament in the seventeenth and early eighteenth centuries. The navy, in contrast, was never regarded as a threat to liberty. Consequently, the Bill of Rights, 1689, expressly forbids the government (i.e. the Crown) to maintain a standing army in time of peace except by the consent of Parliament. The raising and maintenance of the air force, however, is authorized by a permanent Statute (the Air Force (Constitution) Act, 1917). The maintenance of a navy requires no statutory authority at all: it is raised and kept up solely by virtue of the common-law prerogative of the Crown.

In practice parliamentary control of all three services is effectively guaranteed by two devices. The first is financial. The money required to maintain the services is requested by Ministers, debated, and granted by Parliament on an annual basis. The second device concerns the discipline of each force. The disciplinary codes of the services, without which neither mutiny nor desertion would be illegal, are made lawful only through statute. The Army and Air Force Acts, and the Naval Discipline Act,

1957, run for five years at a stretch before requiring a new statute from Parliament; but they would automatically expire within this five-year period unless Parliament expressly approved an annual Order in Council to permit the renewal of the Act.

The Commonwealth and the Dependencies. The Commonwealth 'is the ghost of the British Empire sitting crowned on the grave thereof': and one might say much the same about the French Community as laid down in the French Constitution. But, like France, Britain still possesses dependencies, as well as maintaining links with former dependencies.

The Commonwealth embraces territories that were, or still are, dependent in some fashion upon the authority of the British Parliament and/or Crown. It comprises independent members, and a number of categories of other territories. The landmark statute is the Statute of Westminster, 1931, whose Section 4 provides that 'No Act of Parliament passed after the commencement of this Act shall extend or be deemed to extend to a Dominion as part of the law of that Dominion unless it is expressly declared in that Act that the Dominion has requested and consented to the enactment thereof'. (The term 'Dominion' has now been dropped in favour of 'full member' or 'independent member' of the Commonwealth.) The effect of this statute has been written into the Acts of the British Parliament which granted independence to former colonies during the period following the Second World War.

In 1931 certain tangible links remained between the (now) independent Dominions and the British polity. They all recognized allegiance to the British Crown, and recognized the Judicial Committee of the Privy Council as the highest court of appeal in respect to their own constitutions. This is no longer so. India, Sri Lanka and a large number of other countries are republics, recognizing the Queen only as the symbolic head of the Commonwealth. Some states are even monarchies: Malaysia, Western Samoa, Swaziland, Tonga, for instance. In addition Canada, Ghana, India, Nigeria and a number of other members of the Commonwealth have abolished the right of appeal to the Privy Council, while others, like Australia, have restricted it.

On the Constitution of Britain

However, two curious anomalies remain in the links between the United Kingdom Parliament, on the one hand, and Canada and Australia respectively, on the other. The Canadian Constitution is, in fact, the British North America Act, 1867, and as subsequently amended especially by the British North America Act (Number 2), 1949. The latter specifies four matters which the federal government of Canada can only amend by getting the British Parliament to make the necessary changes in the British North America Act itself. There is no doubt that the British Parliament would agree to this. The problem is what number of Canada's Provinces, acting through what process, would be regarded by the British Parliament as authorization to alter the Act. So far the Federal Government of Canada and the governments of its Provinces have not been able to agree on this. As to Australia, constitutional change in the federal sphere is entirely an internal matter. However, unlike the federal legislature, the legislatures of the six component states are still subject to the British statute known as the Colonial Laws Validity Act, 1865. In consequence any law made by the legislature of any of these states which is repugnant to a British statute is void.

There remain, outside the independent and 'full' members of the Commonwealth, a variety of territories which are not fully independent. *Associated states* have full control of their internal affairs, while the British government controls their external relations and defence matters; but their constitutions provide them with an internal means of moving to full independence (e.g. Canada, 1967–74). *Colonies* comprise territories like Hong Kong: the population owes allegiance to the British Crown, and its members are automatically British citizens. All colonies have governors, representing the Crown, and most have legislative assemblies, some of which may possess the power to make the colony self-governing in internal matters (e.g. Bermuda). The constitutions of such colonies are embodied either in a British statute or in letters patent or an Order in Council of the British Crown. Protectorates are not territories of the Crown at all. These states have their own rulers but they are subject to varied degrees of control by the British government while their external relations are fully controlled by it (e.g. the Solomon Islands).

Protected states are fully self-governing countries under their own native rulers, while their external relations are managed by Britain. Brunei was the last state to belong to this category, becoming independent in 1971.

The EEC. The question of the relationship between the domestic laws of a country (its 'municipal law') and international law is complex.

The German Constitution provides expressly that international law is an integral part of its municipal law (Article 25). The French Constitution states (Article 55) only that duly approved and ratified *treaties or agreements* shall have an authority superior to domestic legislation on the relevant matters. However, in the Preamble to the Constitution of the Fourth Republic, 1946, which is adhered to by the 1958 Constitution, it is stipulated that the Republic 'shall conform to the rules of international public law'. British law is unclear on this important matter. If the sovereignty of Parliament be taken as axiomatic there is a *prima facie* contradiction between it and the overriding nature of international law or treaty obligations. Parliament, as sovereign, could ignore these in framing domestic legislation.

This question was raised in acute form by the United Kingdom's accession to the European Economic Community, which took place in 1973. A distinction must be made between the practical and the legal consequences of this accession. On the practical plane, the European Economic Commission (the Community's executive organ) may make regulations which bind every member state, and which will not in the normal way have received the assent of the British Parliament; conversely, the Commission can only operate in so far as the Council of Ministers of the nine member states permits, and in this council each state has a full veto. Hence the British executive can, in practice, veto the passage of any decision or regulation it dislikes, so that implicitly the Queen-in-Parliament may be said to have been a consenting party to any such decisions or regulations that it has not vetoed.

However, decisions of the Community Court are binding law in the courts of every member state. This raises the question: if

Parliament disliked a judicial decision of the British courts which was founded on such a Community Court decision and passed a statute overriding the court's judgment, would the British courts accept this statute as binding on them or would they declare it void as repugnant to the European Community Court's judgment?

The answer seems to be that they would not declare it void but accept it as valid law: at least, they would do so in the immediate future. Successive Lords Chancellors have stated that, if it wished, Parliament could repeal the European Communities Act, 1972. This would be a breach of Britain's international obligations but fully within the sovereign competence of Parliament. Similarly, 'If the Queen-in-Parliament were to make laws which were in conflict with [Britain's] obligations under the Treaty of Rome, those laws and not the conflicting provisions of the Treaty would be given effect to as the domestic law of the United Kingdom.'[16]

Citizens and the State

The five constitutions all mention citizens, but do not state, or not in any detail, how citizenship is acquired and what constitute the distinguishing characteristics of a citizen as contrasted with an alien. A written constitution for Britain would presumably, like these other constitutions, refer the reader to the ordinary laws of the land. Suffice it to say therefore that citizenship may be acquired in three main ways in Britain. The first, corresponding to a highly general, indeed universal, concept, is that citizenship may be acquired by birth in the country or by descent from persons born in the country. Second – and again, as is almost universal elsewhere – citizenship may be acquired by naturalization, the appropriate Minister in this case being the Home Secretary. Finally, citizenship may also be acquired by registration with the Home Secretary. This process is particularly relevant to that special category of citizens of a Commonwealth country called 'Patrials' – persons who, at the time of their birth, had a parent who was either a citizen of the UK by birth, or the wife of such a citizen.

Introduction

The Electorate. We have already specified how the electorate is composed. Manifestly, one of the privileges of being a British citizen is the right to vote and to hold parliamentary office. Curiously, and anomalously, this privilege is shared by citizens of the Irish Republic and by citizens of any Commonwealth country, provided they have satisfied the residence requirements.

The Political Parties. Elections are contested by political parties. Some constitutions, like the German, contain general clauses regulating the status of such organizations. No such provision appears in the American Constitution, and in Britain, the laws that relate to parties are rare and parenthetical. Certainly there is no general 'Statute of Parties' concerned with their aims, organization, finances and procedures. In law they are treated as essentially private bodies.

Rights and Duties of Citizens. Each of the five constitutions contains a recitation of the rights (sometimes, also of the duties) of citizens – whoever these may be. True, the French Constitution refers to these rights parenthetically, by means of its Preamble, which in its turn refers to the Preamble to the Constitution of 1946 and to the 1789 Declaration of the Rights of Man and the Citizen. Such recitations are usually known nowadays as so many 'Bills of Rights'. No such document exists among the laws of Britain.

Yet the British citizen unquestionably enjoys a large number of individual rights in his capacity as a citizen of his country. As far as the application of the law is concerned it may fairly be argued that he enjoys much wider personal freedom than his Soviet counterpart, for all that both the Soviet constitutions contain a large number of articles specifying the citizens' rights. By the same token while he appears to enjoy freedoms comparable with those of his American, French and German counterparts, in the constitutions of these countries the rights are expressed in the written constitution and are reviewable by a court or (in a limited range of circumstances) a specially appointed constitutional tribunal (as in the case of France).

Britain, like Germany and France, is a signatory of the European Convention on Human Rights (1950) and in 1966 accepted the compulsory jurisdiction of the European Commission on Human Rights and the European Court of Human Rights to which, therefore, an aggrieved individual can appeal. From this it may be inferred that the rights of the citizen in either Britain, France or Germany are all subsumable under the Declaration of Human Rights, since the first seventeen Articles of the European Convention are those of the Declaration.

From these equivalences and differences we may deduce the following. First, it is possible to express the rights of British citizens in such general language and subject to so many qualifications and escape clauses that, at a certain level of abstraction, they may appear identical with those of their European neighbours. One could even go further and assert that, at this level, and with similar qualifications, they are not significantly different from those of their Soviet counterparts. Second, the detailed and precise import of these generally expressed rights in Britain, *vis-à-vis* Germany and France, can only be understood by examining the specific laws and the judicial decisions thereon in Britain compared with these other countries. Such a task is beyond the scope of this Introduction. A catalogue of rights such as freedom of expression, assembly, petition, association and election would be too equivocal; a particularization would, conversely, be tantamount to a volume on civil liberties in Britain and would, indeed, take us beyond even that into the fields of judicial procedure, police powers and of social and economic legislation. Third, the scope and effectiveness of the laws relating to civil liberty are not affected *in principle* by whether or not they are embodied in a charter which has the force of fundamental and superior law; witness the insubstantiality of rights in such a document as the Constitution of the USSR on the one hand and the practical effectiveness of the American Constitution's 'Bill of Rights' on the other.

The most that can be done here, therefore, is not to describe the substance of citizens' rights but their *status*. And the following observations may be made about this:

(1) The rights of the British citizen are not codified into statements of general principle like the clauses in the Preamble to the

French 1946 Constitution, the first twenty Articles of the German Constitution, or Amendments I–X, XIV and XV of the American Constitution. Nor are they guaranteed any greater legal sanctity than that enjoyed by, for example, a Lotteries and Gaming Act. These liberties are founded in the common law of the kingdom, or in statutes, and in either case they are interpreted by the ordinary courts of the country; and both these and subsequent judicial decisions thereon can be overridden or altered by subsequent parliamentary statutes. In a word: the rights of the British citizen are not 'entrenched'.

(2) Furthermore, these rights are residual. To know one's rights is to know what matters or actions the law forbids. Thus a citizen is free to express his opinion in speech or writing or other visual means, subject, however, to a long train of restrictions including, *inter alia*, the laws relating to treason, the Official Secrets Act, sedition, defamation, incitement to mutiny or to disaffection, obscene publication or blasphemy; and to those also that relate to incitement to a criminal offence, or to provoking public discord or incitement to racial hatred. And each of these qualifying restrictions is defined by statute, common law and the judicial decisions thereon.

(3) Finally, for every wrongful encroachment on the citizens' liberties, there exists a legal remedy, ascertainable and enforceable by the ordinary courts of the land.

A number of eminent lawyers have increasingly found this situation unsatisfactory. They have called for a Bill of Rights enshrined in a written constitution on lines similar to the American or the German constitutions. Their dissatisfaction has arisen from recent developments in the parliamentary system. Parliament is sovereign: this is the key axiom of the Constitution, and consequently Lord Justice Scarman is able to write: 'Its sovereign power [is] more often than not exercised at the will of an executive sustained by an impregnable majority . . . The less internal control Parliament is prepared to accept, the greater the need for a constitutional settlement protecting entrenched provisions in the field of fundamental human rights.'[17]

To establish such a 'constitutional settlement' is far more easily said than done. The chief difficulties seem to be the following.

First, it is difficult to envisage such a novel situation arising as long as the sovereignty of Parliament remains the fundamental axiom of the law. If this is not to remain, how can Parliament divest itself of such a power?

Second, it is sometimes argued that the desired result could be brought about by Parliament passing a statute which is, somehow, 'entrenched'. That is to say, the statute would prescribe a procedure for altering itself which is more elaborate than that required for ordinary statutes, e.g. that it might be amended only by a two-thirds majority, or a two-thirds majority in each House, and/or by a popular referendum. But constitutional lawyers are divided as to whether such entrenchment is legally feasible, i.e. as to whether Parliament could not, under its ordinary procedure, simply wipe from the book the 'entrenching' statute.

Third, some (including the Labour Party) would settle for a Statute of Rights that was not entrenched but passed by Parliament in the ordinary way, similar to the Canadian Bill of Rights, 1960.

In our opinion, entrenchment in the ways suggested is legally feasible. After all, the provision that Parliament's life must not exceed five years is 'entrenched' under the Parliament Act, 1911, in that it requires the consent of both the Lords and the Commons; whereas other Commons Bills can be passed into law without the consent of the Lords provided they follow the procedure of the 1911 Act, as described on page 65 above. It is hard to see why a similar procedure or, indeed, an analogous line of reasoning should not apply to a Statute of Rights.

However, it is one thing to guarantee that such a statute shall not be simply repealed or suspended every time a government finds that it stands in the way of its intended legislation, and another to ensure that the courts will treat it as superior law to statutes that are challenged on the grounds that they are contrary to the Statute of Rights. The experience of Canada, with its Bill of Rights, is instructive. It is true that this is an ordinary and not an entrenched statute and that the Ottawa Parliament could repeal it if it wanted to. But it has not wanted to, and yet, despite that, the Bill has proved ineffective. With the exception of one rather minor case in 1969 the Supreme Court of Canada has taken

Introduction

the line that when Parliament has passed a statute it must, *ipso facto*, have had this Bill of Rights in mind and has consequently upheld the statute which has been challenged. A British Parliament is likely to defend its sovereignty more ferociously than its Canadian offspring. The latter has long been habituated to a degree of judicial control by its Supreme Court and, indeed, until 1934 (for federal cases) and 1947 (for provincial cases) by the Judicial Committee of the Privy Council. The tradition of independent review and the annulment of statutes by the courts has been lost in Britain since the early seventeenth century.

This argument can be taken more widely, too. On the one hand, it seems that the mechanism of the entrenched Bill of Rights *plus* judicial review only operates effectively in countries whose legislatures have long been habituated to the arrangement: the American experience dates from *Marbury* v. *Madison*, 1803, while the German system takes up the centuries-old *Rechtsstaat* tradition. On the other hand, the absence of entrenched clauses in the Australian and Canadian constitutions has not restricted civil liberties in those countries as compared with, say, the USA or Germany, and has demonstrably restricted them far less than in the great majority of states which have such entrenched Bills of Rights. The situation recalls a wry joke which goes the rounds of Soviet-controlled Eastern Europe: 'In England everything that is not prohibited is permitted. In Germany everything that is not permitted is prohibited. In France everything that is prohibited is permitted. In the USSR everything that is permitted is prohibited.' In short, there are more ways than one of negating civil liberties and more ways than one of guaranteeing it.

References

1. K. Wheare, *Modern Constitutions*, Oxford, 1964, Ch. III; L. Wolff-Philips, *Comparative Constitutions*, Macmillan, 1972, Ch. 4.
2. cf. A. Vishinsky, *The Law of the Soviet State*, Macmillan, New York, 1948, pp. 312–22.
3. J. Cadart, *Institutions politiques et droit constitutionnel*, Paris, 1975, Vol. II, p. 886.
4. P. S. Romashkin, 'Proposals for a New Constitution ... 1960', in: J. F. Triska (ed.), *Constitutions of the Communist States*, Hoover Institute, Stanford, 1970, pp. 77–87.

5. A. V. Dicey, *Law of the Constitution*, 9th ed., Macmillan, 1939, p. 4.
6. See, for instance: A. V. Dicey, *Introduction to the Study of the Law of the Constitution* (ed. E. C. S. Wade), 10th ed., London, 1961, Chs. I, II, III, and the Introduction (by E. C. S. Wade), pp. xxxiv–xcvi, cxciv–v; Sir W. Ivor Jennings, *The Law and the Constitution*, 5th ed., University of London Press, 1959, Ch. IV; G. Marshall, *Parliamentary Sovereignty and the Commonwealth*, Oxford, 1957; O. Hood-Phillips, *Constitutional Law of Great Britain and the Commonwealth*, 5th ed., London, 1973, Chs. 3, 4; S. A. de Smith, *Constitutional and Administrative Law*, Penguin Books, Harmondsworth, 1971, Ch. 3; G. Marshall, *Constitutional Theory*, Oxford, 1971.
7. Sir William Blackstone, *Commentary on the Laws of England*, 1765–9, Bk I, Ch. 2.
8. For a more detailed account, including some of the problems that have arisen in the relationship between the islands and the United Kingdom, see: *The Royal Commission on the Constitution* (Kilbrandon), CMND 5460, 1973, Vol. I, pp. 407–13.
9. Jennings, op. cit., p. 138. For a commentary on this view and its implications see de Smith, op. cit., p. 85 ff.
10. Henri Benjamin Constant de Rebecque, 'Principes de politique', in: *Oeuvres*, Ed. La Pléiade, Paris, 1937, p. 1079.
11. S. E. Finer, *A Primer of Public Administration*, London, 1950, p. 30.
12. S. E. Finer, 'One Out, All Out', *New Society*, 25 August 1977, pp. 397–8.
13. S. E. Finer, 'The Individual Responsibility of Ministers', *Public Administration*, Winter 1956, pp. 377–96.
14. Cadart, op. cit., Vol. II, p. 886.
15. *Select Committee on Privileges: Case of A. J. Brown*, 1947, p. 83 ff.
16. *The Common Market and the Common Law*, 1972 (6. *Law Teacher* 3·5).
17. Sir Leslie Scarman, *English Law: The New Dimensions*, Stevens, London, 1974, pp. 74–5.

The Constitution of the

UNITED STATES
OF
AMERICA
1787

We the People of the United States, in Order to form a more perfect Union, establish Justice, insure domestic Tranquility, provide for the common defence, promote the general Welfare, and secure the Blessings of Liberty to ourselves and our Posterity, do ordain and establish this Constitution for the United States of America.

ARTICLE I

Section 1. All legislative Powers herein granted shall be vested in a Congress of the United States, which shall consist of a Senate and House of Representatives.

Section 2. [1] The House of Representatives shall be composed of Members chosen every second Year by the People of the several States, and the Electors in each State shall have the Qualifications requisite for Electors of the most numerous Branch of the State Legislature.

[2] No person shall be a Representative who shall not have attained to the Age of twenty five Years, and been seven Years a Citizen of the United States, and who shall not, when elected, be an Inhabitant of that State in which he shall be chosen.

[3] [Representatives and direct Taxes shall be apportioned among the several States which may be included within this Union, according to their respective Numbers, which shall be determined by adding to the whole Number of free Persons, including those bound to Service for a Term of Years, and excluding Indians not taxed, three fifths of all other Persons.].* The actual Enumeration

NOTE. This text of the Constitution follows the engrossed copy signed by Gen. Washington and the deputies from twelve States. The superior number preceding the paragraphs designates the number of the clause; it was not in the original.

*The part included in square brackets was changed by section 2 of the fourteenth amendment.

shall be made within three Years after the first Meeting of the Congress of the United States, and within every subsequent Term of ten Years, in such Manner as they shall by Law direct. The Number of Representatives shall not exceed one for every thirty Thousand, but each State shall have at Least one Representative; and until such enumeration shall be made, the State of New Hampshire shall be entitled to chuse three, Massachusetts eight, Rhode-Island and Providence Plantations one, Connecticut five, New-York six, New Jersey four, Pennsylvania eight, Delaware one, Maryland six, Virginia ten, North Carolina five, South Carolina five, and Georgia three.

[4] When vacancies happen in the Representation from any State, the Executive Authority thereof shall issue Writs of Election to fill such Vacancies.

[5] The House of Representatives shall chuse their Speaker and other Officers; and shall have the sole Power of Impeachment.

Section 3. [1] The Senate of the United States shall be composed of two Senators from each State, [chosen by the Legislature thereof,] * for six Years; and each Senator shall have one Vote.

[2] Immediately after they shall be assembled in Consequence of the first Election, they shall be divided as equally as may be into three Classes. The Seats of the Senators of the first Class shall be vacated at the Expiration of the second Year, of the second Class at the Expiration of the fourth Year, and of the third Class at the Expiration of the sixth Year, so that one third may be chosen every second Year; [and if Vacancies happen by Resignation, or otherwise, during the Recess of the Legislature of any State, the Executive thereof may make temporary Appointments until the next Meeting of the Legislature, which shall then fill such Vacancies].†

[3] No Person shall be a Senator who shall not have attained to the Age of thirty Years, and been nine Years a Citizen of the United States, and who shall not, when elected, be an Inhabitant of that State for which he shall be chosen.

---

*The part included in square brackets was changed by section 1 of the seventeenth amendment.

†The part included in square brackets was changed by clause 2 of the seventeenth amendment.

⁴ The Vice President of the United States shall be President of the Senate, but shall have no Vote, unless they be equally divided.

⁵ The Senate shall chuse their other Officers, and also a President pro tempore, in the Absence of the Vice-President, or when he shall exercise the Office of President of the United States.

⁶ The Senate shall have the sole Power to try all Impeachments. When sitting for that Purpose, they shall be on Oath or Affirmation. When the President of the United States is tried, the Chief Justice shall preside: And no Person shall be convicted without the Concurrence of two thirds of the Members present.

⁷ Judgment in Cases of Impeachment shall not extend further than to removal from Office, and disqualification to hold and enjoy any Office of honor, Trust or Profit under the United States: but the Party convicted shall nevertheless be liable and subject to Indictment, Trial, Judgment and Punishment, according to Law.

Section 4. ¹ The Times, Places and Manner of holding Elections for Senators and Representatives, shall be prescribed in each State by the Legislature thereof; but the Congress may at any time by Law make or alter such Regulations, except as to the Places of chusing Senators.

² The Congress shall assemble at least once in every Year, and such Meeting shall [be on the first Monday in December,]* unless they shall by Law appoint a different Day.

Section 5. ¹ Each House shall be the Judge of the Elections, Returns and Qualifications of its own Members, and a Majority of each shall constitute a Quorum to do Business; but a smaller Number may adjourn from day to day, and may be authorized to compel the Attendance of absent Members, in such Manner, and under such Penalties as each House may provide.

² Each House may determine the Rules of its Proceedings, punish its Members for disorderly Behaviour, and, with the Concurrence of two thirds, expel a Member.

³ Each House shall keep a Journal of its Proceedings, and from time to time publish the same, excepting such Parts as may in their Judgment require Secrecy; and the Yeas and Nays of the

*The part included in square brackets was changed by section 2 of the seventeenth amendment.

Members of either House on any question shall, at the Desire of one fifth of those Present, be entered on the Journal.

[4] Neither House, during the Session of Congress, shall, without the Consent of the other, adjourn for more than three days, nor to any other Place than that in which the two Houses shall be sitting.

Section 6. [1] The Senators and Representatives shall receive a Compensation for their Services, to be ascertained by Law, and paid out of the Treasury of the United States. They shall in all Cases, except Treason, Felony and Breach of the Peace, be privileged from Arrest during their Attendance at the Session of their respective Houses, and in going to and returning from the same; and for any Speech or Debate in either House, they shall not be questioned in any other Place.

[2] No Senator or Representative shall, during the Time for which he was elected, be appointed to any civil Office under the Authority of the United States, which shall have been created, or the Emoluments whereof shall have been encreased during such time; and no Person holding any Office under the United States, shall be a Member of either House during his Continuance in Office.

Section 7. [1] All Bills for raising Revenue shall originate in the House of Representatives; but the Senate may propose or concur with Amendments as on other Bills.

[2] Every Bill which shall have passed the House of Representatives and the Senate, shall, before it become a Law, be presented to the President of the United States; If he approve he shall sign it, but if not he shall return it, with his Objections to that House in which it shall have originated, who shall enter the Objections at large on their Journal, and proceed to reconsider it. If after such Reconsideration two thirds of that House shall agree to pass the Bill, it shall be sent, together with the Objections, to the other House, by which it shall likewise be reconsidered, and if approved by two thirds of that House, it shall become a Law. But in all such Cases the Votes of both Houses shall be determined by Yeas and Nays, and the Names of the Persons voting for and against the Bill shall be entered on the Journal of each House respectively. If any Bill shall not be returned by the President within ten Days

(Sundays excepted) after it shall have been presented to him, the Same shall be a Law, in like Manner as if he had signed it, unless the Congress by their Adjournment prevent its Return, in which Case it shall not be a Law.

[3] Every Order, Resolution, or Vote to which the Concurrence of the Senate and House of Representatives may be necessary (except on a question of Adjournment) shall be presented to the President of the United States; and before the Same shall take Effect, shall be approved by him, or being disapproved by him, shall be repassed by two thirds of the Senate and House of Representatives, according to the Rules and Limitations prescribed in the Case of a Bill.

Section 8. [1] The Congress shall have Power To lay and collect Taxes, Duties, Imposts and Excises, to pay the Debts and provide for the common Defence and general Welfare of the United States; but all Duties, Imposts and Excises shall be uniform throughout the United States;

[2] To borrow Money on the credit of the United States;

[3] To regulate Commerce with foreign Nations, and among the several States, and with the Indian Tribes;

[4] To establish an uniform Rule of Naturalization, and uniform Laws on the subject of Bankruptcies throughout the United States;

[5] To coin Money, regulate the Value thereof, and of foreign Coin, and fix the Standard of Weights and Measures;

[6] To provide for the Punishment of counterfeiting the Securities and current Coin of the United States;

[7] To establish Post Offices and post Roads;

[8] To promote the Progress of Science and useful Arts, by securing for limited Times to Authors and Inventors the exclusive Right to their respective Writings and Discoveries;

[9] To constitute Tribunals inferior to the supreme Court;

[10] To define and punish Piracies and Felonies committed on the high Seas, and Offences against the Law of Nations;

[11] To declare War, grant Letters of Marque and Reprisal, and make Rules concerning Captures on Land and Water;

[12] To raise and support Armies, but no Appropriation of Money to that Use shall be for a longer Term than two Years;

[13] To provide and maintain a Navy;

[14] To make Rules for the Government and Regulation of the land and naval Forces;

[15] To provide for calling forth the Militia to execute the Laws of the Union, suppress Insurrections and repel Invasions;

[16] To provide for organizing, arming, and disciplining, the Militia, and for governing such Part of them as may be employed in the Service of the United States, reserving to the States respectively, the Appointment of the Officers, and the Authority of training the Militia according to the discipline prescribed by Congress;

[17] To exercise exclusive Legislation in all Cases whatsoever, over such District (not exceeding ten Miles square) as may, by Cession of particular States, and the Acceptance of Congress, become the Seat of the Government of the United States, and to exercise like Authority over all Places purchased by the Consent of the Legislature of the State in which the Same shall be, for the Erection of Forts, Magazines, Arsenals, dock-Yards, and other needful Buildings; – And

[18] To make all Laws which shall be necessary and proper for carrying into Execution the foregoing Powers, and all other Powers vested by this Constitution in the Government of the United States, or in any Department or Officer thereof.

Section 9. [1] The Migration or Importation of such Persons as any of the States now existing shall think proper to admit, shall not be prohibited by the Congress prior to the Year one thousand eight hundred and eight, but a Tax or duty may be imposed on such Importation, not exceeding ten dollars for each Person.

[2] The Privilege of the Writ of Habeas Corpus shall not be suspended, unless when in Cases of Rebellion or Invasion the public Safety may require it.

[3] No Bill of Attainder or ex post facto Law shall be passed.

*[4] No Capitation, or other direct, Tax shall be laid, unless in Proportion to the Census or Enumeration herein before directed to be taken.

[5] No Tax or Duty shall be laid on Articles exported from any State.

---

*See also the sixteenth amendment.

[6] No Preference shall be given by any Regulation of Commerce or Revenue to the Ports of one State over those of another: nor shall Vessels bound to, or from, one State, be obliged to enter, clear, or pay Duties in another.

[7] No Money shall be drawn from the Treasury, but in Consequence of Appropriations made by Law; and a regular Statement and Account of the Receipts and Expenditures of all public Money shall be published from time to time.

[8] No Title of Nobility shall be granted by the United States: And no Person holding any Office of Profit or Trust under them, shall, without the Consent of the Congress, accept of any present, Emolument, Office, or Title, of any kind whatever, from any King, Prince, or foreign State.

Section 10. [1] No State shall enter into any Treaty, Alliance, or Confederation; grant Letters of Marque and Reprisal; coin Money; emit Bills of Credit; make any Thing but gold and silver Coin a Tender in Payment of Debts; pass any Bill of Attainder, ex post facto Law, or Law impairing the Obligation of Contracts, or grant any Title of Nobility.

[2] No State shall, without the Consent of the Congress, lay any Imposts or Duties on Imports or Exports, except what may be absolutely necessary for executing it's inspection Laws: and the net Produce of all Duties and Imposts, laid by any State on Imports or Exports, shall be for the Use of the Treasury of the United States; and all such Laws shall be subject to the Revision and Controul of the Congress.

[3] No State shall, without the Consent of Congress, lay any Duty of Tonnage, keep Troops, or Ships of War in time of Peace, enter into any Agreement or Compact with another State, or with a foreign Power, or engage in War, unless actually invaded, or in such imminent Danger as will not admit of delay.

ARTICLE II

Section 1. [1] The executive Power shall be vested in a President of the United States of America. He shall hold his Office during the Term of four Years, and, together with the Vice-President, chosen for the same Term, be elected, as follows

² Each State shall appoint, in such Manner as the Legislature thereof may direct, a Number of Electors, equal to the whole Number of Senators and Representatives to which the State may be entitled in the Congress: but no Senator or Representative, or Person holding an Office of Trust or Profit under the United States, shall be appointed an Elector.

[The Electors shall meet in their respective States, and vote by Ballot for two Persons, of whom one at least shall not be an Inhabitant of the same State with themselves. And they shall make a List of all the Persons voted for, and of the Number of Votes for each; which List they shall sign and certify, and transmit sealed to the Seat of the Government of the United States, directed to the President of the Senate. The President of the Senate shall, in the Presence of the Senate and House of Representatives, open all the Certificates, and the Votes shall then be counted. The Person having the greatest Number of Votes shall be the President, if such Number be a Majority of the whole Number of Electors appointed; and if there be more than one who have such Majority, and have an equal Number of Votes, then the House of Representatives shall immediately chuse by Ballot one of them for President; and if no Person have a Majority, then from the five highest on the List the said House shall in like Manner chuse the President. But in chusing the President, the Votes shall be taken by States, the Representation from each State having one Vote; A quorum for this Purpose shall consist of a Member or Members from two thirds of the States, and a Majority of all the Senates shall be necessary to a Choice. In every Case, after the Choice of the President, the Person having the greatest Number of Votes of the Electors shall be the Vice-President. But if there should remain two or more who have equal Votes, the Senate shall chuse from them by Ballot the Vice-President.]*

³ The Congress may determine the Time of chusing the Electors, and the Day on which they shall give their Votes; which Day shall be the same throughout the United States.

⁴ No Person except a natural born Citizen, or a Citizen of the United States, at the time of the Adoption of this Constitution, shall be eligible to the Office of President; neither shall any

*This paragraph has been superseded by the twelfth amendment.

Person be eligible to that Office who shall not have attained to the Age of thirty five Years, and been fourteen Years a Resident within the United States.

[5] In Case of the Removal of the President from Office, or of his Death, Resignation, or Inability to discharge the Powers and Duties of the said Office,* the Same shall devolve on the Vice-President, and the Congress may by Law provide for the Case of Removal, Death, Resignation or Inability, both of the President and Vice-President, declaring what Officer shall then act as President, and such Officer shall act accordingly, until the Disability be removed, or a President shall be elected.

[6] The President shall, at stated Times, receive for his Services, a Compensation, which shall neither be encreased nor diminished during the Period for which he shall have been elected, and he shall not receive within that Period any other Emolument from the United States, or any of them.

[7] Before he enter on the Execution of his Office, he shall take the following Oath or Affirmation: – 'I do solemnly swear (or affirm) that I will faithfully execute the Office of President of the United States, and will to the best of my Ability, preserve, protect and defend the Constitution of the United States.'

Section 2. [1] The President shall be Commander in Chief of the Army and Navy of the United States, and of the Militia of the several States, when called into the actual Service of the United States; he may require the Opinion, in writing, of the principal Officer in each of the executive Departments, upon any Subject relating to the Duties of their respective Offices, and he shall have Power to grant Reprieves and Pardons for Offences against the United States, except in Cases of Impeachment.

[2] He shall have Power, by and with the Advice and Consent of the Senate, to make Treaties, provided two thirds of the Senators present concur; and he shall nominate, and by and with the Advice and Consent of the Senate, shall appoint Ambassadors, other public Ministers and Consuls, Judges of the supreme Court, and all other Officers of the United States, whose Appointments are not herein otherwise provided for, and which shall be established by Law: but the Congress may by Law vest the Appoint-

*This provision has been affected by the twenty-fifth amendment.

ment of such inferior Officers, as they think proper, in the President alone, in the Courts of Law, or in the Heads of Departments.

[3] The President shall have Power to fill up all Vacancies that may happen during the Recess of the Senate, by granting Commissions which shall expire at the End of their next Session.

Section 3. He shall from time to time give to the Congress Information of the State of the Union, and recommend to their Consideration such Measures as he shall judge necessary and expedient; he may, on extraordinary Occasions, convene both Houses, or either of them, and in Case of Disagreement between them, with Respect to the Time of Adjournment, he may adjourn them to such Time as he shall think proper; he shall receive Ambassadors and other public Ministers; he shall take Care that the Laws be faithfully executed, and shall Commission all the Officers of the United States.

Section 4. The President, Vice-President and all civil Officers of the United States, shall be removed from Office on Impeachment for, and Conviction of, Treason, Bribery, or other high Crimes and Misdemeanors.

ARTICLE III

Section 1. The judicial Power of the United States, shall be vested in one supreme Court, and in such inferior Courts as the Congress may from time to time ordain and establish. The Judges, both of the supreme and inferior Courts, shall hold their Offices during good Behaviour, and shall, at stated Times, receive for their Services, a Compensation, which shall not be diminished during their Continuance in Office.

Section 2. [1] The judicial Power shall extend to all Cases, in Law and Equity, arising under this Constitution, the Laws of the United States, and Treaties made, or which shall be made, under their Authority; – to all Cases affecting Ambassadors, other public Ministers and Consuls; – to all Cases of admiralty and maritime Jurisdiction; – to Controversies to which the United States shall be a Party; – to Controversies between two or more States; – between a State and Citizens of another State;* – be-

*This clause has been affected by the eleventh amendment.

tween Citizens of different States, – between Citizens of the same State claiming Lands under Grants of different States, and between a State, or the Citizens thereof, and foreign States, Citizens or Subjects.

[2] In all Cases affecting Ambassadors, other public Ministers and Consuls, and those in which a State shall be Party, the supreme Court shall have original Jurisdiction. In all the other Cases before mentioned, the supreme Court shall have appellate Jurisdiction, both as to Law and Fact, with such Exceptions, and under such Regulations as the Congress shall make.

[3] The Trial of all Crimes, except in Cases of Impeachment, shall be by Jury; and such Trial shall be held in the State where the said Crimes shall have been committed; but when not committed within any State, the Trial shall be at such Place or Places as the Congress may by Law have directed.

Section 3. [1] Treason against the United States, shall consist only in levying War against them, or in adhering to their Enemies, giving them Aid and Comfort. No Person shall be convicted of Treason unless on the Testimony of two Witnesses to the same overt Act, or on Confession in open Court.

[2] The Congress shall have Power to declare the Punishment of Treason, but no Attainder of Treason shall work Corruption of Blood, or Forfeiture except during the Life of the Person attained.

ARTICLE IV

Section 1. Full Faith and Credit shall be given in each State to the public Acts, Records, and judicial Proceedings of every other State. And the Congress may by general Laws prescribe the Manner in which such Acts, Records and Proceedings shall be proved, and the Effect thereof.

Section 2. [1] The Citizens of each State shall be entitled to all Privileges and Immunities of Citizens in the several States.

[2] A Person charged in any State with Treason, Felony, or other Crime, who shall flee from Justice, and be found in another State, shall on Demand of the executive Authority of the State from which he fled, be delivered up, to be removed to the State having Jurisdiction of the Crime.

[3] [No Person held to Service or Labour in one State, under the Laws thereof, escaping into another, shall, in Consequence of any Law or Regulation therein, be discharged from such Service or Labour, but shall be delivered up on Claim of the Party to whom such Service or Labour may be due.]*

Section 3. [1] New States may be admitted by the Congress into this Union; but no new State shall be formed or erected within the Jurisdiction of any other State; nor any State be formed by the Junction of two or more States, or Parts of States, without the Consent of the Legislatures of the States concerned as well as of the Congress.

[2] The Congress shall have Power to dispose of and make all needful Rules and Regulations respecting the Territory or other Property belonging to the United States; and nothing in this Constitution shall be so construed as to Prejudice any Claims of the United States, or of any particular State.

Section 4. The United States shall guarantee to every State in this Union a Republican Form of Government, and shall protect each of them against Invasion; and on Application of the Legislature, or of the Executive (when the Legislature cannot be convened) against domestic Violence.

ARTICLE V

The Congress, whenever two thirds of both Houses shall deem it necessary, shall propose Amendments to this Constitution, or, on the Application of the Legislatures of two thirds of the several States, shall call a Convention for proposing Amendments, which, in either Case, shall be valid to all Intents and Purposes, as Part of this Constitution, when ratified by the Legislatures of three fourths of the several States, or by Conventions in three fourths thereof, as the one or the other Mode of Ratification may be proposed by the Congress; Provided [that no Amendment which may be made prior to the Year One thousand eight hundred and eight shall in any Manner affect the first and fourth Clauses in the Ninth Section of the first Article; and]† that no State, with-

*This paragraph has been superseded by the thirteenth amendment.
†Obsolete.

out its Consent, shall be deprived of its equal Suffrage in the Senate.

ARTICLE VI

[1] All Debts contracted and Engagements entered into, before the Adoption of this Constitution, shall be as valid against the United States under this Constitution, as under the Confederation.

[2] This Constitution, and the Laws of the United States which shall be made in Pursuance thereof; and all Treaties made, or which shall be made, under the Authority of the United States, shall be the supreme Law of the Land; and the Judges in every State shall be bound thereby, any Thing in the Constitution or Laws of any State to the Contrary notwithstanding.

[3] The Senators and Representatives before mentioned, and the Members of the several State Legislatures, and all executive and judicial Officers, both of the United States and of the several States, shall be bound by Oath or Affirmation, to support this Constitution; but no religious Test shall ever be required as a Qualification to any Office or public Trust under the United States.

ARTICLE VII

The Ratification of the Conventions of nine States, shall be sufficient for the Establishment of this Constitution between the States so ratifying the Same.

DONE in Convention by the Unanimous Consent of the States present the Seventeenth Day of September in the Year of our Lord one thousand seven hundred and Eighty seven and of the Independence of the United States of America the Twelfth, IN WITNESS whereof We have hereunto subscribed our Names.

GEORGE WASHINGTON,
President and deputy from Virginia

[Signed also by the deputies of twelve States:]

New Hampshire. John Langdon, Nicholas Gilman

Massachusetts. Nathaniel Gorham, Rufus King

Connecticut. Wm Saml Johnson, Roger Sherman

New York. Alexander Hamilton

New Jersey. Wil. Livingston, David Brearley, Wm Paterson, Jona. Dayton

Pennsylvania. B. Franklin, Robt Morris, Thos FitzSimons, James Wilson, Thomas Mifflin, Geo. Clymer, Jared Ingersoll, Gouv Morris

Delaware. Geo. Read, John Dickinson, Jaco. Broom, Gunning Bedford, jun., Richard Bassett

Maryland. James McHenry, Danl Carroll, Dan of St Thos Jenifer

Virginia. John Blair, James Madison Jr

North Carolina. Wm Blount, Hu Williamson, Rich'd Dobbs Spaight

South Carolina. J. Rutledge, Charles Pinckney, Charles Cotesworth Pinckney, Pierce Butler

Georgia. William Few, Abr Baldwin

Attest: William Jackson, *Secretary*

RATIFICATION OF THE CONSTITUTION

The Constitution was adopted by a convention of the States on 17 September 1787, and was subsequently ratified by the several States, on the following dates: Delaware, 7 December 1787; Pennsylvania, 12 December 1787; New Jersey, 18 December 1787; Georgia, 2 January 1788; Connecticut, 9 January 1788; Massachusetts, 6 February 1788; Maryland, 28 April 1788; South Carolina, 23 May 1788; New Hampshire, 21 June 1788.

Ratification was completed on 21 June 1788.

The Constitution was subsequently ratified by Virginia, 25 June 1788; New York, 26 July 1788; North Carolina, 21 November 1789; Rhode Island, 29 May 1790; and Vermont, 10 January 1791.

ARTICLES IN ADDITION TO, AND IN AMENDMENT OF, THE CONSTITUTION OF THE UNITED STATES OF AMERICA, PROPOSED BY CONGRESS, AND RATIFIED BY THE LEGISLATURES OF THE SEVERAL STATES PURSUANT TO THE FIFTH ARTICLE OF THE ORIGINAL CONSTITUTION

ARTICLE [I]*[1]

Congress shall make no law respecting an establishment of religion, or prohibiting the free exercise thereof; or abridging the freedom of speech, or of the press; or the right of the people peaceably to assemble, and to petition the Government for a redress of grievances.

ARTICLE [II]

A well regulated Militia, being necessary to the security of a free State, the right of the people to keep and bear Arms, shall not be infringed.

ARTICLE [III]

No Soldier shall, in time of peace be quartered in any house, without the consent of the Owner, nor in time of war, but in a manner to be prescribed by law.

---

*Only the 13th, 14th, 15th and 16th articles of amendment had numbers assigned to them at the time of ratification.

1. The first ten amendments were duly ratified, thus becoming effective in 1791.

ARTICLE [IV]

The right of the people to be secure in their persons, houses, papers, and effects, against unreasonable searches and seizures, shall not be violated, and no Warrants shall issue, but upon probable cause, supported by Oath or affirmation, and particularly describing the place to be searched, and the persons or things to be seized.

ARTICLE [V]

No person shall be held to answer for a capital, or otherwise infamous crime, unless on a presentment or indictment of a Grand Jury, except in cases arising in the land or naval forces, or in the Militia, when in actual service in time of War or public danger; nor shall any person be subject for the same offence to be twice put in jeopardy of life or limb; nor shall be compelled in any criminal case to be a witness against himself, nor be deprived of life, liberty, or property, without due process of law; nor shall private property be taken for public use without just compensation.

ARTICLE [VI]

In all criminal prosecutions, the accused shall enjoy the right to a speedy and public trial, by an impartial jury of the State and district wherein the crime shall have been committed, which district shall have been previously ascertained by law, and to be informed of the nature and cause of the accusation; to be confronted with the witnesses against him; to have compulsory process for obtaining Witnesses in his favor, and to have the assistance of counsel for his defence.

ARTICLE [VII]

In Suits at common law, where the value in controversy shall exceed twenty dollars, the right of trial by jury shall be preserved, and no fact tried by a jury, shall be otherwise reexamined in any

Court of the United States, than according to the rules of the common law.

ARTICLE [VIII]

Excessive bail shall not be required, nor excessive fines imposed, nor cruel and unusual punishments inflicted.

ARTICLE [IX]

The enumeration in the Constitution, of certain rights, shall not be construed to deny or disparage others retained by the people.

ARTICLE [X]

The powers not delegated to the United States by the Constitution, nor prohibited by it to the States, are reserved to the States respectively, or to the people.

ARTICLE [XI][1]

The Judicial power of the United States shall not be construed to extend to any suit in law or equity, commenced or prosecuted against one of the United States by Citizens of another State, or by Citizens or Subjects of any Foreign State.

ARTICLE [XII][2]

The electors shall meet in their respective states and vote by ballot for President and Vice-President, one of whom, at least, shall not be an inhabitant of the same state with themselves; they shall name in their ballots the person voted for as President, and in distinct ballots the person voted for as Vice-President, and they shall make distinct lists of all persons voted for as President, and of all persons voted for as Vice-President, and of the number of votes for each, which lists they shall sign and certify, and transmit

1. 1795.
2. 1804.

sealed to the seat of the government of the United States, directed
to the President of the Senate; – The President of the Senate shall,
in the presence of the Senate and House of Representatives, open
all the certificates and the votes shall then be counted; – The
person having the greatest number of votes for President, shall be
the President, if such number be a majority of the whole number
of Electors appointed; and if no person have such majority, then
from the persons having the highest numbers not exceeding three
on the list of those voted for as President, the House of Representatives shall choose immediately, by ballot, the President. But
in choosing the President, the votes shall be taken by states, the
representation from each state having one vote; a quorum for
this purpose shall consist of a member or members from two-
thirds of the states, and a majority of all the states shall be necessary to a choice. [And if the House of Representatives shall not
choose a President whenever the right of choice shall devolve
upon them, before the fourth day of March next following, then
the Vice-President shall act as President, as in the case of the
death or other constitutional disability of the President.]* The
person having the greatest number of votes as Vice-President,
shall be the Vice-President, if such number be a majority of the
whole number of Electors appointed, and if no person have a
majority, then from the two highest numbers on the list, the
Senate shall choose the Vice-President; a quorum for the purpose
shall consist of two-thirds of the whole number of Senators, and
a majority of the whole number shall be necessary to a choice.
But no person constitutionally ineligible to the office of President
shall be eligible to that of Vice-President of the United States.

ARTICLE XIII[1]

Section 1. Neither slavery nor involuntary servitude, except as
a punishment for crime whereof the party shall have been duly
convicted, shall exist within the United States, or any place subject to their jurisdiction.

*The part included in square brackets has been superseded by section 3
of the twentieth amendment.
1. 1865.

Section 2. Congress shall have power to enforce this article by appropriate legislation.

ARTICLE XIV[1]

Section 1. All persons born or naturalized in the United States, and subject to the jurisdiction thereof, are citizens of the United States and of the State wherein they reside. No State shall make or enforce any law which shall abridge the privileges or immunities of citizens of the United States; nor shall any State deprive any person of life, liberty, or property, without due process of law; nor deny to any person within its jurisdiction the equal protection of the laws.

Section 2. Representatives shall be apportioned among the several States according to their respective numbers, counting the whole number of persons in each State, excluding Indians not taxed. But when the right to vote at any election for the choice of electors for President and Vice-President of the United States, Representatives in Congress, the Executive and Judicial officers of a State, or the members of the Legislature thereof, is denied to any of the male inhabitants of such State, being twenty-one years of age, and citizens of the United States, or in any way abridged, except for participation in rebellion, or other crime, the basis of representation therein shall be reduced in the proportion which the number of such male citizens shall bear to the whole number of male citizens twenty-one years of age in such State.

Section 3. No person shall be a Senator or Representative in Congress, or elector of President and Vice-President, or hold any office, civil or military, under the United States, or under any State, who, having previously taken an oath, as a member of Congress, or as an officer of the United States, or as a member of any State legislature, or as an executive or judicial officer of any State, to support the Constitution of the United States, shall have engaged in insurrection or rebellion against the same, or given aid or comfort to the enemies thereof. But Congress may by a vote of two-thirds of each House, remove such disability.

Section 4. The validity of the public debt of the United States,

1. 1868.

authorized by law, including debts incurred for payment of pensions and bounties for services in suppressing insurrection or rebellion, shall not be questioned. But neither the United States nor any State shall assume or pay any debt or obligation incurred in aid of insurrection or rebellion against the United States, or any claim for the loss or emancipation of any slave; but all such debts, obligations and claims shall be held illegal and void.

Section 5. The Congress shall have power to enforce, by appropriate legislation, the provisions of this article.

ARTICLE XV[1]

Section 1. The right of citizens of the United States to vote shall not be denied or abridged by the United States or by any State on account of race, color, or previous condition of servitude.

Section 2. The Congress shall have power to enforce this article by appropriate legislation.

ARTICLE XVI[2]

The Congress shall have power to lay and collect taxes on incomes, from whatever source derived, without apportionment among the several States, and without regard to any census or enumeration.

ARTICLE [XVII][3]

The Senate of the United States shall be composed of two Senators from each State, elected by the people thereof, for six years; and each Senator shall have one vote. The electors in each State shall have the qualifications requisite for electors of the most numerous branch of the State legislatures.

When vacancies happen in the representation of any State in the Senate, the executive authority of such State shall issue writs of election to fill such vacancies: *Provided,* That the legislature of

1. 1870.
2. 1913.
3. 1913.

any State may empower the executive thereof to make temporary appointments until the people fill the vacancies by election as the legislature may direct.

This amendment shall not be so construed as to affect the election or term of any Senator chosen before it becomes valid as part of the Constitution.

ARTICLE [XVIII][1]

[Section 1. After one year from the ratification of this article the manufacture, sale, or transportation of intoxicating liquors within, the importation thereof into, or the exportation thereof from the United States and all territory subject to the jurisdiction thereof for beverage purposes is hereby prohibited.

[Section 2. The Congress and the several States shall have concurrent power to enforce this article by appropriate legislation.

[Section 3. This article shall be inoperative unless it shall have been ratified as an amendment to the Constitution by the legislatures of the several States, as provided in the Constitution, within seven years from the date of the submission hereof to the States by the Congress.]*

ARTICLE [XIX][2]

The right of citizens of the United States to vote shall not be denied or abridged by the United States or by any State on account of sex.

Congress shall have power to enforce this article by appropriate legislation.

ARTICLE [XX][3]

Section 1. The terms of the President and Vice-President shall end at noon on the 20th day of January, and the terms of Senators

*Repealed by section 1 of the twenty-first amendment.
1. 1919.
2. 1919.
3. 1933.

and Representatives at noon on the 3d day of January, of the years in which such terms would have ended if this article had not been ratified; and the terms of their successors shall then begin.

Section 2. The Congress shall assemble at least once in every year, and such meetings shall begin at noon on the 3d day of January, unless they shall by law appoint a different day.

Section 3.* If, at the time fixed for the beginning of the term of the President, the President elect shall have died, the Vice-President elect shall become President. If a President shall not have been chosen before the time fixed for the beginning of his term, or if the President elect shall have failed to qualify, then the Vice-President elect shall act as President until a President shall have qualified; and the Congress may by law provide for the case wherein neither a President elect nor a Vice-President elect shall have qualified, declaring who shall then act as President, or the manner in which one who is to act shall be selected, and such person shall act accordingly until a President or Vice-President shall have qualified.

Section 4. The Congress may by law provide for the case of the death of any of the persons from whom the House of Representatives may choose a President whenever the right of choice shall have devolved upon them, and for the case of the death of any of the persons from whom the Senate may choose a Vice-President whenever the right of choice shall have devolved upon them.

Section 5. Sections 1 and 2 shall take effect on the 15th day of October following the ratification of this article.

Section 6. This article shall be inoperative unless it shall have been ratified as an amendment to the Constitution by the legislatures of three-fourths of the several States within seven years from the date of its submission.

ARTICLE [XXI][1]

Section 1. The eighteenth article of amendment to the Constitution of the United States is hereby repealed.

Section 2. The transportation or importation into any State,

*See, the twenty-fifth amendment.
1. 1933.

Territory, or possession of the United States for delivery or use therein of intoxicating liquors, in violation of the laws thereof, is hereby prohibited.

Section 3. This article shall be inoperative unless it shall have been ratified as an amendment to the Constitution by conventions in the several States, as provided in the Constitution, within seven years from the date of the submission hereof to the States by the Congress.

ARTICLE [XXII][1]

Section 1. No person shall be elected to the office of the President more than twice, and no person who has held the office of President, or acted as President, for more than two years of a term to which some other person was elected President shall be elected to the office of the President more than once. But this Article shall not apply to any person holding the office of President when this Article was proposed by the Congress, and shall not prevent any person who may be holding the office of President, or acting as President, during the term within which this Article becomes operative from holding the office of President or acting as President during the remainder of such term.

Section 2. This article shall be inoperative unless it shall have been ratified as an amendment to the Constitution by the legislatures of three-fourths of the several States within seven years from the date of its submission to the States by the Congress.

ARTICLE [XXIII][2]

Section 1. The District constituting the seat of Government of the United States shall appoint in such manner as the Congress may direct:

A number of electors of President and Vice-President equal to the whole number of Senators and Representatives in Congress to which the District would be entitled if it were a State, but in no event more than the least populous State; they shall be in addition

1. 1951.
2. 1960.

113

to those appointed by the States, but they shall be considered, for the purposes of the election of President and Vice-President, to be electors appointed by a State; and they shall meet in the District and perform such duties as provided by the twelfth article of amendment.

Section 2. The Congress shall have power to enforce this article by appropriate legislation.

ARTICLE [XXIV][1]

Section 1. The right of citizens of the United States to vote in any primary or other election for President or Vice-President, for electors for President or Vice-President, or for Senator or Representative in Congress, shall not be denied or abridged by the United States or any State by reason of failure to pay any poll tax or other tax.

Section 2. The Congress shall have power to enforce this article by appropriate legislation.

ARTICLE [XXV][2]

Section 1. In case of the removal of the President from office or of his death or resignation, the Vice-President shall become President.

Section 2. Whenever there is a vacancy in the office of the Vice-President, the President shall nominate a Vice-President who shall take office upon confirmation by a majority vote of both Houses of Congress.

Section 3. Whenever the President transmits to the President pro tempore of the Senate and the Speaker of the House of Representatives his written declaration that he is unable to discharge the powers and duties of his office, and until he transmits to them a written declaration to the contrary, such powers and duties shall be discharged by the Vice-President as Acting President.

Section 4. Whenever the Vice-President and a majority of either

1. 1964.
2. 1967.

the principal officers of the executive departments or of such other body as Congress may by law provide, transmit to the President pro tempore of the Senate and the Speaker of the House of Representatives their written declaration that the President is unable to discharge the powers and duties of his office, the Vice-President shall immediately assume the powers and duties of the office as Acting President.

Thereafter, when the President transmits to the President pro tempore of the Senate and the Speaker of the House of Representatives his written declaration that no inability exists, he shall resume the powers and duties of his office unless the Vice-President and a majority of either the principal officers of the executive department or of such other body as Congress may by law provide, transmit within four days to the President pro tempore of the Senate and the Speaker of the House of Representatives their written declaration that the President is unable to discharge the powers and duties of his office. Thereupon Congress shall decide the issue, assembling within forty-eight hours for that purpose if not in session. If the Congress, within twenty-one days after receipt of the latter written declaration, or, if Congress is not in session, within twenty-one days after Congress is required to assemble, determines by two-thirds vote of both Houses that the President is unable to discharge the powers and duties of his office, the Vice-President shall continue to discharge the same as Acting President; otherwise, the President shall resume the powers and duties of his office.

ARTICLE [XXVI][1]

Section 1. The right of citizens of the United States, who are eighteen years of age or older, to vote shall not be denied or abridged by the United States or by any State on account of age.

Section 2. The Congress shall have power to enforce this article by appropriate legislation.

1. 1971.

The Constitution (Fundamental Law) of the

UNION OF
SOVIET SOCIALIST
REPUBLICS
1936

CONTENTS

CHAPTER I. THE SOCIAL STRUCTURE

Article 1. The Union of Soviet Socialist Republics shall be a socialist state of workers and peasants.

Article 2. The Soviets of Working People's Deputies, which arose and developed as a result of the overthrow of the landowners and capitalists and of the attainment of the dictatorship of the proletariat, shall constitute the political foundation of the USSR.

Article 3. All power in the USSR shall be vested in the working people of town and country as represented by the Soviets of Working People's Deputies.

Article 4. The socialist economic system and socialist property in the instruments and means of production, firmly established as a result of the abolition of the capitalist economic system, private ownership of the instruments and means of production, and the exploitation of man by man, shall constitute the economic foundation of the USSR.

Article 5. Socialist property in the USSR shall exist either as state property (belonging to the whole people) or as cooperative and collective-farm property (belonging to collective farms or cooperative societies).

Article 6. State property, that is property belonging to the whole people, shall comprise the land, its mineral wealth, waters, forests, the factories, mills, mines, railways, water and air transport, the banks, means of communication, large state-run agricultural enterprises (state farms, machine-and-tractor stations, etc.), municipal institutions and the bulk of urban housing.

Article 7. The common, socialist property of the collective farms and cooperative organizations shall comprise the communal enterprises of collective farms and cooperative organizations with their livestock and implements, the output of the collective farms and cooperative organizations, as well as their communal buildings.

In addition to its basic income from communal farming, every collective-farm household shall have a small plot of land attached to the house for its own use and, as its personal property, a subsidiary husbandry – a house, livestock, poultry and minor agricultural implements – in conformity with the rules of the agricultural artel.

Article 8. The land occupied by collective farms shall be allocated to them for their free use for an unlimited time, that is for ever.

Article 9. In addition to the socialist economic system, which is the predominant economic form in the USSR, the law shall permit small private undertakings of individual peasants and handicraftsmen, based on their own labour and precluding the exploitation of the labour of others.

Article 10. The law shall protect the right of citizens to have personal property in the form of earned income and savings, a house and a house-and-garden plot, articles of household and personal use and convenience, and also the right of citizens to inherit personal property.

Article 11. The state economic plan shall determine and guide the economic affairs of the USSR for the purpose of increasing the wealth of society, steadily raising the material and cultural standards of the working people, and strengthening the independence of the USSR and its defence potential.

Article 12. It shall be the duty and honour of every able-bodied citizen in the USSR to work according to the principle 'he who would not work, neither shall he eat'.

The USSR shall apply the socialist principle of 'from each according to his ability, to each according to his work'.

CHAPTER II. THE STATE STRUCTURE

Article 13. The Union of Soviet Socialist Republics shall be a federal state, formed on the basis of a voluntary union of the following Soviet Socialist Republics enjoying equal rights:

Russian Soviet Federative Socialist Republic,

Ukrainian Soviet Socialist Republic,

Byelorussian Soviet Socialist Republic,

Uzbek Soviet Socialist Republic,
Kazakh Soviet Socialist Republic,
Georgian Soviet Socialist Republic,
Azerbaijan Soviet Socialist Republic,
Lithuanian Soviet Socialist Republic,
Moldavian Soviet Socialist Republic,
Latvian Soviet Socialist Republic,
Kirghiz Soviet Socialist Republic,
Tajik Soviet Socialist Republic,
Armenian Soviet Socialist Republic,
Turkmen Soviet Socialist Republic,
Estonian Soviet Socialist Republic.

Article 14. The jurisdiction of the Union of Soviet Socialist Republics, as represented by its higher organs of state power and organs of state administration, shall extend to:

(i) Representation of the USSR in international relations, conclusion, ratification and denunciation of treaties of the USSR with other states, establishment of general procedure governing the relations of the Union Republics with foreign states;

(ii) Issues of war and peace;

(iii) Admission of new Republics into the USSR;

(iv) Control over the observance of the Constitution of the USSR, and ensuring conformity of the Constitutions of the Union Republics with the Constitution of the USSR;

(v) Approval of changes to boundaries between the Union Republics;

(vi) Approval of the formation of new Autonomous Republics and Autonomous Regions within Union Republics;

(vii) Organization of the defence of the USSR, direction of its Armed Forces, formulation of principles guiding the organization of the military formations of the Union Republics;

(viii) Foreign trade on the basis of state monopoly;

(ix) State security;

(x) Approval of the economic plans of the USSR;

(xi) Approval of the consolidated state budget of the USSR and of the report on its execution, determination of taxes and other revenues that go to the Union, Republican and local budgets;

(xii) Administration of the banks and industrial, agricultural and trading enterprises and institutions under Union jurisdiction; general direction of industry and construction under Union-Republican jurisdiction;

(xiii) Administration of transport and communications of all-Union importance;

(xiv) Direction of the monetary and credit system;

(xv) Organization of state insurance;

(xvi) Contracting and granting of loans;

(xvii) Definition of the basic principles of land tenure and of the use of mineral wealth, forests and waters;

(xviii) Definition of the basic principles of public education and health protection;

(xix) Organization of a uniform system of national economic statistics;

(xx) Definition of the fundamentals of labour legislation;

(xxi) Definition of the fundamentals of legislation on the judicial system and judicial procedure and the fundamentals of civil, criminal and corrective labour legislation;

(xxii) Legislation on Union citizenship; legislation on rights of foreign nationals;

(xxiii) Definition of the fundamentals of legislation on marriage and the family;

(xxiv) Promulgation of all-Union acts of amnesty.

Article 15. The sovereignty of the Union Republics shall be limited only in the spheres defined in Article 14 of the Constitution of the USSR. Outside of these spheres each Union Republic shall exercise state authority independently. The USSR shall protect the sovereign powers of the Union Republics.

Article 16. Every Union Republic shall have its own Constitution with due account for the specific features of the Republic and drawn up in full conformity with the Constitution of the USSR.

Article 17. Every Union Republic shall have the right freely to secede from the USSR.

Article 18. The territory of a Union Republic may not be altered without its consent.

Article 18a. Every Union Republic shall have the right to enter into direct relations with foreign states and to conclude agreements and exchange diplomatic and consular representatives with them.

Article 18b. Every Union Republic shall have its own republican military formations.

Article 19. The laws of the USSR shall have the same force within the territory of every Union Republic.

Article 20. In the event of any discrepancy between a law of a Union Republic and a law of the Union, the Union law shall prevail.

Article 21. Uniform citizenship shall be established for the citizens of the USSR.

Every citizen of a Union Republic shall be a citizen of the USSR.

Article 22. The Russian Soviet Federative Socialist Republic shall include the Bashkirian, Buryat, Checheno-Ingush, Chuvash, Daghestan, Kabardinian-Balkar, Kalmyk, Karelian, Komi, Mari, Mordovian, North Ossetian, Tatar, Tuva, Udmurt and Yakut Autonomous Soviet Socialist Republics; and the Adygei, Gorno-Altai, Jewish, Karachai-Circassian and Khakass Autonomous Regions.

Article 23. Repealed.

Article 24. The Azerbaijan Soviet Socialist Republic shall include the Nakhichevan Autonomous Soviet Socialist Republic and the Nagorno-Karabakh Autonomous Region.

Article 25. The Georgian Soviet Socialist Republic shall include the Abkhazian and Ajarian Autonomous Soviet Socialist Republics and the South Ossetian Autonomous Region.

Article 26. The Uzbek Soviet Socialist Republic shall include the Karakalpak Autonomous Soviet Socialist Republic.

Article 27. The Tajik Soviet Socialist Republic shall include the Gorno-Badakhshan Autonomous Region.

Article 28. The settlement of questions pertaining to the administrative division of the Union Republics into regions and territories shall come within the jurisdiction of the Union Republics.

Article 29. Repealed.

CHAPTER III. HIGHER ORGANS OF STATE POWER IN THE UNION OF SOVIET SOCIALIST REPUBLICS

Article 30. The USSR Supreme Soviet shall be the highest organ of state power in the USSR.

Article 31. The USSR Supreme Soviet shall exercise all rights vested in the Union of Soviet Socialist Republics in accordance with Article 14 of the Constitution, in so far as they do not, by virtue of the Constitution, come within the jurisdiction of the USSR organs which are accountable to the USSR Supreme Soviet, e.g. the Presidium of the USSR Supreme Soviet, the USSR Council of Ministers and the USSR Ministries.

Article 32. The legislative power of the USSR shall be exercised exclusively by the USSR Supreme Soviet.

Article 33. The USSR Supreme Soviet shall consist of two chambers: the Soviet of the Union and the Soviet of Nationalities.

Article 34. The Soviet of the Union shall be elected by USSR citizens voting by constituencies on the basis of one deputy for every 300,000 peoples.

Article 35. The Soviet of Nationalities shall be elected by USSR citizens voting by Union Republics, Autonomous Republics, Autonomous Regions, and National Areas on the basis of 32 deputies from each Union Republic, 11 deputies from each Autonomous Republic, 5 deputies from each Autonomous Region, and one deputy from each National Area.

Article 36. The USSR Supreme Soviet shall be elected for a term of four years.

Article 37. The two chambers of the USSR Supreme Soviet, the Soviet of the Union and the Soviet of Nationalities, shall have equal rights.

Article 38. The Soviet of the Union and the Soviet of Nationalities shall have equal powers to initiate legislation.

Article 39. A law shall be deemed enacted if passed by both chambers of the USSR Supreme Soviet by a simple majority vote in each.

Article 40. Laws passed by the USSR Supreme Soviet shall be published in the languages of the Union Republics over the signatures of the President and Secretary of the Presidium of the USSR Supreme Soviet.

Article 41. Sessions of the Soviet of the Union and of the Soviet of Nationalities shall begin and terminate simultaneously.

Article 42. The Soviet of the Union shall elect a Chairman of the Soviet of the Union and four Vice-Chairmen.

Article 43. The Soviet of Nationalities shall elect a Chairman of the Soviet of Nationalities and four Vice-Chairmen.

Article 44. The Chairmen of the Soviet of the Union and the Soviet of Nationalities shall preside over sittings of the respective chambers and have charge of the conduct of their business and proceedings.

Article 45. Joint sittings of the two chambers of the USSR Supreme Soviet shall be presided over alternately by the Chairman of the Soviet of the Union and the Chairman of the Soviet of Nationalities.

Article 46. Sessions of the USSR Supreme Soviet shall be convened by the Presidium of the USSR Supreme Soviet twice a year.

Extraordinary sessions shall be convened by the Presidium of the USSR Supreme Soviet at its discretion or at the bidding of one of the Union Republics.

Article 47. In the event of disagreement between the Soviet of the Union and the Soviet of Nationalities, the question at issue shall be referred for settlement to a conciliation commission formed by the chambers on a parity basis. If the conciliation commission fails to arrive at an agreement or if its decision fails to satisfy one of the chambers, the question is considered for a second time by the chambers. Failing agreement between the two chambers, the Presidium of the USSR Supreme Soviet shall dissolve the USSR Supreme Soviet and appoint new elections.

Article 48. The USSR Supreme Soviet at a joint sitting of the two chambers shall elect the Presidium of the USSR Supreme Soviet, consisting of the Presidium President of the USSR

Supreme Soviet, fifteen Vice-Presidents – one representing each Union Republic, the Presidium Secretary and twenty Presidium members.

The Presidium of the USSR Supreme Soviet shall be accountable to the USSR Supreme Soviet in all its activities.

Article 49. The Presidium of the USSR Supreme Soviet shall:

(i) Convene sessions of the USSR Supreme Soviet;

(ii) Issue ordinances;

(iii) Interpret the laws of the USSR in operation;

(iv) Dissolve the USSR Supreme Soviet in conformity with Article 47 of the USSR Constitution and appoint new elections;

(v) Conduct nation-wide polls (referendums) on its initiative or at the bidding of one of the Union Republics;

(vi) Revoke decisions and orders of the USSR Council of Ministers and of the Councils of Ministers of the Union Republics where they do not conform to the law;

(vii) Release or appoint USSR Ministers in the recesses of the USSR Supreme Soviet, on the recommendation of the Chairman of the USSR Council of Ministers, subject to confirmation by the USSR Supreme Soviet;

(viii) Institute decorations (Orders and Medals) and titles of honour of the USSR;

(ix) Award Orders and Medals and confer titles of honour of the USSR;

(x) Exercise the right of pardon;

(xi) Institute military titles, diplomatic ranks and other special titles;

(xii) Appoint and remove the supreme command of the Armed Forces of the USSR;

(xiii) In the recesses of the USSR Supreme Soviet, proclaim a state of war in the event of an armed attack on the USSR, or where necessary to fulfil international treaty obligations providing for mutual defence against aggression;

(xiv) Order general or partial mobilization;

(xv) Ratify and denounce USSR international treaties;

(xvi) Appoint or recall plenipotentiary representatives of the USSR to foreign states;

(xvii) Receive the letters of credence and recall of diplomatic representatives accredited to it by foreign states;

(xviii) Proclaim martial law in separate localities or throughout the USSR in the interest of its defence or of the maintenance of public order and state security.

Article 50. The Soviet of the Union and the Soviet of Nationalities shall elect Credentials Committees which shall verify the credentials of the members of the respective chambers.

On the strength of the Credentials Committees' reports, the chambers shall decide whether to recognize the credentials of deputies or to declare their election void.

Article 51. The USSR Supreme Soviet shall appoint investigation and audit commissions on any matter, when it so chooses.

It shall be the duty of all institutions and officials to comply with the demands of these commissions and to submit to them all the necessary materials and documents.

Article 52. A member of the USSR Supreme Soviet may not be prosecuted or arrested without the authorization of the USSR Supreme Soviet, or, when the USSR Supreme Soviet is not in session, without the authorization of the Presidium of the USSR Supreme Soviet.

Article 53. On the expiry of the term of the USSR Supreme Soviet, or on its dissolution prior to the expiry of its term, the Presidium of the USSR Supreme Soviet shall retain its powers until the newly elected USSR Supreme Soviet has formed a new Presidium.

Article 54. On the expiry of the term of the USSR Supreme Soviet, or in the event of its dissolution prior to the expiry of its term, the Presidium of the USSR Supreme Soviet shall appoint new elections to be held within a period not exceeding two months from the date of expiry or dissolution.

Article 55. The newly elected USSR Supreme Soviet shall be convened by the outgoing Presidium of the USSR Supreme Soviet not later than three months after the elections.

Article 56. The USSR Supreme Soviet, at a joint sitting of the two chambers, shall form the Government of the USSR, namely the Council of Ministers of the USSR.

CHAPTER IV. HIGHER ORGANS OF STATE POWER IN THE UNION REPUBLICS

Article 57. The Supreme Soviet of a Union Republic shall be the highest organ of state power in the Union Republic.

Article 58. The Supreme Soviet of a Union Republic shall be elected for a term of four years by the citizens of the Union Republic.

The rate of representation shall be established by the Constitution of the Union Republic.

Article 59. The Supreme Soviet of a Union Republic shall be the sole legislative organ of the Republic.

Article 60. The Supreme Soviet of a Union Republic shall:

(i) Adopt the Constitution of the Republic and amend it in conformity with Article 16 of the USSR Constitution;

(ii) Confirm the Constitutions of the Autonomous Republics forming part of it and define the boundaries of their territory;

(iii) Approve the economic plan and the budget of the Republic;

(iv) Exercise the right of amnesty and pardon of citizens sentenced by the judicial bodies of the Union Republic;

(v) Decide upon the representation of the Union Republic in international relations;

(vi) Determine the organization of the Republic's military formations.

Article 61. The Supreme Soviet of a Union Republic shall elect the Presidium of the Supreme Soviet of the Union Republic, which shall consist of the Presidium President of the Supreme Soviet, Vice-Presidents, the Presidium Secretary and Presidium members.

The Power of the Presidium of the Supreme Soviet of a Union Republic shall be defined by the Constitution of the Union Republic.

Article 62. The Supreme Soviet of a Union Republic shall elect a Chairman and Vice-Chairman to conduct its sittings.

Article 63. The Supreme Soviet of a Union Republic shall form the Government of the Union Republic, namely, the Council of Ministers of the Union Republic.

CHAPTER V. ORGANS OF STATE ADMINISTRATION IN THE UNION OF SOVIET SOCIALIST REPUBLICS

Article 64. The USSR Council of Ministers shall be the highest executive and administrative organ of state power in the Union of Soviet Socialist Republics.

Article 65. The USSR Council of Ministers shall be responsible and accountable to the USSR Supreme Soviet, or, in the recesses of the Supreme Soviet, it shall be accountable to the Presidium of the USSR Supreme Soviet.

Article 66. The USSR Council of Ministers shall issue decisions and orders on the basis and in pursuance of the laws in operation and shall verify their execution.

Article 67. Decisions and orders of the USSR Council of Ministers shall be binding throughout the territory of the USSR.

Article 68. The USSR Council of Ministers shall:

(i) Coordinate and direct the work of the all-Union and Union-Republican Ministries of the USSR, the State Committees of the USSR Council of Ministers and of other bodies under its jurisdiction;

(ii) Adopt measures to fulfil the national economic plan, execute the state budget, and strengthen the credit and monetary system;

(iii) Adopt measures to maintain public order, protect state interests and safeguard the rights of citizens;

(iv) Exercise general guidance in the sphere of relations with foreign states;

(v) Fix the annual contingent of citizens to be called up for active military service and direct the general organization of the Armed Forces of the country;

(vi) Set up State Committees of the USSR and, where necessary, special Committees and Central Boards under the USSR Council of Ministers for economic and cultural affairs and defence.

Article 69. The USSR Council of Ministers shall have the right in respect of those branches of administration and economy which come within the jurisdiction of the USSR, to suspend decisions and orders of the Councils of Ministers of the Union Republics and to revoke orders and instructions of the Ministers of the USSR and also statutory acts of other bodies under its jurisdiction.

Article 70. The USSR Council of Ministers shall be formed by the USSR Supreme Soviet and consist of:

Chairman of the USSR Council of Ministers;

First Vice-Chairmen of the USSR Council of Ministers;

Vice-Chairmen of the USSR Council of Ministers;

Ministers of the USSR;

Chairman of the State Planning Committee of the USSR Council of Ministers;

Chairman of the State Building Committee of the USSR Council of Ministers;

Chairman of the State Committee of the USSR Council of Ministers for Material and Technical Supply;

Chairman of the People's Control Committee of the USSR;

Chairman of the State Labour and Wages Committee of the USSR Council of Ministers;

Chairman of the State Committee of the USSR Council of Ministers for Science and Technology;

Chairman of the State Committee of the USSR Council of Ministers for Inventions and Discoveries;

Chairman of the State Price Committee of the USSR Council of Ministers;

Chairman of the State Standards Committee of the USSR Council of Ministers;

Chairman of the State Committee of the USSR Council of Ministers for Vocational Training;

Chairman of the State Television and Radio Committee of the USSR Council of Ministers;

Chairman of the State Committee of the USSR Council of Ministers for Cinematography;

Chairman of the State Committee of the USSR Council of Ministers for the Publishing, Printing and Sale of Books;

Chairman of the State Forestry Committee of the USSR Council of Ministers;

Chairman of the State Foreign Economic Relations Committee of the USSR Council of Ministers;

Chairman of the State Security Committee under the USSR Council of Ministers;

Chairman of the All-Union Board of the USSR Council of Ministers for the Supply of Farm Machinery, Fuel and Fertilizers;

Chairman of the Administrative Board of the USSR State Bank;

Chief of the Central Statistical Board under the USSR Council of Ministers;

The USSR Council of Ministers shall include the Chairmen of the Councils of Ministers of the Union Republics by virtue of their office.

Article 71. The USSR Government or a Minister of the USSR who receives a question from a member of the USSR Supreme Soviet, shall give a verbal or written reply on the floor of the respective chamber within no more than three days.

Article 72. Ministers of the USSR shall direct the state administrative sectors which come within the jurisdiction of the USSR.

Article 73. Within the terms of reference of their respective Ministries, the Ministers of the USSR shall issue orders and instructions on the basis and in pursuance of the laws in operation, and also of decisions and orders of the USSR Council of Ministers, and shall verify their execution.

Article 74. USSR Ministries shall be either all-Union or Union-Republican.

Article 75. The all-Union Ministries shall direct the state administrative sectors entrusted to them throughout the territory of the USSR either directly or through bodies appointed by them.

Article 76. The Union-Republican Ministries shall direct the state administrative sectors entrusted to them chiefly through the relevant Ministries of the Union Republics and shall administer directly only a certain limited number of enterprises according to a list approved by the Presidium of the USSR Supreme Soviet.

Article 77. The following Ministries shall be all-Union Ministries:

Ministry of: Aircraft Industry; Automobile Industry; Building,

Road and Communal Machinery; Chemical and Oil Machine-Building; Chemical Industry; Civil Aviation; Construction of Oil and Gas Enterprises; Defence Industry; Electronic Industry; Electrotechnical Industry; Engineering; Foreign Trade; Gas Industry; General Engineering; Heavy and Transport Engineering; Instrument-Making, Means of Automation and Control Systems; Machine-Building for Animal Husbandry and Fodder Production; Machine-Building for Light and Food Industries and Household Appliances; Machine-Tool and Tool-Making Industry; Manufacture of Means of Communications; Medical Industry; Medium Machine-Building; Merchant Marine; Oil Industry; Power Engineering; Pulp and Paper Industry; Radio Industry; Railways; Shipbuilding; Tractor and Agricultural Machine-Building; Transport Building.

Article 78. The following Ministries shall be Union-Republican Ministries:

Ministry of: Agriculture; Building; Building Materials; Coal Industry; Communications; Culture; Defence; Education; Ferrous Metallurgy; Finance; Fisheries; the Food Industry; Foreign Affairs; Geological Surveys; Health; Heavy Industry Building; Higher and Specialized Secondary Education; Industrial Building; Justice; Land-Improvement and Water Conservancy; Light Industry; Meat and Dairy Produce; Assembly and Specialized Building; Non-Ferrous Metallurgy; Oil Refining and Petrochemical Industry; Power and Electrification; Rural Construction; State Purchases; the Interior; Timber and Woodworking Industry; Trade.

CHAPTER VI. ORGANS OF STATE ADMINISTRATION IN THE UNION REPUBLICS

Article 79. The Council of Ministers of a Union Republic shall be the highest executive and administrative organ of state power in the Union Republic.

Article 80. The Council of Ministers of a Union Republic shall be responsible and accountable to the Supreme Soviet of the Union Republic, or, in recesses of the Republican Supreme Soviet, it shall be accountable to the Presidium of the Supreme Soviet of the Union Republic.

Article 81. The Council of Ministers of a Union Republic shall issue decisions and orders on the basis and in pursuance of the laws of the USSR and of the Union Republic, and of the decisions and orders of the USSR Council of Ministers, and shall verify their execution.

Article 82. The Council of Ministers of a Union Republic shall have the right to suspend decisions and orders of the Councils of Ministers of its Autonomous Republics, and to revoke decisions and orders of the Executive Committees of the Soviets of Working People's Deputies of its Territories, Regions and Autonomous Regions.

Article 83. The Council of Ministers of a Union Republic shall be formed by the Supreme Soviet of the Union Republic and consist of:

Chairman of the Council of Ministers of the Union Republic;

Vice-Chairmen of the Council of Ministers of the Union Republic;

Ministers;

Chairmen of State Committees, Commissions, and the heads of other departments of the Council of Ministers set up by the Supreme Soviet of the Union Republic, in conformity with the Constitution of the Union Republic.

Article 84. The Ministers of a Union Republic shall direct the state administrative sectors which come within the jurisdiction of the Union Republic.

Article 85. Within the terms of reference of their respective Ministries, the Ministers of a Union Republic shall issue orders and instructions on the basis and in pursuance of the laws of the USSR and of the Union Republic, of the decisions and orders of the USSR Council of Ministers and the Council of Ministers of the Union Republic, and of the orders and instructions of the Union-Republican Ministries of the USSR.

Article 86. The Ministries of a Union Republic shall be either Union-Republican or Republican.

Article 87. The Union-Republican Ministries shall direct the state administrative sectors entrusted to them, and shall be subordinate both to the Council of Ministers of the Union Republic and to the corresponding Union-Republican Ministry of the USSR.

Article 88. The Republican Ministries shall direct the state administrative sectors entrusted to them and shall be directly subordinate to the Council of Ministers of the Union Republic.

CHAPTER VII. HIGHER ORGANS OF STATE POWER IN THE AUTONOMOUS SOVIET SOCIALIST REPUBLICS

Article 89. The Supreme Soviet of an Autonomous Soviet Socialist Republic shall be the highest organ of state power in the Republic.

Article 90. The Supreme Soviet of an Autonomous Republic shall be elected by the citizens of the Republic for a term of four years on the basis of representation rates established by the Constitution of the Autonomous Republic.

Article 91. The Supreme Soviet of an Autonomous Republic shall be its sole legislature.

Article 92. Every Autonomous Republic shall have its own Constitution with due account for the specific features of the Autonomous Republic and drawn up in full conformity with the Constitution of the respective Union Republic.

Article 93. The Supreme Soviet of an Autonomous Republic shall elect the Presidium of its Supreme Soviet and shall form the Council of Ministers of the Autonomous Republic, in accordance with its Constitution.

CHAPTER VIII. LOCAL ORGANS OF STATE POWER

Article 94. Soviets of Working People's Deputies shall be the organs of state power in Territories, Regions, Autonomous Regions, National Areas, districts, towns and rural localities (stanitsas, villages, hamlets, kishlaks, auls).

Article 95. Soviets of Working People's Deputies of Territories, Regions, Autonomous Regions, National Areas, districts, towns and rural localities (stanitsas, villages, hamlets, kishlaks, auls) shall be elected for a term of two years by the working people of the respective Territories, Regions, Autonomous Regions, National Areas, districts, towns and rural localities.

Article 96. The rate of representation in Soviets of Working People's Deputies shall be determined by the Constitutions of the Union Republics.

Article 97. Soviets of Working People's Deputies shall guide the work of the organs of administration subordinate to them, ensure the maintenance of law and order, the observance of the laws, the protection of the rights of citizens, direct local economic and cultural affairs, draw up and approve local budgets.

Article 98. Soviets of Working People's Deputies shall adopt decisions and issue orders within the powers vested in them by the laws of the USSR and the Union Republic.

Article 99. The Executive Committees elected by Soviets of Working People's Deputies and consisting of a Chairman, Vice-Chairmen, a Secretary and members shall be executive and administrative organs of the Soviets of Working People's Deputies of Territories, Regions, Autonomous Regions, National Areas, districts, towns and rural localities.

Article 100. The Chairman, Vice-Chairman and Secretary elected by a Soviet of Working People's Deputies shall make up the executive and administrative organ of the Soviet of Working People's Deputies in a small locality, in accordance with the Constitution of the respective Union Republic.

Article 101. The executive organ of a Soviet of Working People's Deputies shall be directly accountable both to the Soviet which elected it and to the executive organ of the superior Soviet.

CHAPTER IX. THE COURTS OF LAW AND THE PROCURATOR'S OFFICE

Article 102. Justice in the USSR shall be administered by the Supreme Court of the USSR, the Supreme Courts of the Union Republics, the courts of the Territories, Regions, Autonomous Republics, Autonomous Regions and National Areas, the special courts of the USSR set up by decision of the USSR Supreme Soviet, and the people's courts.

Article 103. Cases in all courts shall be heard with the participation of people's assessors, except in cases specially provided for by law.

Article 104. The Supreme Court of the USSR shall be the highest judicial organ. It shall be charged with the supervision of the judicial activities of the judicial organs of the USSR and of the Union Republics within statutory limits.

Article 105. The Supreme Court of the USSR shall be elected by the USSR Supreme Soviet for a term of five years.

The Supreme Court of the USSR shall include the Chairmen of the Supreme Courts of the Union Republics by virtue of their office.

Article 106. The Supreme Courts of the Union Republics shall be elected by the Supreme Soviets of these Republics for a term of five years.

Article 107. The Supreme Courts of the Autonomous Republics shall be elected by the Supreme Soviets of these Republics for a term of five years.

Article 108. The courts of Territories, Regions, Autonomous Regions and National Areas shall be elected by the Soviets of Working People's Deputies of the respective Territories, Regions, Autonomous Regions and National Areas for a term of five years.

Article 109. People's judges of district (town) people's courts shall be elected for a term of five years by the citizens of the respective district (town) on the basis of universal, equal and direct suffrage by secret ballot.

People's assessors of the district (town) people's courts shall be elected for a term of two years at general meetings of industrial, office and professional workers, and of peasants at their place of work or residence, and of servicemen in military units.

Article 110. Judicial proceedings shall be conducted in the language of the Union Republic, or the Autonomous Republic, or the Autonomous Region, as the case may be; persons who do not know that language shall be guaranteed an opportunity to acquaint themselves fully with the material of a case through an interpreter, and likewise the right to use their own language in court.

Article 111. In all courts of the USSR, cases shall be heard in public, unless the law provides otherwise, [and] the accused person shall be guaranteed the right to defence.

Article 112. Judges shall be independent and subject only to the law.

Article 113. Supreme supervisory power to ensure the strict observance of the law by all Ministries and the institutions subordinated to them, as also by officials and other citizens within the USSR, shall be exercised by the Procurator-General of the USSR.

Article 114. The Procurator-General of the USSR shall be appointed by the USSR Supreme Soviet for a term of seven years.

Article 115. The Procurators of Republics, Territories, Regions, and also Autonomous Republics and Autonomous Regions shall be appointed by the Procurator-General of the USSR for a term of five years.

Article 116. The Procurators of National Areas, districts and towns shall be appointed for a term of five years by the Procurators of the Union Republics, subject to approval by the Procurator-General of the USSR.

Article 117. The agencies of the Procurator's Office shall perform their duties independently of all local bodies, being subordinate solely to the Procurator-General of the USSR.

CHAPTER X. FUNDAMENTAL RIGHTS AND DUTIES OF CITIZENS

Article 118. The citizens of the USSR shall have the right to work, that is, the right to guaranteed employment and payment for their work in accordance with its quantity and quality.

The right to work shall be ensured by the socialist organization of the national economy, the steady growth in the productive forces of Soviet society, the removal of any possibility of economic crises, and the abolition of unemployment.

Article 119. The citizens of the USSR shall have the right to rest and leisure.

The right to rest and leisure shall be ensured by the establishment of a seven-hour working day for industrial, office and professional workers and the reduction of the working day to six hours for arduous trades and to four hours in workshops with particularly arduous conditions of work; by the institution of annual holidays with full pay for industrial, office and professional workers; by the provision of a large number of sanatoriums, holiday homes and clubs for use by the working people.

Article 120. The citizens of the USSR shall have the right to maintenance in old age and also in the event of sickness or disability.

This right shall be ensured by the extensive development of social insurance of industrial, office and professional workers at state expense, by free medical service for the working people, and by placing a large number of health resorts at the disposal of the working people.

Article 121. The citizens of the USSR shall have the right to education.

This right shall be ensured by universal compulsory eight-year education; by extensive development of general secondary polytechnical education, vocational and technical education, secondary specialized and higher education, based on close ties between the school, real life and production; by extensive development of evening and correspondence education; by free education in all schools; by provision of state scholarship grants; by instruction in schools in the native language; and by the organization of free vocational, technical and agronomic training for the working people at factories, state farms and collective farms.

Article 122. Women in the USSR shall be accorded equal rights with men in economic, government, cultural, political and other public activities.

These rights shall be ensured by women being accorded the same rights as men in work, remuneration, rest and leisure, social insurance and education, and by state protection of the interests of mother and child, state aid to mothers of large families and to unmarried mothers, maternity leave with full pay, and by provision of a large number of maternity homes, nurseries and kindergartens.

Article 123. Equality of rights of citizens of the USSR, irrespective of their nationality or race, in economic, government,

cultural, political and other public activities, shall be an in-
defeasible law.

Any direct or indirect restriction of the rights of, or, conversely, the establishment of direct or indirect privileges for citizens
on grounds of race or nationality, likewise any advocacy of racial
or national exclusiveness, or hatred and contempt, shall be
punishable by law.

Article 124. The church in the USSR shall be separated from
the state, and the school from the church to ensure freedom
of conscience for all citizens. Freedom of religious worship
and of anti-religious propaganda shall be recognized for all
citizens.

Article 125. In conformity with the interests of the working
people, and for the purpose of strengthening the socialist system,
the citizens of the USSR shall be guaranteed by law:

  (i) Freedom of speech;

 (ii) Freedom of the press;

(iii) Freedom of assembly and rallies;

(iv) Freedom of street processions and demonstrations.

These rights of citizens shall be ensured by putting at the
disposal of the working people and their organizations printing
presses, stocks of paper, public buildings, streets, communication facilities and other material requisites for the exercise of
these rights.

Article 126. In conformity with the interests of the working
people and for the purpose of developing public initiative in organization and political activity, the citizens of the USSR shall
be guaranteed the right to unite in mass organizations – trade
unions, cooperative societies, youth organizations, sports and
defence organizations, cultural, technical and scientific societies;
the most active and politically conscious citizens among the
working class, working peasants and working intelligentsia
voluntarily unite in the Communist Party of the Soviet Union,
which is the vanguard of the working people in their struggle to
build communist society and is the leading core of all organizations of the working people, both governmental and non-
governmental.

Article 127. The citizens of the USSR shall be guaranteed inviolability of the person. No person shall be placed under arrest except by decision of a court of law or with the sanction of a procurator.

Article 128. The inviolability of the citizens' homes and privacy of correspondence shall be protected by law.

Article 129. The USSR shall afford the right of asylum to foreign nationals persecuted for upholding the interests of the working people, or for scientific activities, or for struggling for national liberation.

Article 130. It shall be the duty of every citizen of the USSR to abide by the Constitution of the Union of Soviet Socialist Republics, to observe the laws, to maintain labour discipline, honestly to perform public duties, and to respect the rules of socialist community.

Article 131. It shall be the duty of every citizen of the USSR to safeguard and fortify public, socialist property as the sacred and inviolable foundation of the Soviet system, as the source of the wealth and might of the country, as the source of the prosperity and culture of all the working people.

Persons committing crimes against public, socialist property shall be enemies of the people.

Article 132. Universal military service shall be statutory.

Military service in the Armed Forces of the USSR shall be an honourable duty of citizens of the USSR.

Article 133. It shall be the sacred duty of every citizen of the USSR to defend the country. Treason to the Motherland – violation of the oath of allegiance, desertion to the enemy, impairing the military power of the state, espionage – shall be punishable with all the severity of the law as the most heinous of crimes.

CHAPTER XI. THE ELECTORAL SYSTEM

Article 134. Members of all Soviets of Working People's Deputies – the Supreme Soviet of the USSR, the Supreme Soviets of the Union Republics, the Soviets of Working People's Deputies of the Territories and Regions, the Supreme Soviets of the Autonomous Republics, the Soviets of Working People's Deputies of the Autonomous Regions, the National Areas, the districts, towns and rural localities (stanitsas, villages, hamlets, kishlaks, auls) – shall be elected by constituents on the basis of universal, equal and direct suffrage by secret ballot.

Article 135. Elections of deputies shall be universal: all citizens of the USSR who have reached the age of eighteen, irrespective of race or nationality, sex, religion, education, domicile, social origin, property status or past activities, shall have the right to vote in the election of deputies, with the exception of persons who have been legally certified insane.

Every citizen of the USSR who has reached the age of twenty-three shall be eligible for election to the USSR Supreme Soviet, irrespective of race or nationality, sex, religion, education, domicile, social origin, property status or past activities.

Article 136. Elections of deputies shall be equal: each citizen shall have one vote; all citizens shall participate in elections on equal terms.

Article 137. Women shall have the right to elect and be elected on equal terms with men.

Article 138. Citizens serving in the Armed Forces of the USSR shall be entitled to elect and be elected on equal terms with all other citizens.

Article 139. Elections of deputies shall be direct: all Soviets of Working People's Deputies, from the rural and town Soviets to the USSR Supreme Soviet, shall be elected by citizens by direct vote.

Article 140. Voting at elections of deputies shall be secret.

Article 141. Candidates for election shall be nominated for each constituency.

The right to nominate candidates shall be ensured for the organizations and societies of working people: Communist Party organizations, trade unions, cooperatives, youth organizations and cultural societies.

Article 142. It shall be the duty of every deputy to report to the electorate on his or her work and on the work of the respective Soviet of Working People's Deputies; every deputy may be recalled at any time upon a decision taken by a majority of constituents in the statutory manner.

CHAPTER XII. ARMS, FLAG AND CAPITAL

Article 143. The arms of the Union of Soviet Socialist Republics shall be a hammer and sickle against a globe depicted in the rays of the sun and surrounded by ears of grain, with the inscription 'Workers of All Countries, Unite!' in the languages of the Union Republics. A five-pointed star shall be at the top of the arms.

Article 144. The state flag of the Union of Soviet Socialist Republics shall be of red cloth with the golden hammer and sickle depicted in the upper corner near the staff, with a five-pointed red star bordered in gold above them. The ratio of width to length shall be 1:2.

Article 145. The City of Moscow shall be the capital of the Union of Soviet Socialist Republics.

CHAPTER XIII. PROCEDURE FOR AMENDMENT TO THE CONSTITUTION

Article 146. Amendment to the Constitution of the USSR may be adopted by a majority of not less than two-thirds of votes in each of the chambers of the USSR Supreme Soviet.

[Incorporating all amendments up to and including 1978]

The Constitution (Fundamental Law) of the

UNION OF
SOVIET SOCIALIST
REPUBLICS
1977

CONTENTS

THE Great October Socialist Revolution, made by the workers and peasants of Russia under the leadership of the Communist Party headed by Lenin, overthrew capitalist and landowner rule, broke the fetters of oppression, established the dictatorship of the proletariat, and created the Soviet state, a new type of state, the basic instrument for defending the gains of the revolution and for building socialism and communism. Humanity thereby began the epoch-making turn from capitalism to socialism.

After achieving victory in the Civil War and repulsing imperialist intervention, the Soviet government carried through far-reaching social and economic transformations, and put an end once and for all to exploitation of man by man, antagonisms between classes, and strife between nationalities. The unification of the Soviet Republics in the Union of Soviet Socialist Republics multiplied the forces and opportunities of the peoples of the country in the building of socialism. Social ownership of the means of production and genuine democracy for the working masses were established. For the first time in the history of mankind a socialist society was created.

The strength of socialism was vividly demonstrated by the immortal feat of the Soviet people and their Armed Forces in achieving their historic victory in the Great Patriotic War. This victory consolidated the influence and international standing of the Soviet Union and created new opportunities for growth of the forces of socialism, national liberation, democracy, and peace throughout the world.

Continuing their creative endeavours, the working people of the Soviet Union have ensured rapid, all-round development of the country and steady improvement of the socialist system. They have consolidated the alliance of the working class, collective-farm peasantry, and people's intelligentsia, and friendship of the nations and nationalities of the USSR. Socio-political and ideological unity of Soviet society, in which the working class is the leading force, has been achieved. The aims of the dictatorship of the proletariat having been fulfilled, the Soviet state has become a state of the whole people. The leading role of the Communist Party, the vanguard of all the people, has grown.

In the USSR a developed socialist society has been built. At this stage, when socialism is developing on its own foundations the creative forces of the new system and the advantages of the socialist way of life are becoming increasingly evident, and the working people are more and more widely enjoying the fruits of their great revolutionary gains.

It is a society in which powerful productive forces and progressive science and culture have been created, in which the well-being of the people is constantly rising, and more and more favourable conditions are being provided for the all-round development of the individual.

It is a society of mature socialist social relations, in which, on the basis of the drawing together of all classes and social strata and of the juridical and factual equality of all its nations and nationalities and their fraternal cooperation, a new historical community of people has been formed – the Soviet people.

It is a society of high organizational capacity, ideological commitment, and consciousness of the working people, who are patriots and internationalists.

It is a society in which the law of life is concern of all for the good of each and concern of each for the good of all.

It is a society of true democracy, the political system of which ensures effective management of all public affairs, ever more active participation of the working people in running the state, and the combining of citizens' real rights and freedoms with their obligations and responsibility to society.

Developed socialist society is a natural, logical stage on the road to communism.

The supreme goal of the Soviet state is the building of a classless communist society in which there will be public, communist self-government. The main aims of the people's socialist state are: to lay the material and technical foundations of communism, to perfect socialist social relations and transform them into communist relations, to mould the citizen of communist society, to raise the people's living and cultural standards, to safeguard the country's security, and to further the consolidation of peace and development of international cooperation.

The Soviet people,

Guided by the ideas of scientific communism and true to their revolutionary traditions,

Relying on the great social, economic, and political gains of socialism,

Striving for the further development of socialist democracy,

Taking into account the international position of the USSR as part of the world system of socialism, and conscious of their internationalist responsibility,

Preserving continuity of the ideas and principles of the first Soviet Constitution of 1918, the 1924 Constitution of the USSR and the 1936 Constitution of the USSR,

Hereby affirm the principles of the social structure and policy of the USSR, and define the rights, freedoms and obligations of citizens, and the principles of the organization of the socialist state of the whole people, and its aims, and proclaim these in this Constitution.

I. PRINCIPLES OF THE SOCIAL STRUCTURE AND POLICY OF THE USSR

CHAPTER 1. THE POLITICAL SYSTEM

Article 1. The Union of Soviet Socialist Republics is a socialist state of the whole people, expressing the will and interests of the workers, peasants, and intelligentsia, the working people of all the nations and nationalities of the country.

Article 2. All power in the USSR belongs to the people.

The people exercise state power through Soviets of People's Deputies, which constitute the political foundation of the USSR.

All other state bodies are under the control of, and accountable to, the Soviets of People's Deputies.

Article 3. The Soviet state is organized and functions on the principle of democratic centralism, namely the electiveness of all bodies of state authority from the lowest to the highest, their accountability to the people, and the obligation of lower bodies to observe the decisions of higher ones. Democratic centralism combines central leadership with local initiative and creative activity and with the responsibility of each state body and official for the work entrusted to them.

Article 4. The Soviet state and all its bodies function on the basis of socialist law, ensure the maintenance of law and order, and safeguard the interests of society and the rights and freedoms of citizens.

State organizations, public organizations and officials shall observe the Constitution of the USSR and Soviet laws.

Article 5. Major matters of state shall be submitted to nationwide discussion and put to a popular vote (referendum).

Article 6. The leading and guiding force of Soviet society and the nucleus of its political system, of all state organizations and public organizations, is the Communist Party of the Soviet Union. The CPSU exists for the people and serves the people.

The Communist Party, armed with Marxism–Leninism, determines the general perspectives of the development of society and the course of the home and foreign policy of the USSR, directs the great constructive work of the Soviet people, and imparts a planned, systematic and theoretically substantiated character to their struggle for the victory of communism.

All Party organizations shall function within the framework of the Constitution of the USSR.

Article 7. Trade unions, the All-Union Leninist Young Communist League, cooperatives, and other public organizations, participate, in accordance with the aims laid down in their rules, in managing state and public affairs, and in deciding political, economic, and social and cultural matters.

Article 8. Work collectives take part in discussing and deciding state and public affairs, in planning production and social development, in training and placing personnel, and in discussing and deciding matters pertaining to the management of enterprises and institutions, the improvement of working and living conditions, and the use of funds allocated both for developing production and for social and cultural purposes and financial incentives.

Work collectives promote socialist emulation, the spread of progressive methods of work, and the strengthening of production discipline, educate their members in the spirit of communist morality, and strive to enhance their political consciousness and raise their cultural level and skills and qualifications.

Article 9. The principal direction in the development of the political system of Soviet society is the extension of socialist democracy, namely ever broader participation of citizens in managing the affairs of society and the state, continuous improvement of the machinery of state, heightening of the activity of public organizations, strengthening of the system of people's control, consolidation of the legal foundations of the functioning of the state and of public life, greater openness and publicity, and constant responsiveness to public opinion.

CHAPTER 2. THE ECONOMIC SYSTEM

Article 10. The foundation of the economic system of the USSR is socialist ownership of the means of production in the form of state property (belonging to all the people), and collective farm-and-cooperative property.

Socialist ownership also embraces the property of trade unions and other public organizations which they require to carry out their purposes under their rules.

The state protects socialist property and provides conditions for its growth.

No one has the right to use socialist property for personal gain or other selfish ends.

Article 11. State property, i.e. the common property of the Soviet people, is the principal form of socialist property.

The land, its minerals, waters, and forests are the exclusive property of the state. The state owns the basic means of production in industry, construction, and agriculture; means of transport and communication; the banks; the property of state-run trade organizations and public utilities, and other state-run undertakings; most urban housing; and other property necessary for state purposes.

Article 12. The property of collective farms and other cooperative organizations, and of their joint undertakings, comprises the means of production and other assets which they require for the purposes laid down in their rules.

The land held by collective farms is secured to them for their free use in perpetuity.

The state promotes development of collective farm-and-cooperative property and its approximation to state property.

Collective farms, like other land users, are obliged to make effective and thrifty use of the land and to increase its fertility.

Article 13. Earned income forms the basis of the personal property of Soviet citizens. The personal property of citizens of the USSR may include articles of everyday use, personal consumption and convenience, the implements and other objects of a small-holding, a house, and earned savings. The personal property of citizens and the right to inherit it are protected by the state.

Citizens may be granted the use of plots of land, in the manner prescribed by law, for a subsidiary small-holding (including the keeping of livestock and poultry), for fruit and vegetable growing or for building an individual dwelling. Citizens are required to make rational use of the land allotted to them. The state, and collective farms, provide assistance to citizens in working their small-holdings.

Property owned or used by citizens shall not serve as a means of deriving unearned income or be employed to the detriment of the interests of society.

Article 14. The source of the growth of social wealth and of the well-being of the people, and of each individual, is the labour, free from exploitation, of Soviet people.

The state exercises control over the measure of labour and of consumption in accordance with the principle of socialism: 'From each according to his ability, to each according to his work.' It fixes the rate of taxation on taxable income.

Socially useful work and its results determine a person's status in society. By combining material and moral incentives and encouraging innovation and a creative attitude to work, the state helps transform labour into the prime vital need of every Soviet citizen.

Article 15. The supreme goal of social production under socialism is the fullest possible satisfaction of the people's growing material, and cultural and intellectual requirements.

Relying on the creative initiative of the working people, socialist emulation, and scientific and technological progress, and by improving the forms and methods of economic management, the state ensures growth of the productivity of labour, raising of the efficiency of production and of the quality of work, and dynamic, planned, proportionate development of the economy.

Article 16. The economy of the USSR is an integral economic complex comprising all the elements of social production, distribution, and exchange on its territory.

The economy is managed on the basis of state plans for economic and social development, with due account of the sectoral and territorial principles, and by combining centralized direction with the managerial independence and initiative of individual and amalgamated enterprises and other organizations, for which active use is made of management accounting, profit, cost, and other economic levers and incentives.

Article 17. In the USSR, the law permits individual labour in handicrafts, farming, the provision of services for the public, and other forms of activity based exclusively on the personal work of individual citizens and members of their families. The state makes regulations for such work to ensure that it serves the interests of society.

Article 18. In the interests of the present and future generations, the necessary steps are taken in the USSR to protect and make scientific, rational use of the land and its mineral and water resources, and the plant and animal kingdoms, to preserve the purity of air and water, ensure reproduction of natural wealth, and improve the human environment.

CHAPTER 3. SOCIAL DEVELOPMENT AND CULTURE

Article 19. The social basis of the USSR is the unbreakable alliance of the workers, peasants, and intelligentsia.

The state helps enhance the social homogeneity of society, namely the elimination of class differences and of the essential distinctions between town and country and between mental and physical labour, and the all-round development and drawing together of all the nations and nationalities of the USSR.

Article 20. In accordance with the communist ideal – 'The free development of each is the condition of the free development of all' – the state pursues the aim of giving citizens more and more real opportunities to apply their creative energies, abilities, and talents, and to develop their personalities in every way.

Article 21. The state concerns itself with improving working conditions, safety and labour protection and the scientific organization of work, and with reducing and ultimately eliminating all arduous physical labour through comprehensive mechanization and automation of production processes in all branches of the economy.

Article 22. A programme is being consistently implemented in the USSR to convert agricultural work into a variety of industrial work, to extend the network of educational, cultural and medical institutions, and of trade, public catering, service and public utility facilities in rural localities, and transform hamlets and villages into well-planned and well-appointed settlements.

Article 23. The state pursues a steady policy of raising people's pay levels and real incomes through increase in productivity.

In order to satisfy the needs of Soviet people more fully social consumption funds are created. The state, with the broad participation of public organizations and work collectives, ensures the growth and just distribution of these funds.

Article 24. In the USSR, state systems of health protection, social security, trade and public catering, communal services and amenities, and public utilities, operate and are being extended.

The state encourages cooperatives and other public organizations to provide all types of services for the population. It encourages the development of mass physical culture and sport.

Article 25. In the USSR there is a uniform system of public education, which is being constantly improved, that provides general education and vocational training for citizens, serves the communist education and intellectual and physical development of the youth, and trains them for work and social activity.

Article 26. In accordance with society's needs the state provides for planned development of science and the training of scientific personnel and organizes introduction of the results of research in the economy and other spheres of life.

Article 27. The state concerns itself with protecting, augmenting and making extensive use of society's cultural wealth for the moral and aesthetic education of the Soviet people, for raising their cultural level.

In the USSR development of the professional, amateur and folk arts is encouraged in every way.

CHAPTER 4. FOREIGN POLICY

Article 28. The USSR steadfastly pursues a Leninist policy of peace and stands for strengthening of the security of nations and broad international cooperation.

The foreign policy of the USSR is aimed at ensuring international conditions favourable for building communism in the USSR, safeguarding the state interests of the Soviet Union, consolidating the positions of world socialism, supporting the struggle of peoples for national liberation and social progress, preventing wars of aggression, achieving universal and complete disarmament, and consistently implementing the principle of the peaceful coexistence of states with different social systems.

In the USSR war propaganda is banned.

Article 29. The USSR's relations with other states are based on observance of the following principles: sovereign equality; mutual renunciation of the use or threat of force; inviolability of frontiers; territorial integrity of states; peaceful settlement of disputes; non-intervention in internal affairs; respect for human rights and fundamental freedoms; the equal rights of peoples and their right to decide their own destiny; cooperation among states; and fulfilment in good faith of obligations arising from the generally recognized principles and rules of international law, and from the international treaties signed by the USSR.

Article 30. The USSR, as part of the world system of socialism and of the socialist community, promotes and strengthens friendship, cooperation, and comradely mutual assistance with other socialist countries on the basis of the principle of socialist internationalism, and takes an active part in socialist economic integration and the socialist international division of labour.

CHAPTER 5. DEFENCE OF THE SOCIALIST MOTHERLAND

Article 31. Defence of the Socialist Motherland is one of the most important functions of the state, and is the concern of the whole people.

In order to defend the gains of socialism, the peaceful labour of the Soviet people, and the sovereignty and territorial integrity of the state, the USSR maintains Armed Forces and has instituted universal military service.

The duty of the Armed Forces of the USSR to the people is to provide reliable defence of the Socialist Motherland and to be in constant readiness, guaranteeing that any aggressor is instantly repulsed.

Article 32. The state ensures the security and defence capability of the country, and supplies the Armed Forces of the USSR with everything necessary for that purpose.

The duties of state bodies, public organizations, officials, and citizens in regard to safeguarding the country's security and strengthening its defence capacity are defined by the legislation of the USSR.

II. THE STATE AND THE INDIVIDUAL

CHAPTER 6. CITIZENSHIP OF THE USSR. EQUALITY OF CITIZENS' RIGHTS

Article 33. Uniform federal citizenship is established for the USSR. Every citizen of a Union Republic is a citizen of the USSR.

The grounds and procedure for acquiring or forfeiting Soviet citizenship are defined by the Law on Citizenship of the USSR.

When abroad, citizens of the USSR enjoy the protection and assistance of the Soviet state.

Article 34. Citizens of the USSR are equal before the law, without distinction of origin, social or property status, race or nationality, sex, education, language, attitude to religion, type and nature of occupation, domicile, or other status.

The equal rights of citizens of the USSR are guaranteed in all fields of economic, political, social, and cultural life.

Article 35. Women and men have equal rights in the USSR.

Exercise of these rights is ensured by according women equal access with men to education and vocational and professional training, equal opportunities in employment, remuneration, and promotion, and in social and political, and cultural activity, and by special labour and health protection measures for women; by providing conditions enabling mothers to work; by legal protection, and material and moral support for mothers and children, including paid leaves and other benefits for expectant mothers and mothers, and gradual reduction of working time for mothers with small children.

Article 36. Citizens of the USSR of different races and nationalities have equal rights.

Exercise of these rights is ensured by a policy of all-round development and drawing together of all the nations and nationalities of the USSR, by educating citizens in the spirit of Soviet patriotism and socialist internationalism, and by the possibility to use their native language and the languages of other peoples of the USSR.

Any direct or indirect limitation of the rights of citizens or establishment of direct or indirect privileges on grounds of race or nationality, and any advocacy of racial or national exclusiveness, hostility or contempt, are punishable by law.

Article 37. Citizens of other countries and stateless persons in the USSR are guaranteed the rights and freedoms provided by law, including the right to apply to a court and other state bodies for the protection of their personal, property, family, and other rights.

Citizens of other countries and stateless persons, when in the USSR, are obliged to respect the Constitution of the USSR and observe Soviet laws.

Article 38. The USSR grants the right of asylum to foreigners persecuted for defending the interests of the working people and the cause of peace, or for participation in the revolutionary and national-liberation movement, or for progressive social and political, scientific or other creative activity.

CHAPTER 7. THE BASIC RIGHTS, FREEDOMS, AND DUTIES OF CITIZENS OF THE USSR

Article 39. Citizens of the USSR enjoy in full the social, economic, political and personal rights and freedoms proclaimed and guaranteed by the Constitution of the USSR and by Soviet laws. The socialist system ensures enlargement of the rights and freedoms of citizens and continuous improvement of their living standards as social, economic, and cultural development programmes are fulfilled.

Enjoyment by citizens of their rights and freedoms must not be to the detriment of the interests of society or the state, or infringe the rights of other citizens.

Article 40. Citizens of the USSR have the right to work (that is, to guaranteed employment and pay in accordance with the quantity and quality of their work, and not below the state-established minimum), including the right to choose their trade or profession, type of job and work in accordance with their inclinations, abilities, training and education, with due account of the needs of society.

This right is ensured by the socialist economic system, steady growth of the productive forces, free vocational and professional training, improvement of skills, training in new trades or professions, and development of the systems of vocational guidance and job placement.

Article 41. Citizens of the USSR have the right to rest and leisure.

This right is ensured by the establishment of a working week not exceeding forty-one hours, for workers and other employees, a shorter working day in a number of trades and industries, and shorter hours for night work; by the provision of paid annual holidays, weekly days of rest, extension of the network of cultural, educational and health-building institutions, and the development on a mass scale of sport, physical culture, and camping and tourism; by the provision of neighbourhood recreational facilities, and of other opportunities for rational use of free time.

The length of collective farmers' working and leisure time is established by their collective farms.

Article 42. Citizens of the USSR have the right to health protection.

This right is ensured by free, qualified medical care provided by state health institutions; by extension of the network of therapeutic and health-building institutions; by the development and improvement of safety and hygiene in industry; by carrying out broad prophylactic measures; by measures to improve the environment; by special care for the health of the rising generation, including prohibition of child labour, excluding the work done by children as part of the school curriculum; and by developing research to prevent and reduce the incidence of disease and ensure citizens a long and active life.

Article 43. Citizens of the USSR have the right to maintenance in old age, in sickness, and in the event of complete or partial disability or loss of the breadwinner.

This right is guaranteed by social insurance of workers and other employees and collective farmers; by allowances for temporary disability; by the provision by the state or by collective farms of retirement pensions, disability pensions, and pensions for loss of the breadwinner; by providing employment for the partially disabled; by care for the elderly and the disabled; and by other forms of social security.

Article 44. Citizens of the USSR have the right to housing.

This right is ensured by the development and upkeep of state and socially owned housing; by assistance for cooperative and individual house building; by fair distribution, under public control, of the housing that becomes available through fulfilment of the programme of building well-appointed dwellings, and by low rents and low charges for utility services. Citizens of the USSR shall take good care of the housing allocated to them.

Article 45. Citizens of the USSR have the right to education.

This right is ensured by free provision of all forms of education, by the institution of universal, compulsory secondary education, and broad development of vocational, specialized secondary, and higher education, in which instruction is oriented towards practical activity and production; by the development of extramural, correspondence and evening courses; by the provision of state scholarships and grants and privileges for students; by the free issue of school textbooks; by the opportunity to attend a school where teaching is in the native language; and by the provision of facilities for self-education.

Article 46. Citizens of the USSR have the right to enjoy cultural benefits.

This right is ensured by broad access to the cultural treasures of their own land and of the world that are preserved in state and other public collections; by the development and fair distribution of cultural and educational institutions throughout the country; by developing television and radio broadcasting and the publishing of books, newspapers and periodicals, and by extending the free library service; and by expanding cultural exchanges with other countries.

Article 47. Citizens of the USSR, in accordance with the aims of building communism, are guaranteed freedom of scientific, technical, and artistic work. This freedom is ensured by broadening scientific research, encouraging invention and innovation, and developing literature and the arts. The state provides the necessary material conditions for this and support for voluntary societies and unions of workers in the arts, organizes introduction of inventions and innovations in production and other spheres of activity.

The rights of authors, inventors and innovators are protected by the state.

Article 48. Citizens of the USSR have the right to take part in the management and administration of state and public affairs and in the discussion and adoption of laws and measures of All-Union and local significance.

This right is ensured by the opportunity to vote and to be elected to Soviets of People's Deputies and other elective state bodies, to take part in nation-wide discussions and referendums, in people's control, in the work of state bodies, public organizations, and local community groups, and in meetings at places of work or residence.

Article 49. Every citizen of the USSR has the right to submit proposals to state bodies and public organizations for improving their activity, and to criticize shortcomings in their work.

Officials are obliged, within established time-limits, to examine citizens' proposals and requests, to reply to them, and to take appropriate action.

Persecution for criticism is prohibited. Persons guilty of such persecution shall be called to account.

Article 50. In accordance with the interests of the people and in order to strengthen and develop the socialist system, citizens of the USSR are guaranteed freedom of speech, of the press, and of assembly, meetings, street processions and demonstrations.

Exercise of these political freedoms is ensured by putting public buildings, streets and squares at the disposal of the working people and their organizations, by broad dissemination of information, and by the opportunity to use the press, television, and radio.

Article 51. In accordance with the aims of building communism, citizens of the USSR have the right to associate in public organizations that promote their political activity and initiative and satisfaction of their various interests.

Public organizations are guaranteed conditions for successfully performing the functions defined in their rules.

Article 52. Citizens of the USSR are guaranteed freedom of conscience, that is, the right to profess or not to profess any religion, and to conduct religious worship or atheistic propaganda. Incitement of hostility or hatred on religious grounds is prohibited.

In the USSR, the church is separated from the state, and the school from the church.

Article 53. The family enjoys the protection of the state.

Marriage is based on the free consent of the woman and the man; the spouses are completely equal in their family relations.

The state helps the family by providing and developing a broad system of child-care institutions, by organizing and improving communal services and public catering, by paying grants on the birth of a child, by providing children's allowances and benefits for large families, and other forms of family allowances and assistance.

Article 54. Citizens of the USSR are guaranteed inviolability of the person. No one may be arrested except by a court decision or on the warrant of a procurator.

Article 55. Citizens of the USSR are guaranteed inviolability of the home. No one may, without lawful grounds, enter a home against the will of those residing in it.

Article 56. The privacy of citizens, and of their correspondence, telephone conversations, and telegraphic communications is protected by law.

Article 57. Respect for the individual and protection of the rights and freedoms of citizens are the duty of all state bodies, public organizations, and officials.

Citizens of the USSR have the right to protection by the courts against encroachments on their honour and reputation, life and health, and personal freedom and property.

Article 58. Citizens of the USSR have the right to lodge a complaint against the actions of officials, state bodies and public bodies. Complaints shall be examined according to the procedure and within the time-limit established by law.

Actions by officials that contravene the law or exceed their powers, and infringe the rights of citizens, may be appealed against in a court in the manner prescribed by law.

Citizens of the USSR have the right to compensation for damage resulting from unlawful actions by state organizations and public organizations, or by officials in the performance of their duties.

Article 59. Citizens' exercise of their rights and freedoms is inseparable from the performance of their duties and obligations.

Citizens of the USSR are obliged to observe the Constitution of the USSR and Soviet laws, comply with the standards of socialist conduct, and uphold the honour and dignity of Soviet citizenship.

Article 60. It is the duty of, and a matter of honour for, every able-bodied citizen of the USSR to work conscientiously in his chosen, socially useful occupation, and strictly to observe labour discipline. Evasion of socially useful work is incompatible with the principles of socialist society.

Article 61. Citizens of the USSR are obliged to preserve and protect socialist property. It is the duty of a citizen of the USSR to combat misappropriation and squandering of state and socially owned property and to make thrifty use of the people's wealth.

Persons encroaching in any way on socialist property shall be punished according to the law.

Article 62. Citizens of the USSR are obliged to safeguard the interests of the Soviet state, and to enhance its power and prestige.

Defence of the Socialist Motherland is the sacred duty of every citizen of the USSR.

Betrayal of the Motherland is the gravest of crimes against the people.

Article 63. Military service in the ranks of the Armed Forces of the USSR is an honourable duty of Soviet citizens.

Article 64. It is the duty of every citizen of the USSR to respect the national dignity of other citizens and to strengthen friendship of the nations and nationalities of the multinational Soviet state.

Article 65. A citizen of the USSR is obliged to respect the rights and lawful interests of other persons, to be uncompromising towards anti-social behaviour, and to help maintain public order.

Article 66. Citizens of the USSR are obliged to concern themselves with the upbringing of children, to train them for socially useful work, and to raise them as worthy members of socialist society. Children are obliged to care for their parents and help them.

Article 67. Citizens of the USSR are obliged to protect nature and conserve its riches.

Article 68. Concern for the preservation of historical monuments and other cultural values is a duty and obligation of citizens of the USSR.

Article 69. It is the internationalist duty of citizens of the USSR to promote friendship and cooperation with peoples of other lands and help maintain and strengthen world peace.

III. THE NATIONAL-STATE STRUCTURE OF THE USSR

CHAPTER 8. THE USSR – A FEDERAL STATE

Article 70. The Union of Soviet Socialist Republics is an integral, federal, multinational state formed on the principle of socialist federalism as a result of the free self-determination of nations and the voluntary association of equal Soviet Socialist Republics.

The USSR embodies the state unity of the Soviet people and draws all its nations and nationalities together for the purpose of jointly building communism.

Article 71. The Union of Soviet Socialist Republics unites the:
Russian Soviet Federative Socialist Republic,
Ukrainian Soviet Socialist Republic,
Byelorussian Soviet Socialist Republic,
Uzbek Soviet Socialist Republic,
Kazakh Soviet Socialist Republic,
Georgian Soviet Socialist Republic,
Azerbaijan Soviet Socialist Republic,
Lithuanian Soviet Socialist Republic,
Moldavian Soviet Socialist Republic,
Latvian Soviet Socialist Republic,
Kirghiz Soviet Socialist Republic,
Tajik Soviet Socialist Republic,
Armenian Soviet Socialist Republic,
Turkmen Soviet Socialist Republic,
Estonian Soviet Socialist Republic.

Article 72. Each Union Republic shall retain the right freely to secede from the USSR.

Article 73. The jurisdiction of the Union of Soviet Socialist Republics, as represented by its highest bodies of state authority and administration, shall cover:

(1) The admission of new republics to the USSR; endorsement

of the formation of new autonomous republics and autonomous regions within Union Republics;

(2) Determination of the state boundaries of the USSR and approval of changes in the boundaries between Union Republics;

(3) Establishment of the general principles for the organization and functioning of republican and local bodies of state authority and administration;

(4) The ensurance of uniformity of legislative norms throughout the USSR and establishment of the fundamentals of the legislation of the Union of Soviet Socialist Republics and Union Republics;

(5) Pursuance of a uniform social and economic policy; direction of the country's economy; determination of the main lines of scientific and technological progress and the general measures for rational exploitation and conservation of natural resources; the drafting and approval of state plans for the economic and social development of the USSR, and endorsement of reports on their fulfilment;

(6) The drafting and approval of the consolidated Budget of the USSR, and endorsement of the report on its execution; management of a single monetary and credit system; determination of the taxes and revenues forming the Budget of the USSR; and the formulation of prices and wages policy;

(7) Direction of the sectors of the economy, and of enterprises and amalgamations under Union jurisdiction, and general direction of industries under Union-Republican jurisdiction;

(8) Issues of war and peace, defence of the sovereignty of the USSR and safeguarding of its frontiers and territory, and organization of defence; direction of the Armed Forces of the USSR;

(9) State security;

(10) Representation of the USSR in international relations; the USSR's relations with other states and with international organizations; establishment of the general procedure for, and coordination of, the relations of Union Republics with other states and with international organizations; foreign trade and other forms of external economic activity on the basis of state monopoly;

(11) Control over observance of the Constitution of the USSR, and ensurance of conformity of the Constitutions of Union Republics to the Constitution of the USSR;

(12) And settlement of other matters of All-Union importance.

Article 74. The laws of the USSR shall have the same force in all Union Republics. In the event of a discrepancy between a Union Republic law and an All-Union law, the law of the USSR shall prevail.

Article 75. The territory of the Union of Soviet Socialist Republics is a single entity and comprises the territories of the Union Republics.

The sovereignty of the USSR extends throughout its territory.

CHAPTER 9. THE UNION SOVIET SOCIALIST REPUBLIC

Article 76. A Union Republic is a sovereign Soviet socialist state that has united with other Soviet Republics in the Union of Soviet Socialist Republics.

Outside the spheres listed in Article 73 of the Constitution of the USSR, a Union Republic exercises independent authority on its territory.

A Union Republic shall have its own Constitution conforming to the Constitution of the USSR with the specific features of the Republic being taken into account.

Article 77. Union Republics take part in decision-making in the Supreme Soviet of the USSR, the Presidium of the Supreme Soviet of the USSR, the Government of the USSR, and other bodies of the Union of Soviet Socialist Republics in matters that come within the jurisdiction of the Union of Soviet Socialist Republics.

A Union Republic shall ensure comprehensive economic and social development on its territory, facilitate exercise of the powers of the USSR on its territory, and implement the decisions of the highest bodies of state authority and administration of the USSR.

In matters that come within its jurisdiction, a Union Republic shall coordinate and control the activity of enterprises, institutions, and organizations subordinate to the Union.

Article 78. The territory of a Union Republic may not be altered without its consent. The boundaries between Union Republics may be altered by mutual agreement of the Republics concerned, subject to ratification by the Union of Soviet Socialist Republics.

Article 79. A Union Republic shall determine its division into territories, regions, areas, and districts, and decide other matters relating to its administrative and territorial structure.

Article 80. A Union Republic has the right to enter into relations with other states, conclude treaties with them, exchange diplomatic and consular representatives, and take part in the work of international organizations.

Article 81. The sovereign rights of Union Republics shall be safeguarded by the USSR.

CHAPTER 10. THE AUTONOMOUS SOVIET SOCIALIST REPUBLIC

Article 82. An Autonomous Republic is a constituent part of a Union Republic.

In spheres not within the jurisdiction of the Union of Soviet Socialist Republics and the Union Republic, an Autonomous Republic shall deal independently with matters within its jurisdiction.

An Autonomous Republic shall have its own Constitution conforming to the Constitutions of the USSR and the Union Republic with the specific features of the Autonomous Republic being taken into account.

Article 83. An Autonomous Republic takes part in decision-making through the highest bodies of state authority and administration of the USSR and of the Union Republic respectively, in matters that come within the jurisdiction of the USSR and the Union Republic.

An Autonomous Republic shall ensure comprehensive economic and social development on its territory, facilitate exercise of the powers of the USSR and the Union Republic on its territory, and implement decisions of the highest bodies of state authority and administration of the USSR and the Union Republic.

In matters within its jurisdiction, an Autonomous Republic shall coordinate and control the activity of enterprises, institutions, and organizations subordinate to the Union or the Union Republic.

Article 84. The territory of an Autonomous Republic may not be altered without its consent.

Article 85. The Russian Soviet Federative Socialist Republic includes the Bashkir, Buryat, Daghestan, Kabardin-Balkar, Kalmyk, Karelian, Komi, Mari, Mordovian, North Ossetian, Tatar, Tuva, Udmurt, Chechen-Ingush, Chuvash, and Yakut Autonomous Soviet Socialist Republics.

The Uzbek Soviet Socialist Republic includes the Kara-Kalpak Autonomous Soviet Socialist Republic.

The Georgian Soviet Socialist Republic includes the Abkhasian and Adzhar Autonomous Soviet Socialist Republics.

The Azerbaijan Soviet Socialist Republic includes the Nakhichevan Autonomous Soviet Socialist Republic.

CHAPTER 11. THE AUTONOMOUS REGION AND AUTONOMOUS AREA

Article 86. An Autonomous Region is a constituent part of a Union Republic or Territory. The Law on an Autonomous Region, upon submission by the Soviet of People's Deputies of the Autonomous Region concerned, shall be adopted by the Supreme Soviet of the Union Republic.

Article 87. The Russian Soviet Federative Socialist Republic includes the Adygei, Gorno-Altai, Jewish, Karachai-Circassian, and Khakass Autonomous Regions.

The Georgian Soviet Socialist Republic includes the South Ossetian Autonomous Region.

The Azerbaijan Soviet Socialist Republic includes the Nagorno-Karabakh Autonomous Region.

The Tajik Soviet Socialist Republic includes the Gorno-Badakhshan Autonomous Region.

Article 88. An Autonomous Area is a constituent part of a Territory or Region. The Law on an Autonomous Area shall be adopted by the Supreme Soviet of the Union Republic concerned.

IV. SOVIETS OF PEOPLE'S DEPUTIES AND ELECTORAL PROCEDURE

CHAPTER 12. THE SYSTEM OF SOVIETS OF PEOPLE'S DEPUTIES AND THE PRINCIPLES OF THEIR WORK

Article 89. The Soviets of People's Deputies, i.e. the Supreme Soviet of the USSR, the Supreme Soviets of Union Republics, the Supreme Soviets of Autonomous Republics, the Soviets of People's Deputies of Territories and Regions, the Soviets of People's Deputies of Autonomous Regions and Autonomous Areas, and the Soviets of People's Deputies of districts, cities, city districts, settlements and villages shall constitute a single system of bodies of state authority.

Article 90. The term of the Supreme Soviet of the USSR, the Supreme Soviets of Union Republics, and the Supreme Soviets of Autonomous Republics shall be five years.

The term of local Soviets of People's Deputies shall be two and a half years.

Elections to Soviets of People's Deputies shall be called not later than two months before expiry of the term of the Soviet concerned.

Article 91. The most important matters within the jurisdiction of the respective Soviets of People's Deputies shall be considered and settled at their sessions.

Soviets of People's Deputies shall elect standing commissions and form executive-administrative, and other bodies accountable to them.

Article 92. Soviets of People's Deputies shall form people's control bodies combining state control with control by the working people at enterprises, collective farms, institutions, and organizations.

People's control bodies shall check on the fulfilment of state plans and assignments, combat breaches of state discipline, localistic tendencies, narrow departmental attitudes, mismanagement, extravagance and waste, red tape and bureaucracy, and help improve the working of the state machinery.

Article 93. Soviets of People's Deputies shall direct all sectors of state, economic and social and cultural development, either directly or through bodies instituted by them, take decisions and ensure their execution, and verify their implementation.

Article 94. Soviets of the People's Deputies shall function publicly on the basis of collective, free, constructive discussion and decision-making, of systematic reporting back to them and the people by their executive-administrative and other bodies, and of involving citizens on a broad scale in their work.

Soviets of People's Deputies and the bodies set up by them shall systematically inform the public about their work and the decisions taken by them.

CHAPTER 13. THE ELECTORAL SYSTEM

Article 95. Deputies to all Soviets shall be elected on the basis of universal, equal, and direct suffrage by secret ballot.

Article 96. Elections shall be universal: all citizens of the USSR who have reached the age of eighteen shall have the right to vote and to be elected, with the exception of persons who have been legally certified insane.

To be eligible for election to the Supreme Soviet of the USSR a citizen of the USSR must have reached the age of twenty-one.

Article 97. Elections shall be equal: each citizen shall have one vote; all voters shall exercise the franchise on an equal footing.

Article 98. Elections shall be direct: Deputies to all Soviets of People's Deputies shall be elected by citizens by direct vote.

Article 99. Voting at elections shall be secret: control over voters' exercise of the franchise is inadmissible.

Article 100. The following shall have the right to nominate candidates: branches and organizations of the Communist Party of the Soviet Union, trade unions, and the All-Union Leninist Young Communist League; cooperatives and other public organizations; work collectives, and meetings of servicemen in their military units.

Citizens of the USSR and public organizations are guaranteed the right to free and all-round discussion of the political and personal qualities and competence of candidates, and the right to campaign for them at meetings, in the press, and on television and radio.

The expenses involved in holding elections to Soviets of People's Deputies shall be met by the state.

Article 101. Deputies to Soviets of People's Deputies shall be elected by constituencies.

A citizen of the USSR may not, as a rule, be elected to more than two Soviets of People's Deputies.

Elections to the Soviets shall be conducted by electoral commissions consisting of representatives of public organizations and work collectives, and of meetings of servicemen in military units.

The procedure for holding elections to Soviets of People's Deputies shall be defined by the laws of the USSR, and of Union and Autonomous Republics.

Article 102. Electors give mandates to their Deputies.

The appropriate Soviets of People's Deputies shall examine electors' mandates, take them into account in drafting economic and social development plans and in drawing up the budget, organize implementation of the mandates, and inform citizens about it.

CHAPTER 14. PEOPLE'S DEPUTIES

Article 103. Deputies are the plenipotentiary representatives of the people in the Soviets of People's Deputies.

In the Soviets, Deputies deal with matters relating to state, economic and social and cultural development, organize implementation of the decisions of the Soviets, and exercise control over the work of state bodies, enterprises, institutions and organizations.

Deputies shall be guided in their activities by the interests of the state, and shall take the needs of their constituents into account and work to implement their electors' mandates.

Article 104. Deputies shall exercise their powers without discontinuing their regular employment or duties.

During sessions of the Soviet, and so as to exercise their Deputy's powers in other cases stipulated by law, Deputies shall be released from their regular employment or duties, with retention of their average earnings at their permanent place of work.

Article 105. A Deputy has the right to address inquiries to the appropriate state bodies and officials, who are obliged to reply to them at a session of the Soviet.

Deputies have the right to approach any state or public body, enterprise, institution, or organization on matters arising from their work as Deputies and to take part in considering the questions raised by them. The heads of the state or public bodies, enterprises, institutions or organizations concerned are obliged to receive Deputies without delay and to consider their proposals within the time-limit established by law.

Article 106. Deputies shall be ensured conditions for the unhampered and effective exercise of their rights and duties.

The immunity of Deputies, and other guarantees of their activity as Deputies, are defined in the Law on the Status of Deputies and other legislative acts of the USSR and of Union and Autonomous Republics.

Article 107. Deputies shall report on their work and on that of the Soviet to their constituents, and to the work collectives and public organizations that nominated them.

Deputies who have not justified the confidence of their constituents may be recalled at any time by decision of a majority of the electors in accordance with the procedure established by law.

V. HIGHER BODIES
OF STATE AUTHORITY
AND ADMINISTRATION
OF THE USSR

CHAPTER 15. THE SUPREME SOVIET
OF THE USSR

Article 108. The highest body of state authority of the USSR shall be the Supreme Soviet of the USSR.

The Supreme Soviet of the USSR is empowered to deal with all matters within the jurisdiction of the Union of Soviet Socialist Republics, as defined by this Constitution.

The adoption and amendment of the Constitution of the USSR; admission of new Republics to the USSR; endorsement of the formation of new Autonomous Republics and Autonomous Regions; approval of the state plans for economic and social development, of the Budget of the USSR, and of reports on their execution; and the institution of bodies of the USSR accountable to it, are the exclusive prerogative of the Supreme Soviet of the USSR.

Laws of the USSR shall be enacted by the Supreme Soviet of the USSR or by a nation-wide vote (referendum) held by decision of the Supreme Soviet of the USSR.

Article 109. The Supreme Soviet of the USSR shall consist of two chambers: the Soviet of the Union and the Soviet of Nationalities.

The two chambers of the Supreme Soviet of the USSR shall have equal rights.

Article 110. The Soviet of the Union and the Soviet of Nationalities shall have equal numbers of deputies.

The Soviet of the Union shall be elected by constituencies with equal populations.

The Soviet of Nationalities shall be elected on the basis of the following representation: thirty-two Deputies from each Union

Republic, eleven Deputies from each Autonomous Republic, five Deputies from each Autonomous Region, and one Deputy from each Autonomous Area.

The Soviet of the Union and the Soviet of Nationalities, upon submission by the credentials commissions elected by them, shall decide on the validity of Deputies' credentials, and, in cases in which the election law has been violated, shall declare the election of the Deputies concerned null and void.

Article 111. Each chamber of the Supreme Soviet of the USSR shall elect a Chairman and four Vice-Chairmen.

The Chairmen of the Soviet of the Union and of the Soviet of Nationalities shall preside over the sittings of the respective chambers and conduct their affairs.

Joint sittings of the chambers of the Supreme Soviet of the USSR shall be presided over alternately by the Chairman of the Soviet of the Union and the Chairman of the Soviet of Nationalities.

Article 112. Sessions of the Supreme Soviet of the USSR shall be convened twice a year.

Special sessions shall be convened by the Presidium of the Supreme Soviet of the USSR at its discretion or on the proposal of a Union Republic, or of not less than one-third of the Deputies of one of the chambers.

A session of the Supreme Soviet of the USSR shall consist of separate and joint sittings of the chambers, and of meetings of the standing commissions of the chambers or commissions of the Supreme Soviet of the USSR held between the sittings of the chambers. A session may be opened and closed at either separate or joint sittings of the chambers.

Article 113. The right to initiate legislation in the Supreme Soviet of the USSR is vested in the Soviet of the Union and the Soviet of Nationalities, the Presidium of the Supreme Soviet of the USSR, the Council of Ministers of the USSR, Union Republics through their higher bodies of state authority, commissions of the Supreme Soviet of the USSR and standing commissions of its chambers, Deputies of the Supreme Soviet of the USSR, the Supreme Court of the USSR, and the Procurator-General of the USSR.

The right to initiate legislation is also vested in public organizations through their All-Union bodies.

Article 114. Bills and other matters submitted to the Supreme Soviet of the USSR shall be debated by its chambers at separate or joint sittings. Where necessary, a Bill or other matter may be referred to one or more commissions for preliminary or additional consideration.

A law of the USSR shall be deemed adopted when it has been passed in each chamber of the Supreme Soviet of the USSR by a majority of the total number of its Deputies. Decisions and other acts of the Supreme Soviet of the USSR are adopted by a majority of the total number of Deputies of the Supreme Soviet of the USSR.

Bills and other very important matters of state may be submitted for nation-wide discussion by a decision of the Supreme Soviet of the USSR or its Presidium taken on their own initiative or on the proposal of a Union Republic.

Article 115. In the event of disagreement between the Soviet of the Union and the Soviet of Nationalities, the matter at issue shall be referred for settlement to a conciliation commission formed by the chambers on a parity basis, after which it shall be considered for a second time by the Soviet of the Union and the Soviet of Nationalities at a joint sitting. If agreement is again not reached, the matter shall be postponed for debate at the next session of the Supreme Soviet of the USSR or submitted by the Supreme Soviet to a nation-wide vote (referendum).

Article 116. Laws of the USSR and decisions and other acts of the Supreme Soviet of the USSR shall be published in the languages of the Union Republics over the signatures of the Chairman and Secretary of the Presidium of the Supreme Soviet of the USSR.

Article 117. A deputy of the Supreme Soviet of the USSR has the right to address inquiries to the Council of Ministers of the USSR, and to Ministers and the heads of other bodies formed by the Supreme Soviet of the USSR. The Council of Ministers of the USSR, or the official to whom the inquiry is addressed, is obliged to give a verbal or written reply within three days at the given session of the Supreme Soviet of the USSR.

Article 118. A Deputy of the Supreme Soviet of the USSR may not be prosecuted, or arrested, or incur a court-imposed penalty, without the sanction of the Supreme Soviet of the USSR or, between its sessions, of the Presidium of the Supreme Soviet of the USSR.

Article 119. The Supreme Soviet of the USSR, at a joint sitting of its chambers, shall elect a Presidium of the Supreme Soviet of the USSR, which shall be a standing body of the Supreme Soviet of the USSR, accountable to it for all its work and exercising the functions of the highest body of state authority of the USSR between sessions of the Supreme Soviet, within the limits prescribed by the Constitution.

Article 120. The Presidium of the Supreme Soviet of the USSR shall be elected from among the Deputies and shall consist of a Chairman, First Vice-Chairman, fifteen Vice-Chairmen (one from each Union Republic), a Secretary, and twenty-one members.

Article 121. The Presidium of the Supreme Soviet of the USSR shall:

(1) Name the date of elections to the Supreme Soviet of the USSR;

(2) Convene sessions of the Supreme Soviet of the USSR;

(3) Coordinate the work of the standing commissions of the chambers of the Supreme Soviet of the USSR;

(4) Ensure observance of the Constitution of the USSR and conformity of the Constitutions and laws of Union Republics to the Constitution and laws of the USSR;

(5) Interpret the laws of the USSR;

(6) Ratify and denounce international treaties of the USSR;

(7) Revoke decisions and ordinances of the Council of Ministers of the USSR and of the Councils of Ministers of Union Republics should they fail to conform to the law;

(8) Institute military and diplomatic ranks and other special titles; and confer the highest military and diplomatic ranks and other special titles;

(9) Institute orders and medals of the USSR, and honorific titles of the USSR; award orders and medals of the USSR; and confer honorific titles of the USSR;

(10) Grant citizenship of the USSR, and rule on matters of the renunciation or deprivation of citizenship of the USSR and of granting asylum;

(11) Issue All-Union acts of amnesty and exercise the right of pardon;

(12) Appoint and recall diplomatic representatives of the USSR to other countries and to international organizations;

(13) Receive the letters of credence and recall of the diplomatic representatives of foreign states accredited to it;

(14) Form the Council of Defence of the USSR and confirm its composition; appoint and dismiss the high command of the Armed Forces of the USSR;

(15) Proclaim martial law in particular localities or throughout the country in the interests of defence of the USSR;

(16) Order general or partial mobilization;

(17) Between sessions of the Supreme Soviet of the USSR, proclaim a state of war in the event of an armed attack on the USSR, or when it is necessary to meet international treaty obligations relating to mutual defence against aggression;

(18) And exercise other powers vested in it by the Constitution and laws of the USSR.

Article 122. The Presidium of the Supreme Soviet of the USSR, between sessions of the Supreme Soviet of the USSR and subject to submission for its confirmation at the next session, shall:

(1) Amend exlsting legislativc acts of the USSR when necessary;

(2) Approve changes in the boundaries between Union Republics;

(3) Form and abolish Ministries and State Committees of the USSR on the recommendation of the Council of Ministers of the USSR;

(4) Relieve individual members of the Council of Ministers of the USSR of their responsibilities and appoint persons to the Council of Ministers on the recommendation of the Chairman of the Council of Ministers of the USSR.

Article 123. The Presidium of the Supreme Soviet of the USSR promulgates decrees and adopts decisions.

Article 124. On expiry of the term of the Supreme Soviet of the USSR, the Presidium of the Supreme Soviet of the USSR shall retain its powers until the newly elected Supreme Soviet of the USSR has elected a new Presidium.

The newly elected Supreme Soviet of the USSR shall be convened by the outgoing Presidium of the Supreme Soviet of the USSR within two months of the elections.

Article 125. The Soviet of the Union and the Soviet of Nationalities shall elect standing commissions from among the Deputies to make a preliminary review of matters coming within the jurisdiction of the Supreme Soviet of the USSR, to promote execution of the laws of the USSR and other acts of the Supreme Soviet of the USSR and its Presidium, and to check on the work of state bodies and organizations. The chambers of the Supreme Soviet of the USSR may also set up joint commissions on a parity basis.

When it deems it necessary, the Supreme Soviet of the USSR sets up commissions of inquiry and audit, and commissions on any other matter.

All state and public bodies, organizations and officials are obliged to meet the requests of the commissions of the Supreme Soviet of the USSR and of its chambers, and submit the requisite materials and documents to them.

The commissions' recommendations shall be subject to consideration by state and public bodies, institutions and organizations. The commissions shall be informed, within the prescribed time-limit, of the results of such consideration or of the action taken.

Article 126. The Supreme Soviet of the USSR shall supervise the work of all state bodies accountable to it.

The Supreme Soviet of the USSR shall form a Committee of People's Control of the USSR to head the system of people's control.

The organization and procedure of people's control bodies are defined by the Law on People's Control in the USSR.

Article 127. The procedure of the Supreme Soviet of the USSR and of its bodies shall be defined in the Rules and Regulations of the Supreme Soviet of the USSR and other laws of the USSR enacted on the basis of the Constitution of the USSR.

CHAPTER 16. THE COUNCIL OF MINISTERS OF THE USSR

Article 128. The Council of Ministers of the USSR, i.e. the Government of the USSR, is the highest executive and administrative body of state authority of the USSR.

Article 129. The Council of Ministers of the USSR shall be formed by the Supreme Soviet of the USSR at a joint sitting of the Soviet of the Union and the Soviet of Nationalities, and shall consist of the Chairman of the Council of Ministers of the USSR, First Vice-Chairmen and Vice-Chairmen, Ministers of the USSR, and Chairmen of State Committees of the USSR.

The Chairmen of the Councils of Ministers of Union Republics shall be *ex officio* members of the Council of Ministers of the USSR.

The Supreme Soviet of the USSR, on the recommendation of the Chairman of the Council of Ministers of the USSR, may include in the Government of the USSR the heads of other bodies and organizations of the USSR.

The Council of Ministers of the USSR shall tender its resignation to a newly elected Supreme Soviet of the USSR at its first session.

Article 130. The Council of Ministers of the USSR shall be responsible and accountable to the Supreme Soviet of the USSR and, between sessions of the Supreme Soviet of the USSR, to the Presidium of the Supreme Soviet of the USSR.

The Council of Ministers of the USSR shall report regularly on its work to the Supreme Soviet of the USSR.

Article 131. The Council of Ministers of the USSR is empowered to deal with all matters of state administration within the jurisdiction of the Union of Soviet Socialist Republics in so far as, under the Constitution, they do not come within the competence of the Supreme Soviet of the USSR or the Presidium of the Supreme Soviet of the USSR.

Within its powers the Council of Ministers of the USSR shall:

(1) Ensure direction of economic, social and cultural development; draft and implement measures to promote the well-being and cultural development of the people, to develop science and engineering, to ensure rational exploitation and conservation of natural resources, to consolidate the monetary and credit system, to pursue a uniform prices, wages, and social security policy, and to organize state insurance and a uniform system of accounting and statistics; and organize the management of industrial, constructional, and agricultural enterprises and amalgamations, transport and communications undertakings, banks, and other organizations and institutions of Union subordination;

(2) Draft current and long-term state plans for the economic and social development of the USSR and the Budget of the USSR, and submit them to the Supreme Soviet of the USSR; take measures to execute the state plans and Budget; and report to the Supreme Soviet of the USSR on the implementation of the plans and Budget;

(3) Implement measures to defend the interests of the state, protect socialist property and maintain public order, and guarantee and protect citizens' rights and freedoms;

(4) Take measures to ensure state security;

(5) Exercise general direction of the development of the Armed Forces of the USSR, and determine the annual contingent of citizens to be called up for active military service;

(6) Provide general direction in regard to relations with other states, foreign trade, and economic, scientific, technical, and cultural cooperation of the USSR with other countries; take measures to ensure fulfilment of the USSR's international treaties; and ratify and denounce intergovernmental international agreements;

(7) And when necessary, form committees, central boards and other departments under the Council of Ministers of the USSR to deal with matters of economic, social and cultural development, and defence.

Article 132. A Presidium of the Council of Ministers of the USSR, consisting of the Chairman, the First Vice-Chairmen, and Vice-Chairmen of the Council of Ministers of the USSR, shall function as a standing body of the Council of Ministers of the USSR to deal with questions relating to guidance of the economy, and with other matters of state administration.

Article 133. The Council of Ministers of the USSR, on the basis of, and in pursuance of, the laws of the USSR and other decisions of the Supreme Soviet of the USSR and its Presidium, shall issue decisions and ordinances and verify their execution. The decisions and ordinances of the Council of Ministers of the USSR shall be binding throughout the USSR.

Article 134. The Council of Ministers of the USSR has the right, in matters within the jurisdiction of the Union of Soviet Socialist Republics, to suspend execution of decisions and ordinances of the Councils of Ministers of Union Republics, and to rescind acts of ministries and state committees of the USSR, and of other bodies subordinate to it.

Article 135. The Council of Ministers of the USSR shall coordinate and direct the work of All-Union and Union-Republican ministries, state committees of the USSR, and other bodies subordinate to it.

All-Union ministries and state committees of the USSR shall direct the work of the branches of administration entrusted to them, or exercise inter-branch administration, throughout the territory of the USSR directly or through bodies set up by them.

Union-Republican ministries and state committees of the USSR direct the work of the branches of administration entrusted to them, or exercise inter-branch administration, as a rule, through the corresponding ministries and state committees, and other bodies of Union Republics, and directly administer individual enterprises and amalgamations of Union subordination. The procedure for transferring enterprises and amalgamations from Republic or local subordination to Union subordination shall be defined by the Presidium of the Supreme Soviet of the USSR.

Ministries and state committees of the USSR shall be responsible for the condition and development of the spheres of administration entrusted to them; within their competence, they issue orders and other acts on the basis of, and in execution of, the laws of the USSR and other decisions of the Supreme

Soviet of the USSR and its Presidium, and of decisions and ordinances of the Council of Ministers of the USSR, and organize and verify their implementation.

Article 136. The competence of the Council of Ministers of the USSR and its Presidium, the procedure for their work, relationships between the Council of Ministers and other state bodies, and the list of All-Union and Union-Republican ministries and state committees of the USSR are defined, on the basis of the Constitution, in the Law on the Council of Ministers of the USSR.

VI. BASIC PRINCIPLES OF THE STRUCTURE OF THE BODIES OF STATE AUTHORITY AND ADMINISTRATION IN UNION REPUBLICS

CHAPTER 17. HIGHER BODIES OF STATE AUTHORITY AND ADMINISTRATION OF A UNION REPUBLIC

Article 137. The highest body of state authority of a Union Republic shall be the Supreme Soviet of that Republic.

The Supreme Soviet of a Union Republic is empowered to deal with all matters within the jurisdiction of the Republic under the Constitutions of the USSR and the Republic.

Adoption and amendment of the Constitution of a Union Republic; endorsement of state plans for economic and social development, of the Republic's Budget, and of reports on their fulfilment; and the formation of bodies accountable to the Supreme Soviet of the Union Republic are the exclusive prerogative of that Supreme Soviet.

Laws of a Union Republic shall be enacted by the Supreme Soviet of the Union Republic or by a popular vote (referendum) held by decision of the Republic's Supreme Soviet.

Article 138. The Supreme Soviet of a Union Republic shall elect a Presidium, which is a standing body of that Supreme Soviet and accountable to it for all its work. The composition and powers of the Presidium of the Supreme Soviet of a Union Republic shall be defined in the Constitution of the Union Republic.

Article 139. The Supreme Soviet of a Union Republic shall form a Council of Ministers of the Union Republic, i.e. the Government of that Republic, which shall be the highest executive and administrative body of state authority in the Republic.

The Council of Ministers of a Union Republic shall be responsible and accountable to the Supreme Soviet of that

Republic or, between sessions of the Supreme Soviet, to its Presidium.

Article 140. The Council of Ministers of a Union Republic issues decisions and ordinances on the basis of, and in pursuance of, the legislative acts of the USSR and of the Union Republic, and of decisions and ordinances of the Council of Ministers of the USSR, and shall organize and verify their execution.

Article 141. The Council of Ministers of a Union Republic has the right to suspend the execution of decisions and ordinances of the Councils of Ministers of Autonomous Republics, to rescind the decisions and orders of the Executive Committees of Soviets of People's Deputies of Territories, Regions, and cities (i.e. cities under Republic jurisdiction) and of Autonomous Regions, and in Union Republics not divided into regions, of the Executive Committees of district and corresponding city Soviets of People's Deputies.

Article 142. The Council of Ministers of a Union Republic shall coordinate and direct the work of the Union-Republican and Republican ministries and of state committees of the Union Republic, and other bodies under its jurisdiction.

The Union-Republican ministries and state committees of a Union Republic shall direct the branches of administration entrusted to them, or exercise inter-branch control, and shall be subordinate to both the Council of Ministers of the Union Republic and the corresponding Union-Republican ministry or state committee of the USSR.

Republican ministries and state committees shall direct the branches of administration entrusted to them, or exercise inter-branch control, and shall be subordinate to the Council of Ministers of the Union Republic.

CHAPTER 18. HIGHER BODIES OF STATE
AUTHORITY AND ADMINISTRATION OF AN
AUTONOMOUS REPUBLIC

Article 143. The highest body of state authority of an Autonomous Republic shall be the Supreme Soviet of that Republic. Adoption and amendment of the Constitution of an Autonomous Republic; endorsement of state plans for economic and social development, and of the Republic's Budget; and the formation of bodies accountable to the Supreme Soviet of the Autonomous Republic are the exclusive prerogative of that Supreme Soviet.

Laws of an Autonomous Republic shall be enacted by the Supreme Soviet of the Autonomous Republic.

Article 144. The Supreme Soviet of an Autonomous Republic shall elect a Presidium of the Supreme Soviet of the Autonomous Republic and shall form a Council of Ministers of the Autonomous Republic, i.e. the Government of that Republic.

CHAPTER 19. LOCAL BODIES OF STATE AUTHORITY AND ADMINISTRATION

Article 145. The bodies of state authority in Territories, Regions, Autonomous Regions, Autonomous Areas, districts, cities, city districts, settlements, and rural communities shall be the corresponding Soviets of People's Deputies.

Article 146. Local Soviets of People's Deputies shall deal with all matters of local significance in accordance with the interests of the whole state and of the citizens residing in the area under their jurisdiction, implement decisions of higher bodies of state authority, guide the work of lower Soviets of People's Deputies, take part in the discussion of matters of Republican and All-Union significance, and submit their proposals concerning them.

Local Soviets of People's Deputies shall direct state, economic, social and cultural development within their territory; endorse plans of economic and social development and the local budget; exercise general guidance over state bodies, enterprises, institutions and organizations subordinate to them; ensure observance of the laws, maintenance of law and order, and protection of citizens' rights, and help strengthen the country's defence capacity.

Article 147. Within their powers, local Soviets of People's Deputies shall ensure the comprehensive, all-round economic and social development of their area; exercise control over the observance of legislation by enterprises, institutions and organizations subordinate to higher authorities and located in their area; and coordinate and supervise their activity as regards land use, nature conservation, building, employment of manpower, production of consumer goods, and social, cultural, communal and other services and amenities for the public.

Article 148. Local Soviets of People's Deputies shall decide matters within the powers accorded them by the legislation of the USSR and of the appropriate Union Republic and Autonomous Republic. Their decisions shall be binding on all enterprises, institutions, and organizations located in their area and on officials and citizens.

Article 149. The executive-administrative bodies of local Soviets shall be the Executive Committees elected by them from among their Deputies.

Executive Committees shall report on their work at least once a year to the Soviets that elected them and to meetings of citizens at their places of work or residence.

Article 150. Executive Committees of local Soviets of People's Deputies shall be directly accountable both to the Soviet that elected them and to the higher executive-administrative body.

VII. JUSTICE, ARBITRATION, AND PROCURATOR'S SUPERVISION

CHAPTER 20. COURTS AND ARBITRATION

Article 151. In the USSR justice is administered only by the courts.

In the USSR there are the following courts: the Supreme Court of the USSR, the Supreme Courts of Union Republics, the Supreme Courts of Autonomous Republics, Territorial, Regional, and city courts, courts of Autonomous Regions, courts of Autonomous Areas, district (city) people's courts, and military tribunals in the Armed Forces.

Article 152. All courts in the USSR shall be formed on the principle of the electiveness of judges and people's assessors.

People's judges of district (city) people's courts shall be elected for a term of five years by the citizens of the district (city) on the basis of universal, equal and direct suffrage by secret ballot. People's assessors of district (city) people's courts shall be elected for a term of two and a half years at meetings of citizens at their places of work or residence by a show of hands.

Higher courts shall be elected for a term of five years by the corresponding Soviet of People's Deputies.

The judges of military tribunals shall be elected for a term of five years by the Presidium of the Supreme Soviet of the USSR and people's assessors for a term of two and a half years by meetings of servicemen.

Judges and people's assessors are responsible and accountable to their electors or the bodies that elected them, shall report to them, and may be recalled by them in the manner prescribed by law.

Article 153. The Supreme Court of the USSR is the highest judicial body in the USSR and supervises the administration of justice by the courts of the USSR and Union Republics within the limits established by law.

The Supreme Court of the USSR shall be elected by the Supreme Soviet of the USSR and shall consist of a Chairman, Vice-Chairmen, members, and people's assessors. The Chairmen of the Supreme Courts of Union Republics are *ex officio* members of the Supreme Court of the USSR.

The organization and procedure of the Supreme Court of the USSR are defined in the Law on the Supreme Court of the USSR.

Article 154. The hearing of civil and criminal cases in all courts is collegial; in courts of first instance cases are heard with the participation of people's assessors. In the administration of justice people's assessors have all the rights of a judge.

Article 155. Judges and people's assessors are independent and subject only to the law.

Article 156. Justice is administered in the USSR on the principle of the equality of citizens before the law and the court.

Article 157. Proceedings in all courts shall be open to the public. Hearings in camera are only allowed in cases provided for by law, with observance of all the rules of judicial procedure.

Article 158. A defendant in a criminal action is guaranteed the right to legal assistance.

Article 159. Judicial proceedings shall be conducted in the language of the Union Republic, Autonomous Republic, Autonomous Region, or Autonomous Area, or in the language spoken by the majority of the people in the locality. Persons participating in court proceedings who do not know the language in which they are being conducted shall be ensured the right to become fully acquainted with the materials in the case; the services of an interpreter during the proceedings; and the right to address the court in their own language.

Article 160. No one may be adjudged guilty of a crime and subjected to punishment as a criminal except by the sentence of a court and in conformity with the law.

Article 161. Colleges of advocates are available to give legal assistance to citizens and organizations. In cases provided for by legislation citizens shall be given legal assistance free of charge.

The organization and procedure of the bar are determined by legislation of the USSR and Union Republics.

Article 162. Representatives of public organizations and of work collectives may take part in civil and criminal proceedings.

Article 163. Economic disputes between enterprises, institutions, and organizations are settled by state arbitration bodies within the limits of their jurisdiction.

The organization and manner of functioning of state arbitration bodies are defined in the Law on State Arbitration in the USSR.

CHAPTER 21. THE PROCURATOR'S OFFICE

Article 164. Supreme power of supervision over the strict and uniform observance of laws by all ministries, state committees and departments, enterprises, institutions and organizations, executive-administrative bodies of local Soviets of People's Deputies, collective farms, cooperatives and other public organizations, officials and citizens is vested in the Procurator-General of the USSR and procurators subordinate to him.

Article 165. The Procurator-General of the USSR is appointed by the Supreme Soviet of the USSR and is responsible and accountable to it and, between sessions of the Supreme Soviet, to the Presidium of the Supreme Soviet of the USSR.

Article 166. The procurators of Union Republics, Autonomous Republics, Territories, Regions and Autonomous Regions are appointed by the Procurator-General of the USSR. The procurators of Autonomous Areas and district and city procurators are appointed by the procurators of Union Republics, subject to confirmation by the Procurator-General of the USSR.

Article 167. The term of office of the Procurator-General of the USSR and all lower-ranking procurators shall be five years.

Article 168. The agencies of the Procurator's Office exercise their powers independently of any local bodies whatsoever, and are subordinate solely to the Procurator-General of the USSR.

The organization and procedure of the agencies of the Procurator's Office are defined in the Law on the Procurator's Office of the USSR.

VIII. THE EMBLEM, FLAG, ANTHEM, AND CAPITAL OF THE USSR

Article 169. The State Emblem of the Union of Soviet Socialist Republics is a hammer and sickle on a globe depicted in the rays of the sun and framed by ears of wheat, with the inscription 'Workers of All Countries, Unite!' in the languages of the Union Republics. At the top of the Emblem is a five-pointed star.

Article 170. The State Flag of the Union of Soviet Socialist Republics is a rectangle of red cloth with a hammer and sickle depicted in gold in the upper corner next to the staff and with a five-pointed red star edged in gold above them. The ratio of the width of the flag to its length is 1:2.

Article 171. The State Anthem of the Union of Soviet Socialist Republics is confirmed by the Presidium of the Supreme Soviet of the USSR.

Article 172. The Capital of the Union of Soviet Socialist Republics is the city of Moscow.

IX. THE LEGAL FORCE OF THE CONSTITUTION OF THE USSR AND PROCEDURE FOR AMENDING THE CONSTITUTION

Article 173. The Constitution of the USSR shall have supreme legal force. All laws and other acts of state bodies shall be promulgated on the basis of and in conformity with it.

Article 174. The Constitution of the USSR may be amended by a decision of the Supreme Soviet of the USSR adopted by a majority of not less than two-thirds of the total number of Deputies of each of its chambers.

[7 October 1977]

The Constitution (Basic Law) of the

FEDERAL REPUBLIC
OF GERMANY
1949

CONTENTS

ANNOUNCEMENT BY THE PARLIAMENTARY COUNCIL

The Parliamentary Council, meeting in public session at Bonn am Rhein on 23 May 1949, confirmed the fact that the Basic Law for the Federal Republic of Germany, which was adopted by the Parliamentary Council on 8 May 1949, was ratified in the week of 16 to 22 May 1949 by the Diets of more than two thirds of the participating constituent states (*Länder*).

By virtue of this fact the Parliamentary Council, represented by its Presidents, has signed and promulgated the Basic Law.

The Basic Law is hereby published in the *Federal Law Gazette* pursuant to paragraph (3) of Article 145.*

PREAMBLE

The German People

In the *Länder* of Baden,** Bavaria, Bremen, Hamburg, Hesse, Lower Saxony, North Rhine-Westphalia, Rhineland-Palatinate, Schleswig-Holstein, Württemberg-Baden** and Württemberg-Hohenzollern,**

Conscious of their responsibility before God and men,

Animated by the resolve to preserve their national and political unity and to serve the peace of the world as an equal partner in a united Europe,

Desiring to give a new order to political life for a transitional period,

Have enacted, by virtue of their constituent power, this Basic Law for the Federal Republic of Germany.

They have also acted on behalf of those Germans to whom participation was denied.

The entire German people are called upon to achieve in free self-determination the unity and freedom of Germany.

*The above notice of publication appeared in the first issue of the *Federal Law Gazette* dated 23 May 1949.

** See footnote * to Article 23.

I. BASIC RIGHTS

Article 1 (Protection of human dignity). (1) The dignity of man shall be inviolable. To respect and protect it shall be the duty of all state authority.

(2) The German people therefore acknowledge inviolable and inalienable human rights as the basis of every community, of peace and of justice in the world.

(3)* The following basic rights shall bind the legislature, the executive and the judiciary as directly enforceable law.

Article 2 (Rights of liberty). (1) Everyone shall have the right to the free development of his personality in so far as he does not violate the rights of others or offend against the constitutional order or the moral code.

(2) Everyone shall have the right to life and to inviolability of his person. The liberty of the individual shall be inviolable. These rights may only be encroached upon pursuant to a law.

Article 3 (Equality before the law). (1) All persons shall be equal before the law.

(2) Men and women shall have equal rights.

(3) No one may be prejudiced or favoured because of his sex, his parentage, his race, his language, his homeland and origin, his faith, or his religious or political opinions.

Article 4 (Freedom of faith and creed). (1) Freedom of faith of conscience, and freedom of creed, religious or ideological (*weltanschaulich*), shall be inviolable.

(2) The undisturbed practice of religion is guaranteed.

(3) No one may be compelled against his conscience to render war service involving the use of arms. Details shall be regulated by a federal law.

Article 5 (Freedom of expression). (1) Everyone shall have the

*As amended by federal law of 19 March 1956 (*Federal Law Gazette*, I, p. 111).

right freely to express and disseminate his opinion by speech, writing and pictures and freely to inform himself from generally accessible sources. Freedom of the press and freedom of reporting by means of broadcasts and films are guaranteed. There shall be no censorship.

(2) These rights are limited by the provisions of the general laws, the provisions of law for the protection of youth, and by the right to inviolability of personal honour.

(3) Art and science, research and teaching, shall be free. Freedom of teaching shall not absolve from loyalty to the constitution.

Article 6 (Marriage, Family, Illegitimate children). (1) Marriage and family shall enjoy the special protection of the state.

(2) The care and upbringing of children are a natural right of, and a duty primarily incumbent on, the parents. The national community shall watch over their endeavours in this respect.

(3) Children may not be separated from their families against the will of the persons entitled to bring them up, except pursuant to a law, if those so entitled fail or the children are otherwise threatened with neglect.

(4) Every mother shall be entitled to the protection and care of the community.

(5) Illegitimate children shall be provided by legislation with the same opportunities for their physical and spiritual development and their place in society as are enjoyed by legitimate children.

Article 7 (Education). (1) The entire educational system shall be under the supervision of the state.

(2) The persons entitled to bring up a child shall have the right to decide whether it shall receive religious instruction.

(3) Religious instruction shall form part of the ordinary curriculum in state and municipal schools, except in secular (*bekenntnisfrei*) schools. Without prejudice to the state's right of supervision, religious instruction shall be given in accordance with the tenets of the religious communities. No teacher may be obliged against his will to give religious instruction.

(4) The right to establish private schools is guaranteed. Private schools, as a substitute for state or municipal schools, shall require the approval of the state and shall be subject to the laws of

the *Länder*. Such approval must be given if private schools are not inferior to the state or municipal schools in their educational aims, their facilities and the professional training of their teaching staff, and if segregation of pupils according to the means of the parents is not promoted thereby. Approval must be withheld if the economic and legal position of the teaching staff is not sufficiently assured.

(5) A private elementary school shall be permitted only if the education authority finds that it serves a special pedagogic interest, or if, on the application of persons entitled to bring up children, it is to be established as an interdenominational or denominational or ideological school and a state or municipal elementary school of this type does not exist in the commune (*Gemeinde*).

(6) Preparatory schools (*Vorschulen*) shall remain abolished.

Article 8 (Freedom of assembly). (1) All Germans shall have the right to assemble peaceably and unarmed without prior notification or permission.

(2) With regard to open-air meetings this right may be restricted by or pursuant to a law.

Article 9 (Freedom of association). (1) All Germans shall have the right to form associations and societies.

(2) Associations, the purposes or activities of which conflict with criminal laws or which are directed against the constitutional order or the concept of international understanding, are prohibited.

(3) The right to form associations to safeguard and improve working and economic conditions is guaranteed to everyone and to all trades, occupations and professions. Agreements which restrict or seek to impair this right shall be null and void; measures directed to this end shall be illegal. Measures taken pursuant to Article 12a, to paragraphs (2) and (3) of Article 35, to paragraph (4) of Article 87a, or to Article 91, may not be directed against any industrial conflicts engaged in by associations within the meaning of the first sentence of this paragraph in order to safeguard and improve working and economic conditions.*

*Last sentence inserted by federal law of 24 June 1968 (*Federal Law Gazette*, I, p. 709).

Article 10* (Privacy of posts and telecommunications). (1) Privacy of posts and telecommunications shall be inviolable.

(2) This right may be restricted only pursuant to a law. Such law may lay down that the person affected shall not be informed of any such restriction if it serves to protect the free democratic basic order or the existence or security of the Federation or a *Land*, and that recourse to the courts shall be replaced by a review of the case by bodies and auxiliary bodies appointed by Parliament.

Article 11 (Freedom of movement). (1) All Germans shall enjoy freedom of movement throughout the federal territory.

(2)* This right may be restricted only by or pursuant to a law and only in cases in which an adequate basis of existence is lacking and special burdens would arise to the community as a result thereof, or in which such restriction is necessary to avert an imminent danger to the existence or the free democratic basic order of the Federation or a *Land*, to combat the danger of epidemics, to deal with natural disasters or particularly grave accidents, to protect young people from neglect or to prevent crime.

Article 12** (Right to choose trade, occupation or profession). (1) All Germans shall have the right freely to choose their trade, occupation, or profession, their place of work and their place of training. The practice of trades, occupations, and professions may be regulated by or pursuant to a law.

(2) No specific occupation may be imposed on any person except within the framework of a traditional compulsory public service that applies generally and equally to all.

(3) Forced labour may be imposed only on persons deprived of their liberty by court sentence.

Article 12a*** (Liability to military and other service). (1) Men who have attained the age of eighteen years may be required to serve in the Armed Forces, in the Federal Border Guard, or in a Civil Defence organization.

*As amended by federal law of 24 June 1968 (*Federal Law Gazette*, I, p. 709).
**As amended by federal laws of 19 March 1956 (*Federal Law Gazette*, I, p. 111) and 24 June 1968 (*Federal Law Gazette*, I, p. 709).
***Inserted by federal law of 24 June 1968 (*Federal Law Gazette*, I, p. 710).

(2) A person who refuses, on grounds of conscience, to render war service involving the use of arms may be required to render a substitute service. The duration of such substitute service shall not exceed the duration of military service. Details shall be regulated by a law which shall not interfere with the freedom of conscience and must also provide for the possibility of a substitute service not connected with units of the Armed Forces or of the Federal Border Guard.

(3) Persons liable to military service who are not required to render service pursuant to paragraph (1) or (2) of this Article may, when a state of defence (*Verteidigungsfall*) exists, be assigned by or pursuant to a law to specific occupations involving civilian services for defence purposes, including the protection of the civilian population; it shall, however, not be permissible to assign persons to an occupation subject to public law except for the purpose of discharging police functions or such other functions of public administration as can only be discharged by persons employed under public law. Persons may be assigned to occupations – as referred to in the first sentence of this paragraph – with the Armed Forces, including the supplying and servicing of the latter, or with public administrative authorities; assignments to occupations connected with supplying and servicing the civilian population shall not be permissible except in order to meet their vital requirements or to guarantee their safety.

(4) If, while a state of defence exists, civilian service requirements in the civilian public health and medical system or in the stationary military hospital organization cannot be met on a voluntary basis, women between eighteen and fifty-five years of age may be assigned to such services by or pursuant to a law. They may on no account render service involving the use of arms.

(5) During the time prior to the existence of any such state of defence, assignments under paragraph (3) of this Article may be effected only if the requirements of paragraph (1) of Article 80a are satisfied. It shall be admissible to require persons by or pursuant to a law to attend training courses in order to prepare them for the performance of such services in accordance with paragraph (3) of this Article as presuppose special knowledge or skills.

To this extent, the first sentence of this paragraph shall not apply.

(6) If, while a state of defence exists, the labour requirements for the purposes referred to in the second sentence of paragraph (3) of this Article cannot be met on a voluntary basis, the right of a German to give up the practice of his trade or occupation or profession, or his place of work, may be restricted by or pursuant to a law in order to meet these requirements. The first sentence of paragraph (5) of this Article shall apply *mutatis mutandis* prior to the existence of a state of defence.

Article 13 (Inviolability of the home). (1) The home shall be inviolable.

(2) Searches may be ordered only by a judge or, in the event of danger in delay, by other organs as provided by law and may be carried out only in the form prescribed by law.

(3) In all other respects, this inviolability may not be encroached upon or restricted except to avert a common danger or a mortal danger to individuals, or, pursuant to a law, to prevent imminent danger to public safety and order, especially to alleviate the housing shortage, to combat the danger of epidemics or to protect endangered juveniles.

Article 14 (Property, Right of inheritance, Expropriation). (1) Property and the right of inheritance are guaranteed. Their content and limits shall be determined by the laws.

(2) Property imposes duties. Its use should also serve the public weal.

(3) Expropriation shall be permitted only in the public weal. It may be effected only by or pursuant to a law which shall provide for the nature and extent of the compensation. Such compensation shall be determined by establishing an equitable balance between the public interest and the interests of those affected. In case of dispute regarding the amount of compensation, recourse may be had to the ordinary courts.

Article 15 (Socialization). Land, natural resources and means of production may for the purpose of socialization be transferred to public ownership or other forms of publicly controlled economy by a law which shall provide for the nature and extent of compensation. In respect of such compensation the third and fourth sentences of paragraph (3) of Article 14 shall apply *mutatis mutandis*.

Article 16 (Deprivation of citizenship, Extradition, Right of asylum). (1) No one may be deprived of his German citizenship. Loss of citizenship may arise only pursuant to a law, and against the will of the person affected only if such person does not thereby become stateless.

(2) No German may be extradited to a foreign country. Persons persecuted on political grounds shall enjoy the right of asylum.

Article 17 (Right of petition). Every one shall have the right individua1ly or jointly with others to address written requests or complaints to the appropriate agencies and to parliamentary bodies.

Article 17a* (Restriction of basic rights for members of the Armed Forces etc.). (1) Laws concerning military service and substitute service may, by provisions applying to members of the Armed Forces and of substitute services during their period of military or substitute service, restrict the basic right freely to express and to disseminate opinions by speech, writing and pictures (first half-sentence of paragraph (1) of Article 5), the basic right of assembly (Article 8), and the right of petition (Article 17) in so far as this right permits the submission of requests or complaints jointly with others.

(2) Laws for defence purposes including the protection of the civilian population may provide for the restriction of the basic rights of freedom of movement (Article 11) and inviolability of the home (Article 13).

Article 18 (Forfeiture of basic rights). Whoever abuses freedom of expression of opinion, in particular freedom of the press (paragraph (1) of Article 5), freedom of teaching [paragraph (3) of Article 5], freedom of assembly (Article 8), freedom of association (Article 9), privacy of posts and telecommunications (Article 10), property (Article 14), or the right of asylum (paragraph (2) of Article 16) in order to combat the free democratic basic order, shall forfeit these basic rights. Such forfeiture and the extent thereof shall be pronounced by the Federal Constitutional Court.

* Inserted by federal law of 19 March 1956 (*Federal Law Gazette*, I, p. 111).

Article 19 (Restriction of basic rights). (1) In so far as a basic right may, under this Basic Law, be restricted by or pursuant to a law, such law must apply generally and not solely to an individual case. Furthermore, such law must name the basic right, indicating the Article concerned.

(2) In no case may the essential content of a basic right be encroached upon.

(3) The basic rights shall apply also to domestic juristic persons to the extent that the nature of such rights permits.

(4) Should any person's right be violated by public authority, recourse to the court shall be open to him. If jurisdiction is not specified, recourse shall be to the ordinary courts. The second sentence of paragraph (2) of Article 10 shall not be affected by the provisions of this paragraph.*

II. THE FEDERATION AND THE CONSTITUENT STATES (*LÄNDER*)

Article 20 (Basic principles of the Constitution – Right to resist). (1) The Federal Republic of Germany is a democratic and social federal state.

(2) All state authority emanates from the people. It shall be exercised by the people by means of elections and voting and by specific legislative, executive, and judicial organs.

(3) Legislation shall be subject to the constitutional order; the executive and the judiciary shall be bound by law and justice.

(4)** All Germans shall have the right to resist any person or persons seeking to abolish that constitutional order, should no other remedy be possible.

Article 21 (Political parties). (1) The political parties shall participate in the forming of the political will of the people. They may be freely established. Their internal organization must conform to democratic principles. They must publicly account for the sources of their funds.

(2) Parties which, by reason of their aims or the behaviour of

---

*Last sentence inserted by federal law of 24 June 1968 (*Federal Law Gazette*, I, p. 710).

**Inserted by federal law of 24 June 1968 (*Federal Law Gazette*, I, p. 710).

their adherents, seek to impair or abolish the free democratic basic order or to endanger the existence of the Federal Republic of Germany, shall be unconstitutional. The Federal Constitutional Court shall decide on the question of unconstitutionality.

(3) Details shall be regulated by federal laws.

Article 22 (Federal flag). The federal flag shall be black-red-gold.

Article 23 (Jurisdiction of the Basic Law). For the time being, this Basic Law shall apply in the territory of the *Länder* of Baden,* Bavaria, Bremen, Greater Berlin, Hamburg, Hesse, Lower Saxony, North Rhine-Westphalia, Rhineland-Palatinate, Schleswig-Holstein, Württemberg-Baden,* and Württemberg-Hohenzollern.* In other parts of Germany it shall be put into force on their accession.**

Article 24 (Entry into a collective security system). (1) The Federation may by legislation transfer sovereign powers to intergovernmental institutions.

(2) For the maintenance of peace, the Federation may enter a system of mutual collective security; in doing so it will consent to such limitations upon its rights of sovereignty as will bring about and secure a peaceful and lasting order in Europe and among the nations of the world.

(3) For the settlement of disputes between states, the Federation will accede to agreements concerning international arbitration of a general, comprehensive and obligatory nature.

Article 25 (International law integral part of federal law). The general rules of public international law shall be an integral part of federal law. They shall take precedence over the laws and shall directly create rights and duties for the inhabitants of the federal territory.

Article 26 (Ban on war of aggression). (1) Acts tending to and undertaken with the intent to disturb the peaceful relations

---

*By federal law of 4 May 1951 (*Federal Law Gazette*, I, p. 284) the Land of Baden-Württemberg was created out of the former *Länder* of Baden, Württemberg-Baden and Württemberg-Hohenzollern.

**This Basic Law became effective in the Saarland by virtue of paragraph (1) of Section 1 of the federal law of 23 December 1956 (*Federal Law Gazette*, I, p. 1011).

between nations, especially to prepare for aggressive war, shall be unconstitutional. They shall be made a punishable offence.

(2) Weapons designed for warfare may not be manufactured, transported or marketed except with the permission of the Federal Government. Details shall be regulated by a federal law.

Article 27 (Merchant fleet). All German merchant vessels shall form one merchant fleet.

Article 28 (Federal guarantee of *Länder* constitutions). (1) The constitutional order in the *Länder* must conform to the principles of republican, democratic and social government based on the rule of law, within the meaning of this Basic Law. In each of the *Länder*, counties (*Kreise*), and communes (*Gemeinden*), the people must be represented by a body chosen in general, direct, free, equal, and secret elections. In the communes the assembly of the commune may take the place of an elected body.

(2) The communes must be guaranteed the right to regulate on their own responsibility all the affairs of the local community within the limits set by law. The associations of communes (*Gemeindeverbände*) shall also have the right of self-government in accordance with the law and within the limits of the functions assigned to them by law.

(3) The Federation shall ensure that the constitutional order of the *Länder* conforms to the basic rights and to the provisions of paragraphs (1) and (2) of this Article.

Article 29 (Reorganization of the federal territory). (1) The federal territory shall be reorganized by federal legislation with due regard to regional ties, historical and cultural connections, economic expediency and social structure. Such reorganization should create *Länder* which by their size and capacity are able effectively to fulfil the functions incumbent upon them.

(2)* In areas which became, upon the reorganization of the *Länder* after 8 May 1945, part of another *Land* without the holding of a plebiscite, a definite change of the decision regarding such incorporation may be demanded by popular initiative within one year of the coming into force of this Basic Law. Such popular

*As amended by federal law of 19 August 1969 (*Federal Law Gazette*, I, p. 1241).

initiative shall require the assent of one tenth of the people entitled to vote in *Land* Diet (Landtag) elections.

(3)* If a popular initiative has received the assent required under paragraph (2) of this Article, a referendum shall be held in the area concerned not later than 31 March 1975, or in the Baden area of the *Land* of Baden-Württemberg not later than 30 June 1970, on whether or not the proposed transfer shall be made. If the transfer is approved by a majority comprising at least one quarter of the people entitled to vote in *Land* Diet elections, the territorial position of the area concerned shall be regulated by a federal law within one year after the referendum has been held. Where several areas within the same *Land* demand to be transferred to another *Land*, the necessary regulations shall be consolidated in one law.

(4)* Such federal law shall be based upon the result of the referendum from which it may depart only to the extent necessary to achieve the purposes of reorganization as specified in paragraph (1) of this Article. Such law shall require the assent of a majority of Bundestag members. If it provides for a transfer, not demanded by a referendum, of an area from one *Land* to another, the law shall require approval by referendum in the entire area to be transferred; this shall not apply if in the event of the separation of areas from an existing *Land* the remaining areas are to continue as a *Land* in themselves.

(5)* Following the adoption of a federal law on the reorganization of the federal territory by a procedure other than that laid down in paragraphs (2) to (4) of this Article, a referendum shall be held in every area to be transferred from one *Land* to another, on those provisions of the law which concern that area. If such provisions are rejected in at least one of the areas concerned, the law must be reintroduced in the Bundestag. Should it be enacted again, the relevant provisions shall require approval by referendum throughout the federal territory.

(6)* A referendum shall be decided by the majority of votes cast; this shall, however, not affect paragraph (3) of this Article. The pertinent procedure shall be laid down by a federal law.

*As amended by federal law of 19 August 1969 (*Federal Law Gazette*, I, p. 1241).

Should reorganization become necessary as a result of the accession of another part of Germany, such reorganization should be concluded within two years of such accession.

(7) The procedure regarding any other change in *Land* boundaries shall be established by a federal law requiring the consent of the Bundesrat and of the majority of the members of the Bundestag.

Article 30 (Functions of the *Länder*). The exercise of governmental powers and the discharge of governmental functions shall be incumbent on the *Länder* (*ist Sache der Länder*)[1] in so far as this Basic Law does not otherwise prescribe or permit.

Article 31 (Priority of federal law). Federal law shall override *Land* law.

Article 32 (Foreign relations). (1) Relations with foreign states shall be conducted by the Federation.

(2) Before the conclusion of a treaty affecting the special circumstances of a *Land*, that *Land* must be consulted in sufficient time.

(3) In so far as the *Länder* have power to legislate, they may, with the consent of the Federal Government, conclude treaties with foreign states.

Article 33 (All Germans have equal political status). (1) Every German shall have in every *Land* the same political (*staatsbürgerlich*) rights and duties.

(2) Every German shall be equally eligible for any public office according to his aptitude, qualifications, and professional achievements.

(3) Enjoyment of civil and political rights, eligibility for public office, and rights acquired in the public service shall be independent of religious denomination. No one may suffer any disadvantage by reason of his adherence or non-adherence to a denomination or ideology.

(4) The exercise of state authority as a permanent function shall as a rule be entrusted to members of the public service whose status, service and loyalty are governed by public law.

(5) The law of the public service shall be regulated with due

---

1. In my view, a mistranslation. More accurately: '. . . is a matter for the *Länder* . . .' S.E.F.

regard to the traditional principles of the professional civil service.

Article 34 (Liability in the event of malfeasance). If any person, in the exercise of a public office entrusted to him, violates his official obligations to a third party, liability shall rest in principle on the state or the public body which employs him. In the event of wilful intent or gross negligence the right of recourse shall be reserved. In respect of the claim for compensation or the right of recourse, the jurisdiction of the ordinary courts must not be excluded.

Article 35* (Legal, administrative and police assistance). (1) All federal and *Land* authorities shall render each other legal and administrative assistance.

(2) In order to maintain or to restore public security or order, a *Land* may, in cases of particular importance, call upon forces and facilities of the Federal Border Guard to assist its police if, without this assistance, the police could not, or only with considerable difficulty, fulfil a task. In order to deal with a natural disaster or an especially grave accident, a *Land* may request the assistance of the police forces of other *Länder* or of forces and facilities of other administrative authorities or of the Federal Border Guard or the Armed Forces.**

(3) If the natural disaster or the accident endangers a region larger than a *Land*, the Federal Government may, in so far as this is necessary effectively to deal with such danger, instruct the *Land* governments to place their police forces at the disposal of other *Länder*, and may commit units of the Federal Border Guard or the Armed Forces to support the police forces. Measures taken by the Federal Government pursuant to the first sentence of this paragraph must be revoked at any time upon the request of the Bundesrat, and in any case without delay upon removal of the danger.

Article 36 (Personnel of the federal authorities). (1) Civil servants employed in the highest federal authorities shall be drawn from

*As amended by federal law of 24 June 1968 (*Federal Law Gazette*, I, p. 710).

**As amended by federal law of 28 July 1972 (*Federal Law Gazette*, I, p. 1305).

all *Länder* in appropriate proportion. Persons employed in other federal authorities should, as a rule, be drawn from the *Land* in which they serve.

(2)* Military laws shall, inter alia, take into account both the division of the Federation into *Länder* and the regional ties of their populations.

Article 37 (Federal enforcement). (1) If a *Land* fails to comply with its obligations of a federal character imposed by this Basic Law or another federal law, the Federal Government may, with the consent of the Bundesrat, take the necessary measures to enforce such compliance by the *Land* by way of federal enforcement.

(2) To carry out such federal enforcement the Federal Government or its commissioner shall have the right to give instructions to all *Länder* and their authorities.

III. THE FEDERAL PARLIAMENT (BUNDESTAG)

Article 38 (Elections). (1) The deputies to the German Bundestag shall be elected in general, direct, free, equal, and secret elections. They shall be representatives of the whole people, not bound by orders and instructions, and shall be subject only to their conscience.

(2) Anyone who has attained the age of eighteen years shall be entitled to vote; anyone who has attained full legal age shall be eligible for election.

(3) Details shall be regulated by a federal law.

Article 39 (Assembly and legislative term). (1) The Bundestag shall be elected for a four-year term. Its legislative term shall end four years after its first meeting or on its dissolution. The new election shall be held during the last three months of the term or within sixty days after dissolution.

(2) The Bundestag shall assemble within thirty days after the election, but not before the end of the term of the previous Bundestag.

(3) The Bundestag shall determine the termination and resumption of its meetings. The President of the Bundestag may convene

*Inserted by federal law of 19 March 1956 (*Federal Law Gazette*, I, p. 111).

it at an earlier date. He must do so if one third of its members or the Federal President or the Federal Chancellor so demand.

Article 40 (President, Rules of procedure). (1) The Bundestag shall elect its President, vice-presidents, and secretaries. It shall draw up its rules of procedure.

(2) The President shall exercise the proprietary and police powers in the Bundestag building. No search or seizure may take place in the premises of the Bundestag without his permission.

Article 41 (Scrutiny of elections). (1) The scrutiny of elections shall be the responsibility of the Bundestag. It shall also decide whether a deputy has lost his seat in the Bundestag.

(2) Complaints against such decisions of the Bundestag may be lodged with the Federal Constitutional Court.

(3) Details shall be regulated by a federal law.

Article 42 (Proceedings, Voting). (1) The meetings of the Bundestag shall be public. Upon a motion of one tenth of its members, or upon a motion of the Federal Government, the public may be excluded by a two-thirds majority. The decision on the motion shall be taken at a meeting not open to the public.

(2) Decisions of the Bundestag shall require a majority of the votes cast unless this Basic Law provides otherwise. The rules of procedure may provide exceptions for elections to be made by the Bundestag.

(3) True and accurate reports on the public meetings of the Bundestag and of its committees shall not give rise to any liability.

Article 43 (Presence of the Federal Government). (1) The Bundestag and its committees may demand the presence of any member of the Federal Government.

(2) The members of the Bundesrat or of the Federal Government as well as persons commissioned by them shall have access to all meetings of the Bundestag and its committees. They must be heard at any time.

Article 44 (Committees of investigation). (1) The Bundestag shall have the right, and upon the motion of one fourth of its members the duty, to set up a committee of investigation which shall take the requisite evidence at public hearings. The public may be excluded.

(2) The rules of criminal procedure shall apply *mutatis mutan-*

dis to the taking of evidence. The privacy of posts and telecommunications shall remain unaffected.

(3) Courts and administrative authorities shall be bound to render legal and administrative assistance.

(4) The decisions of committees of investigation shall not be subject to judicial consideration. The courts shall be free to evaluate and judge the facts on which the investigation is based.

Article 45 (Standing Committee). (1) The Bundestag shall appoint a Standing Committee which shall safeguard the rights of the Bundestag as against the Federal Government in the intervals between any two legislative terms. The Standing Committee shall also have the rights of a committee of investigation.

(2) Wider powers, such as the right to legislate, to elect the Federal Chancellor, or to impeach the Federal President, shall not be within the competence of the Standing Committee.

Article 45a* (Committees on Foreign Affairs and Defence). (1) The Bundestag shall appoint a Committee on Foreign Affairs and a Committee on Defence. Both committees shall function also in the intervals between any two legislative terms.

(2) The Committee on Defence shall also have the rights of a committee of investigation. Upon the motion of one fourth of its members it shall have the duty to make a specific matter the subject of investigation.

(3) Paragraph (1) of Article 44 shall not be applied in matters of defence.

Article 45b* (Defence Commissioner of the Bundestag). A Defence Commissioner of the Bundestag shall be appointed to safeguard the basic rights and to assist the Bundestag in exercising parliamentary control. Details shall be regulated by a federal law.

Article 46 (Indemnity and immunity of deputies). (1) A deputy may not at any time be prosecuted in the courts or subjected to disciplinary action or otherwise called to account outside the Bundestag for a vote cast or a statement made by him in the Bundestag or any of its committees. This shall not apply to defamatory insults.

(2) A deputy may not be called to account or arrested for a

*Inserted by federal law of 19 March 1956 (*Federal Law Gazette*, I, p. 111).

punishable offence except by permission of the Bundestag, unless he is apprehended in the commission of the offence or in the course of the following day.

(3) The permission of the Bundestag shall also be necessary for any other restriction of the personal liberty of a deputy or for the initiation of proceedings against a deputy under Article 18.

(4) Any criminal proceedings or any proceedings under Article 18 against a deputy, any detention or any other restriction of his personal liberty shall be suspended upon the request of the Bundestag.

Article 47 (Right of deputies to refuse to give evidence). Deputies may refuse to give evidence concerning persons who have confided facts to them in their capacity as deputies, or to whom they have confided facts in such capacity, as well as concerning these facts themselves. To the extent that this right to refuse to give evidence exists, no seizure of documents shall be permissible.

Article 48 (Entitlements of deputies). (1) Any candidate for election to the Bundestag shall be entitled to the leave necessary for his election campaign.

(2) No one may be prevented from accepting and exercising the office of deputy. He may not be given notice of dismissal nor dismissed from employment on this ground.

(3) Deputies shall be entitled to a remuneration adequate to ensure their independence. They shall be entitled to the free use of all state-owned means of transport. Details shall be regulated by a federal law.

Article 49* (Interim between legislative terms). In respect of the members of the Presidency, the Standing Committee, the Committee on Foreign Affairs, and the Committee on Defence, as well as their principal substitutes, Articles 46, 47, and paragraphs (2) and (3) of Article 48, shall apply also in the intervals between any two legislative terms.

---

*As amended by federal law of 19 March 1956 (*Federal Law Gazette*, I, p. 111).

IV. THE COUNCIL OF CONSTITUENT
STATES (BUNDESRAT)

Article 50 (Function). The *Länder* shall participate through the Bundesrat in the legislation and administration of the Federation.

Article 51 (Composition). (1) The Bundesrat shall consist of members of the *Land* governments which appoint and recall them. Other members of such governments may act as substitutes.

(2) Each *Land* shall have at least three votes; *Länder* with more than 2 million inhabitants shall have four, *Länder* with more than 6 million inhabitants five votes.

(3) Each *Land* may delegate as many members as it has votes. The votes of each *Land* may be cast only as a block vote and only by members present or their substitutes.

Article 52 (President, Rules of procedure). (1) The Bundesrat shall elect its President for one year.

(2) The President shall convene the Bundesrat. He must convene it if the members for at least two *Länder* or the Federal Government so demand.

(3) The Bundesrat shall take its decisions with at least the majority of its votes. It shall draw up its rules of procedure. Its meetings shall be public. The public may be excluded.

(4) Other members of, or persons commissioned by, *Land* governments may serve on the committees of the Bundesrat.

Article 53 (Participation of the Federal Government). The members of the Federal Government shall have the right, and on demand the duty, to attend the meetings of the Bundesrat and of its committees. They must be heard at any time. The Bundesrat must be currently kept informed by the Federal Government of the conduct of affairs.

IVa.* THE JOINT COMMITTEE

Article 53a. (1) Two thirds of the members of the Joint Committee shall be deputies of the Bundestag and one third shall be members of the Bundesrat. The Bundestag shall delegate its deputies in proportion to the sizes of its parliamentary groups;

* Inserted by federal law of 24 June 1968 (*Federal Law Gazette*, I, p. 710).

such deputies must not be members of the Federal Government. Each *Land* shall be represented by a Bundesrat member of its choice; these members shall not be bound by instructions. The establishment of the Joint Committee and its procedures shall be regulated by rules of procedure to be adopted by the Bundestag and requiring the consent of the Bundesrat.

(2) The Federal Government must inform the Joint Committee about its plans in respect of a state of defence. The rights of the Bundestag and its committees under paragraph (1) of Article 43 shall not be affected by the provision of this paragraph.

V. THE FEDERAL PRESIDENT

Article 54 (Election by the Federal Convention). (1) The Federal President shall be elected, without debate, by the Federal Convention (*Bundesversammlung*). Every German shall be eligible who is entitled to vote for Bundestag candidates and has attained the age of forty years.

(2) The term of office of the Federal President shall be five years. Re-election for a consecutive term shall be permitted only once.

(3) The Federal Convention shall consist of the members of the Bundestag and an equal number of members elected by the Diets of the *Länder* according to the principles of proportional representation.

(4) The Federal Convention shall meet not later than thirty days before the expiration of the term of office of the Federal President or, in the case of premature termination, not later than thirty days after that date. It shall be convened by the President of the Bundestag.

(5) After the expiration of a legislative term, the period specified in the first sentence of paragraph (4) of this Article shall begin with the first meeting of the Bundestag.

(6) The person receiving the votes of the majority of the members of the Federal Convention shall be elected. If such majority is not obtained by any candidate in two ballots, the candidate who receives the largest number of votes in the next ballot shall be elected.

(7) Details shall be regulated by a federal law.

Article 55 (No secondary occupation). (1) The Federal President may not be a member of the government nor of a legislative body of the Federation or of a *Land*.

(2) The Federal President may not hold any other salaried office, nor engage in a trade or occupation, nor practise a profession, nor belong to the management or the board of directors of an enterprise carried on for profit.

Article 56 (Oath of office). On assuming his office the Federal President shall take the following oath before the assembled members of the Bundestag and the Bundesrat:

'I swear that I will dedicate my efforts to the well-being of the German people, enhance its benefits, ward harm from it, uphold and defend the Basic Law and the laws of the Federation, fulfil my duties conscientiously, and do justice to all. So help me God.'

The oath may also be taken without religious affirmation.

Article 57 (Representation). If the Federal President is prevented from acting, or if his office falls prematurely vacant, his powers shall be exercised by the President of the Bundesrat.

Article 58 (Countersignature). Orders and decrees of the Federal President shall require for their validity the countersignature of the Federal Chancellor or the appropriate Federal Minister. This shall not apply to the appointment and dismissal of the Federal Chancellor, the dissolution of the Bundestag under Article 63 and the request under paragraph (3) of Article 69.

Article 59 (Authority to represent the Federation in international relations). (1) The Federal President shall represent the Federation in its international relations. He shall conclude treaties with foreign states on behalf of the Federation. He shall accredit and receive envoys.

(2) Treaties which regulate the political relations of the Federation or relate to matters of federal legislation shall require the consent or participation, in the form of a federal law, of the bodies competent in any specific case for such federal legislation. As regards administrative agreements, the provisions concerning the federal administration shall apply *mutatis mutandis*.

Article 59a* (Repealed).

*Inserted by federal law of 19 March 1956 (*Federal Law Gazette*, I, p. 111) and repealed by federal law of 24 June 1968 (*Federal Law Gazette*, I, p. 711).

Article 60 (Appointment of federal civil servants and officers).
(1)* The Federal President shall appoint and dismiss the federal
judges, the federal civil servants, the officers and non-commis-
sioned officers, unless otherwise provided for by law.

(2) He shall exercise the right of pardon in individual cases on
behalf of the Federation.

(3) He may delegate these powers to other authorities.

(4) Paragraphs (2) to (4) of Article 46 shall apply *mutatis
mutandis* to the Federal President.

**Article 61 (Impeachment before the Federal Constitutional
Court).** (1) The Bundestag or the Bundesrat may impeach the
Federal President before the Federal Constitutional Court for
wilful violation of this Basic Law or any other federal law. The
motion for impeachment must be brought forward by at least one
fourth of the members of the Bundestag or one fourth of the votes
of the Bundesrat. The decision to impeach shall require a majority
of two thirds of the members of the Bundestag or of two thirds of
the votes of the Bundesrat. The impeachment shall be substantiated by a person commissioned by the impeaching body.

(2) If the Federal Constitutional Court finds the Federal President guilty of a wilful violation of this Basic Law or of another
federal law, it may declare him to have forfeited his office. After
impeachment, it may issue an interim order preventing the
Federal President from exercising his functions.

VI. THE FEDERAL GOVERNMENT

Article 62 (Composition). The Federal Government shall consist of the Federal Chancellor and the Federal Ministers.

**Article 63 (Election of the Federal Chancellor – Dissolution of
the Bundestag).** (1) The Federal Chancellor shall be elected, without debate, by the Bundestag upon the proposal of the Federal
President.

(2) The person obtaining the votes of the majority of the members of the Bundestag shall be elected. The person elected must be
appointed by the Federal President.

*As amended by federal law of 19 March 1956 (*Federal Law Gazette*, I,
p. 111).

(3) If the person proposed is not elected, the Bundestag may elect within fourteen days of the ballot a Federal Chancellor by more than one half of its members.

(4) If no candidate has been elected within this period, a new ballot shall take place without delay, in which the person obtaining the largest number of votes shall be elected. If the person elected has obtained the votes of the majority of the members of the Bundestag, the Federal President must appoint him within seven days of the election. If the person elected did not obtain such a majority, the Federal President must within seven days either appoint him or dissolve the Bundestag.

Article 64 (Appointment of Federal Ministers). (1) The Federal Ministers shall be appointed and dismissed by the Federal President upon the proposal of the Federal Chancellor.

(2) The Federal Chancellor and the Federal Ministers, on assuming office, shall take before the Bundestag the oath provided for in Article 56.

Article 65 (Distribution of responsibility). The Federal Chancellor shall determine, and be responsible for, the general policy guidelines. Within the limits set by these guidelines, each Federal Minister shall conduct the affairs of his department autonomously and on his own responsibility. The Federal Government shall decide on differences of opinion between Federal Ministers. The Federal Chancellor shall conduct the affairs of the Federal Government in accordance with rules of procedure adopted by it and approved by the Federal President.

Article 65a* (Power of command over Armed Forces). Power of command in respect of the Armed Forces shall be vested in the Federal Minister of Defence.

Article 66 (No secondary occupation). The Federal Chancellor and the Federal Ministers may not hold any other salaried office, nor engage in a trade or occupation, nor practise a profession, nor belong to the management or, without the consent of the Bundestag, to the board of directors of an enterprise carried on for profit.

Article 67 (Vote of no-confidence). (1) The Bundestag can

*Inserted by federal law of 19 March 1956 (*Federal Law Gazette*, I, p. 111) and amended by federal law of 24 June 1968 (*Federal Law Gazette*, I, p. 711).

express its lack of confidence in the Federal Chancellor only by electing a successor with the majority of its members and by requesting the Federal President to dismiss the Federal Chancellor. The Federal President must comply with the request and appoint the person elected.

(2) Forty-eight hours must elapse between the motion and the election.

Article 68 (Vote of confidence – Dissolution of the Bundestag). (1) If a motion of the Federal Chancellor for a vote of confidence is not assented to by the majority of the members of the Bundestag, the Federal President may, upon the proposal of the Federal Chancellor, dissolve the Bundestag within twenty-one days. The right to dissolve shall lapse as soon as the Bundestag with the majority of its members elects another Federal Chancellor.

(2) Forty-eight hours must elapse between the motion and the vote thereon.

Article 69 (Deputy of the Federal Chancellor). (1) The Federal Chancellor shall appoint a Federal Minister as his deputy.

(2) The tenure of office of the Federal Chancellor or a Federal Minister shall end in any event on the first meeting of a new Bundestag; the tenure of office of a Federal Minister shall also end on any other termination of the tenure of office of the Federal Chancellor.

(3) At the request of the Federal President the Federal Chancellor, or at the request of the Federal Chancellor or of the Federal President a Federal Minister, shall be bound to continue to transact the affairs of his office until the appointment of a successor.

VII. LEGISLATIVE POWERS OF THE FEDERATION

Article 70 (Legislation of the Federation and the *Länder*). (1) The *Länder* shall have the right to legislate in so far as this Basic Law does not confer legislative power on the Federation.

(2) The division of competence between the Federation and the *Länder* shall be determined by the provisions of this Basic Law concerning exclusive and concurrent legislative powers.

Article 71 (Exclusive legislation of the Federation, definition). In matters within the exclusive legislative power of the Federation the *Länder* shall have power to legislate only if, and to the extent that, a federal law explicitly so authorizes them.

Article 72 (Concurrent[1] legislation of the Federation, definition). (1) In matters within concurrent legislative powers the *Länder* shall have power to legislate as long as, and to the extent that, the Federation does not exercise its right to legislate.

(2) The Federation shall have the right to legislate in these matters to the extent that a need for regulation by federal legislation exists because:

1. A matter cannot be effectively regulated by the legislation of individual *Länder*, or
2. The regulation of a matter by a *Land* law might prejudice the interests of other *Länder* or of the people as a whole, or
3. The maintenance of legal or economic unity, especially the maintenance of uniformity of living conditions beyond the territory of any one *Land*, necessitates such regulation.

Article 73 (Exclusive legislation, catalogue). The Federation shall have exclusive power to legislate in the following matters:

1.* Foreign affairs as well as defence including the protection of the civilian population;
2. Citizenship in the Federation;
3. Freedom of movement, passport matters, immigration, emigration, and extradition;
4. Currency, money and coinage, weights and measures, as well as the determination of standards of time;
5. The unity of the customs and commercial territory, treaties on commerce and on navigation, the freedom of movement of goods, and the exchanges of goods and payments with foreign countries, including customs and other frontier protection;
6. Federal railroads and air transport;
7. Postal and telecommunication services;
8. The legal status of persons employed by the Federation and by federal corporate bodies under public law;
9. Industrial property rights, copyrights and publishers' rights;

1. German: *Konkurrierende*. In my view, this ought to be translated as 'competing', or 'alternative', and not as 'concurrent'. [S.E.F.]

*As amended by federal laws of 26 March 1954 (*Federal Law Gazette*, I, p. 45) and 24 June 1968 (*Federal Law Gazette*, I, p. 711).

10.* Cooperation of the Federation and the *Länder* in matters of:
   (a) Criminal police,
   (b) Protection of the free democratic basic order, of the existence and the security of the Federation or of a *Land* (protection of the constitution) and
   (c) Protection against efforts in the federal territory which, by the use of force or actions in preparation for the use of force, endanger the foreign interests of the Federal Republic of Germany,

   As well as the establishment of a Federal Criminal Police Office and the international control of crime.
11. Statistics for federal purposes.

   Article 74 (Concurrent legislation, catalogue). Concurrent legislative powers shall extend to the following matters:
   1. Civil law, criminal law and execution of sentences, the organization and procedure of courts, the legal profession, notaries, and legal advice (*Rechtsberatung*);
   2. Registration of births, deaths, and marriages;
   3. The law of association and assembly;
   4. The law relating to residence and establishment of aliens;
   4a.* The law relating to weapons;
   5. The protection of German cultural treasures against removal abroad;
   6. Refugee and expellee matters;
   7. Public welfare;
   8. Citizenship in the *Länder*;
   9. War damage and reparations;
   10.** Benefits to war-disabled persons and to dependants of those killed in the war as well as assistance to former prisoners of war;
   10a.*** War graves of soldiers, graves of other victims of war and of victims of despotism;

---

*As amended by federal law of 28 July 1972 (*Federal Law Gazette*, I, p. 1305).
**As amended by federal law of 16 June 1965 (*Federal Law Gazette*, I, p. 513).
***Inserted by federal law of 16 June 1965 (*Federal Law Gazette*, I, p. 513).

11. The law relating to economic matters (mining, industry, supply of power, crafts, trades, commerce, banking, stock exchanges, and private insurance);

11a.* The production and utilization of nuclear energy for peaceful purposes, the construction and operation of installations serving such purposes, protection against hazards arising from the release of nuclear energy or from ionizing radiation, and the disposal of radioactive substances;

12. Labour law, including the legal organization of enterprises, protection of workers, employment exchanges and agencies, as well as social insurance, including unemployment insurance;

13.** The regulation of educational and training grants and the promotion of scientific research;

14. The law regarding expropriation, to the extent that matters enumerated in Articles 73 and 74 are concerned;

15. Transfer of land, natural resources and means of production to public ownership or other forms of publicly controlled economy;

16. Prevention of the abuse of economic power;

17. Promotion of agricultural and forest production, safeguarding of the supply of food, the importation and exportation of agricultural and forest products, deep-sea and coastal fishing, and preservation of the coasts;

18. Real-estate transactions, land law and matters concerning agricultural leases, as well as housing, settlement and homestead matters;

19. Measures against human and animal diseases that are communicable or otherwise endanger public health, admission to the medical profession and to other health occupations or practices, as well as trade in medicines, curatives, narcotics, and poisons;

19a.*** The economic viability of hospitals and the regulation of hospitalization fees;

*Inserted by federal law of 23 December 1959 (*Federal Law Gazette*, I, p. 813).

**As amended by federal law of 12 May 1969 (*Federal Law Gazette*, I, p. 363).

***Inserted by federal law of 12 May 1969 (*Federal Law Gazette*, I, p. 363).

20.* Protection regarding the marketing of food, drink and tobacco, of necessities of life, fodder, agricultural and forest seeds and seedlings, and protection of plants against diseases and pests, as well as the protection of animals;

21. Ocean and coastal shipping as well as aids to navigation, inland navigation, meteorological services, sea routes, and inland waterways used for general traffic;

22.** Road traffic, motor transport, construction and maintenance of long-distance highways as well as the collection of charges for the use of public highways by vehicles and the allocation of revenue therefrom;

23. Non-federal railroads, except mountain railroads;

24.*** Disposal of waste, keeping the air pure, and combating noise.

Article 74a† (Wider competence of Federation for pay scales).
(1) Concurrent legislation shall further extend to the pay scales and pensions of members of the public service whose service and loyalty are governed by public law, in so far as the Federation does not have exclusive power to legislate pursuant to item 8 of Article 73.

(2) Federal laws enacted pursuant to paragraph (1) of this Article shall require the consent of the Bundesrat.

(3) Federal laws enacted pursuant to item 8 of Article 73 shall likewise require the consent of the Bundesrat, in so far as they prescribe for the structure and computation of pay scales and pensions, including the appraisal of posts, criteria or minimum or maximum rates other than those provided for in federal laws enacted pursuant to paragraph (1) of this Article.

(4) Paragraphs (1) and (2) of this Article shall apply *mutatis mutandis* to the pay scales and pensions for judges in the *Länder*.

---

*As amended by federal law of 18 March 1971 (*Federal Law Gazette*, I, p. 207).

**As amended by federal law of 12 May 1969 (*Federal Law Gazette*, I, p. 363).

***As amended by federal law of 14 April 1972 (*Federal Law Gazette*, I, p. 593).

†As inserted by federal law of 18 March 1971 (*Federal Law Gazette*, I, p. 206).

Paragraph (3) of this Article shall apply *mutatis mutandis* to laws enacted pursuant to paragraph (1) of Article 98.

Article 75* (General provisions of the Federation, catalogue). Subject to the conditions laid down in Article 72 the Federation shall have the right to enact skeleton provisions concerning:

1.** The legal status of persons in the public service of the *Länder*, communes, or other corporate bodies under public law, in so far as Article 74a does not provide otherwise;

1a.*** The general principles governing higher education;

2. The general legal status of the press and the film industry;

3. Hunting, protection of nature, and care of the countryside;

4. Land distribution, regional planning, and water management;

5. Matters relating to the registration of changes of residence or domicile (*Meldewesen*) and to identity cards.

Article 76 (Bills). (1) Bills shall be introduced in the Bundestag by the Federal Government or by members of the Bundestag or by the Bundesrat.

(2)† Bills of the Federal Government shall be submitted first to the Bundesrat. The Bundesrat shall be entitled to state its position on such bills within six weeks. A bill exceptionally submitted to the Bundesrat as being particularly urgent by the Federal Government may be submitted by the latter to the Bundestag three weeks later, even though the Federal Government may not yet have received the statement of the Bundesrat's position; such statement shall be transmitted to the Bundestag by the Federal Government without delay upon its receipt.

(3)**** Bills of the Bundesrat shall be submitted to the Bundestag by the Federal Government within three months. In doing so, the Federal Government must state its own view.

---

*As amended by federal law of 12 May 1969 (*Federal Law Gazette*, I, p. 363).

**As amended by federal law of 18 March 1971 (*Federal Law Gazette*, I, p. 206).

***Inserted by federal law of 12 May 1969 (*Federal Law Gazette*, I, p. 363).

†As amended by federal law of 15 November 1969 (*Federal Law Gazette*, I, p. 1177).

****As amended by federal law of 17 July 1969 (*Federal Law Gazette*, I, p. 817).

Article 77 (Procedure concerning adopted bills – Objection of the Bundesrat). (1) Bills intended to become federal laws shall require adoption by the Bundestag. Upon their adoption they shall, without delay, be transmitted to the Bundesrat by the President of the Bundestag.

(2)* The Bundesrat may, within three weeks of the receipt of the adopted bill, demand that a committee for joint consideration of bills, composed of members of the Bundestag and members of the Bundesrat, be convened. The composition and the procedure of this committee shall be regulated by rules of procedure to be adopted by the Bundestag and requiring the consent of the Bundesrat. The members of the Bundesrat on this committee shall not be bound by instructions. If the consent of the Bundesrat is required for a bill to become a law, the convening of this committee may also be demanded by the Bundestag or the Federal Government. Should the committee propose any amendment to the adopted bill, the Bundestag must again vote on the bill.

(3)* In so far as the consent of the Bundesrat is not required for a bill to become a law, the Bundesrat may, when the proceedings under paragraph (2) of this Article are completed, enter an objection within two weeks against a bill adopted by the Bundestag. This period shall begin, in the case of the last sentence of paragraph (2) of this Article, on the receipt of the bill as re-adopted by the Bundestag, and in all other cases on the receipt of a communication from the chairman of the committee provided for in paragraph (2) of this Article, to the effect that the committee's proceedings have been concluded.

(4) If the objection was adopted with the majority of the votes of the Bundesrat, it can be rejected by a decision of the majority of the members of the Bundestag. If the Bundesrat adopted the objection with a majority of at least two thirds of its votes, its rejection by the Bundestag shall require a majority of two thirds, including at least the majority of the members of the Bundestag.

Article 78 (Conditions for passing of federal laws). A bill adopted by the Bundestag shall become a law if the Bundesrat consents to

*As amended by federal law of 15 November 1968 (*Federal Law Gazette*, I, p. 1177).

it, or fails to make a demand pursuant to paragraph (2) of Article 77, or fails to enter an objection within the period stipulated in paragraph (3) of Article 77, or withdraws such objection, or if the objection is overridden by the Bundestag.

Article 79 (Amendment of the Basic Law). (1) This Basic Law can be amended only by laws which expressly amend or supplement the text thereof. In respect of international treaties the subject of which is a peace settlement, the preparation of a peace settlement, or the abolition of an occupation regime, or which are designed to serve the defence of the Federal Republic, it shall be sufficient, for the purpose of clarifying that the provisions of this Basic Law do not preclude the conclusion and entry into force of such treaties, to effect a supplementation of the text of this Basic Law confined to such clarification.*

(2) Any such law shall require the affirmative vote of two thirds of the members of the Bundestag and two thirds of the votes of the Bundesrat.

(3) Amendments of this Basic Law affecting the division of the Federation into *Länder*, the participation on principle of the *Länder* in legislation, or the basic principles laid down in Articles 1 and 20, shall be inadmissible.

Article 80 (Issue of ordinances having force of law). (1) The Federal Government, a Federal Minister or the *Land* governments may be authorized by a law to issue ordinances having the force of law (*Rechtsverordnungen*). The content, purpose, and scope of the authorization so conferred must be set forth in such law. This legal basis must be stated in the ordinance. If a law provides that such authorization may be delegated, such delegation shall require another ordinance having the force of law.

(2) The consent of the Bundesrat shall be required, unless otherwise provided by federal legislation, for ordinances having the force of law issued by the Federal Government or a Federal Minister concerning basic rules for the use of facilities of the federal railroads and of postal and telecommunication services, or charges therefor, or concerning the construction and operation

---

* Second sentence inserted by federal law of 26 March 1954 (*Federal Law Gazette*, I, p. 45).

of railroads, as well as for ordinances having the force of law issued pursuant to federal laws that require the consent of the Bundesrat or that are executed by the *Länder* as agents of the Federation or as matters of their own concern.

Article 80a* (State of tension). (1) Where this Basic Law or a federal law on defence, including the protection of the civilian population, stipulates that legal provisions may only be applied in accordance with this Article, their application shall, except when a state of defence exists, be admissible only after the Bundestag has determined that a state of tension (*Spannungsfall*) exists or if it has specifically approved such application. In respect of the cases mentioned in the first sentence of paragraph (5) and the second sentence of paragraph (6) of Article 12a, such determination of a state of tension and such specific approval shall require a two-thirds majority of the votes cast.

(2) Any measures taken by virtue of legal provisions enacted under paragraph (1) of this Article shall be revoked whenever the Bundestag so requests.

(3) In derogation of paragraph (1) of this Article, the application of such legal provisions shall also be admissible by virtue of, and in accordance with, a decision taken with the consent of the Federal Government by an international organ within the framework of a treaty of alliance. Any measures taken pursuant to this paragraph shall be revoked whenever the Bundestag so requests with the majority of its members.

Article 81 (State of legislative emergency). (1) Should, in the circumstances of Article 68, the Bundestag not be dissolved, the Federal President may, at the request of the Federal Government and with the consent of the Bundesrat, declare a state of legislative emergency with respect to a bill, if the Bundestag rejects the bill although the Federal Government has declared it to be urgent. The same shall apply if a bill has been rejected although the Federal Chancellor had combined with it the motion under Article 68.

(2) If, after a state of legislative emergency has been declared, the Bundestag again rejects the bill or adopts it in a version stated to be unacceptable to the Federal Government, the bill shall be

*Inserted by federal law of 24 June 1968 (*Federal Law Gazette*, I, p. 711).

deemed to have become a law to the extent that the Bundesrat consents to it. The same shall apply if the bill is not passed by the Bundestag within four weeks of its reintroduction.

(3) During the term of office of a Federal Chancellor, any other bill rejected by the Bundestag may become a law in accordance with paragraphs (1) and (2) of this Article within a period of six months after the first declaration of a state of legislative emergency. After the expiration of this period, a further declaration of a state of legislative emergency shall be inadmissible during the term of office of the same Federal Chancellor.

(4) This Basic Law may not be amended nor repealed nor suspended in whole or in part by a law enacted pursuant to paragraph (2) of this Article.

Article 82 (Promulgation and effective date of laws). (1) Laws enacted in accordance with the provisions of this Basic Law shall, after countersignature, be signed by the Federal President and promulgated in the *Federal Law Gazette*. Ordinances having the force of law shall be signed by the agency which issues them, and, unless otherwise provided by law, shall be promulgated in the *Federal Law Gazette*.

(2) Every law or every ordinance having the force of law should specify its effective date. In the absence of such a provision, it shall become effective on the fourteenth day after the end of the day on which the *Federal Law Gazette* containing it was published.

VIII. THE EXECUTION OF FEDERAL LAWS AND THE FEDERAL ADMINISTRATION

Article 83 (Execution of federal laws by the *Länder*). The *Länder* shall execute federal laws as matters of their own concern in so far as this Basic Law does not otherwise provide or permit.

Article 84 (*Land* administration and Federal Government supervision). (1) Where the *Länder* execute federal laws as matters of their own concern, they shall provide for the establishment of the requisite authorities and the regulation of administrative procedures in so far as federal laws consented to by the Bundesrat do not otherwise provide.

(2) The Federal Government may, with the consent of the Bundesrat, issue pertinent general administrative rules.

(3) The Federal Government shall exercise supervision to ensure that the *Länder* execute the federal laws in accordance with applicable law. For this purpose the Federal Government may send commissioners to the highest *Land* authorities and with their consent or, if such consent is refused, with the consent of the Bundesrat, also to subordinate authorities.

(4) Should any shortcomings which the Federal Government has found to exist in the execution of federal laws in the *Länder* not be corrected, the Bundesrat shall decide, on the application of the Federal Government or the *Land* concerned, whether such *Land* has violated applicable law. The decision of the Bundesrat may be challenged in the Federal Constitutional Court.

(5) With a view to the execution of federal laws, the Federal Government may be authorized by a federal law requiring the consent of the Bundesrat to issue individual instructions for particular cases. They shall be addressed to the highest *Land* authorities unless the Federal Government considers the matter urgent.

Article 85 (Execution by *Länder* as agents of the Federation).
(1) Where the *Länder* execute federal laws as agents of the Federation, the establishment of the requisite authorities shall remain the concern of the *Länder* except in so far as federal laws consented to by the Bundesrat otherwise provide.

(2) The Federal Government may, with the consent of the Bundesrat, issue pertinent general administrative rules. It may regulate the uniform training of civil servants (*Beamte*) and other salaried public employees (*Angestellte*). The heads of authorities at the intermediate level shall be appointed with its agreement.

(3) The *Land* authorities shall be subject to the instructions of the appropriate highest federal authorities. Such instructions shall be addressed to the highest *Land* authorities unless the Federal Government considers the matter urgent. Execution of the instructions shall be ensured by the highest *Land* authorities.

(4) Federal supervision shall extend to conformity with law and appropriateness of execution. The Federal Government may, for

this purpose, require the submission of reports and documents and send commissioners to all authorities.

Article 86 (Direct federal administration). Where the Federation executes laws by means of direct federal administration or by federal corporate bodies or institutions under public law, the Federal Government shall, in so far as the law concerned contains no special provision, issue pertinent general administrative rules. The Federal Government shall provide for the establishment of the requisite authorities in so far. as the law concerned does not otherwise provide.

Article 87* (Matters of direct federal administration). (1) The foreign service, the federal finance administration, the federal railroads, the federal postal service, and, in accordance with the provisions of Article 89, the administration of federal waterways and of shipping shall be conducted as matters of direct federal administration with their own administrative substructures. **Federal frontier protection authorities, central offices for police information and communications, for the criminal police and for the compilation of data for the purposes of protection of the constitution and protection against efforts in the Federal territory which, by the use of force or actions in preparation for the use of force, endanger the foreign interests of the Federal Republic of Germany may be established by federal legislation.

(2) Social insurance institutions whose sphere of competence extends beyond the territory of one *Land* shall be administered as federal corporate bodies under public law.

(3) In addition, autonomous federal higher authorities as well as federal corporate bodies and institutions under public law may be established by federal legislation for matters in which the Federation has the power to legislate. If new functions arise for the Federation in matters in which it has the power to legislate, federal authorities at the intermediate and lower levels may be established, in case of urgent need, with the consent of the

*Inserted by federal law of 19 March 1956 (*Federal Law Gazette*, I, p. 111) and amended by federal law of 24 June 1968 (*Federal Law Gazette*, I, p. 711).

**As amended by federal law of 28 July 1972 (*Federal Law Gazette*, I, p. 1305).

Bundesrat and of the majority of the members of the Bundestag.

Article 87a* (Build-up, strength, use and functions of the Armed Forces). (1) The Federation shall build up Armed Forces for defence purposes. Their numerical strength and general organizational structure shall be shown in the budget.

(2) Apart from defence, the Armed Forces may only be used to the extent explicitly permitted by this Basic Law.

(3) While a state of defence or a state of tension exists, the Armed Forces shall have the power to protect civilian property and discharge functions of traffic control in so far as this is necessary for the performance of their defence mission. Moreover, the Armed Forces may, when a state of defence or a state of tension exists, be entrusted with the protection of civilian property in support of police measures; in this event the Armed Forces shall cooperate with the competent authorities.

(4) In order to avert any imminent danger to the existence or to the free democratic basic order of the Federation or a *Land*, the Federal Government may, should conditions as envisaged in paragraph (2) of Article 91 obtain and the police forces and the Federal Border Guard be inadequate, use the Armed Forces to support the police and the Federal Border Guard in the protection of civilian property and in combating organized and militarily armed insurgents. Any such use of Armed Forces must be discontinued whenever the Bundestag or the Bundesrat so requests.

Article 87b* (Administration of the Armed Forces). (1) The Federal Armed Forces Administration shall be conducted as a direct federal administration with its own administrative substructure. Its function shall be to administer personnel matters and directly to meet the material requirements of the Armed Forces. Tasks connected with benefits to injured persons or with construction work shall not be assigned to the Federal Armed Forces Administration except by federal legislation requiring the consent of the Bundesrat. Such consent shall also be required for any laws to the extent that they empower the Federal Armed Forces Administration to interfere with rights of third parties;

*Inserted by federal law of 19 March 1956 (*Federal Law Gazette*, I, p. 111).

this shall, however, not apply in the case of laws concerning personnel.

(2) Moreover, federal laws concerning defence including recruitment for military service and protection of the civilian population may, with the consent of the Bundesrat, provide that they shall be carried out, wholly or in part, either by means of direct federal administration having its own administrative substructure or by the *Länder* acting as agents of the Federation. If such laws are executed by the *Länder* acting as agents of the Federation, they may, with the consent of the Bundesrat, provide that the powers vested in the Federal Government or appropriate highest federal authorities by virtue of Article 85 shall be transferred wholly or in part to higher federal authorities; in such an event it may be enacted that these authorities shall not require the consent of the Bundesrat in issuing general administrative rules as referred to in the first sentence of paragraph (2) of Article 85.

Article 87c* (Production and utilization of nuclear energy). Laws enacted under item 11a of Article 74 may, with the consent of the Bundesrat, provide that they shall be executed by the *Länder* acting as agents of the Federation.

Article 87d** (Aviation Administration). (1) The Aviation Administration shall be conducted as a direct federal administration.

(2) By means of federal legislation requiring the consent of the Bundesrat, functions of the Aviation Administration may be delegated to the *Länder* acting as agents of the Federation.

Article 88 (Federal Bank). The Federation shall establish a note-issuing and currency bank as the Federal Bank.

Article 89 (Federal waterways). (1) The Federation shall be the owner of the former *Reich* waterways.

(2) The Federation shall administer the federal waterways through its own authorities. It shall exercise those governmental functions relating to inland shipping which extend beyond the territory of one *Land*, and those governmental functions relating to maritime shipping which are conferred on it by law. Upon

*Inserted by federal law of 23 December 1959 (*Federal Law Gazette*, I, p. 813).
**Inserted by federal law of 6 February 1961 (*Federal Law Gazette*, I, p. 65).

request, the Federation may transfer the administration of federal waterways, in so far as they lie within the territory of one *Land*, to that *Land* as its agent. If a waterway touches the territories of several *Länder*, the Federation may designate one *Land* as its agent if so requested by the *Länder* concerned.

(3) In the administration, development, and new construction of waterways the needs of soil cultivation and of water management shall be safeguarded in agreement with the *Länder*.

Article 90 (Federal highways). (1) The Federation shall be the owner of the former *Reich* motorways (*Reichsautobahnen*) and *Reich* highways.

(2) The *Länder*, or such self-governing corporate bodies as are competent under *Land* law, shall administer as agents of the Federation the federal motorways and other federal highways used for long-distance traffic.

(3) At the request of a *Land*, the Federation may take under direct federal administration federal motorways and other federal highways used for long-distance traffic, in so far as they lie within the territory of that *Land*.

Article 91* (Aversion of dangers to the existence of the Federation or of a *Land*). (1) In order to avert any imminent danger to the existence or to the free democratic basic order of the Federation or a *Land*, a *Land* may request the services of the police forces of other *Länder*, or of the forces** and facilities of other administrative authorities and of the Federal Border Guard.

(2) If the *Land* where such danger is imminent is not itself willing or able to combat the danger, the Federal Government may place the police in that *Land* and the police forces of other *Länder* under its own instructions and commit units of the Federal Border Guard. The order for this shall be rescinded after the removal of the danger or else at any time upon the request of the Bundesrat. If the danger extends to a region larger than a *Land*, the Federal Government may, in so far as is necessary for effectively combating such danger, issue instructions to the *Land*

*As amended by federal law of 24 June 1968 (*Federal Law Gazette*, I, p. 711).
** e.g. civil defence corps, emergency civil engineering corps, fire brigades, etc.

governments; the first and second sentences of this paragraph shall not be affected by this provision.

VIIIa. JOINT TASKS*

Article 91a* (Definition of joint tasks). (1) The Federation shall participate in the discharge of the following responsibilities of the *Länder*, provided that such responsibilities are important to society as a whole and that federal participation is necessary for the improvement of living conditions (joint tasks):

1. Expansion and construction of institutions of higher education including university clinics;
2. Improvement of regional economic structures;
3. Improvement of the agrarian structure and of coast preservation.

(2) Joint tasks shall be defined in detail by federal legislation requiring the consent of the Bundesrat. Such legislation should include general principles governing the discharge of joint tasks.

(3) Such legislation shall provide for the procedure and the institutions required for joint overall planning. The inclusion of a project in the overall planning shall require the consent of the *Land* in which it is to be carried out.

(4) In cases to which items 1 and 2 of paragraph (1) of this Article apply, the Federation shall meet one half of the expenditure in each *Land*. In cases to which item 3 of paragraph (1) of this Article applies, the Federation shall meet at least one half of the expenditure, and such proportion shall be the same for all the *Länder*. Details shall be regulated by legislation. Provision of funds shall be subject to appropriation in the budgets of the Federation and the *Länder*.

(5) The Federal Government and the Bundesrat shall be informed about the execution of joint tasks, should they so demand.

Article 91b* (Cooperation of Federation and *Länder* in educational planning and in research). The Federation and the *Länder* may pursuant to agreements cooperate in educational planning and in the promotion of institutions and projects of scientific

*Inserted by federal law of 12 May 1969 (*Federal Law Gazette*, I, p. 359).

research of supraregional importance. The apportionment of costs shall be regulated in the pertinent agreements.

IX. THE ADMINISTRATION OF JUSTICE

Article 92* (Court organization). Judicial power shall be vested in the judges; it shall be exercised by the Federal Constitutional Court, by the federal courts provided for in this Basic Law, and by the courts of the *Länder*.

Article 93 (Federal Constitutional Court, competency). (1) The Federal Constitutional Court shall decide:

1. On the interpretation of this Basic Law in the event of disputes concerning the extent of the rights and duties of a highest federal organ or of other parties concerned who have been vested with rights of their own by this Basic Law or by rules of procedure of a highest federal organ;
2. In case of differences of opinion or doubts on the formal and material compatibility of federal law or *Land* law with this Basic Law, or on the compatibility of *Land* law with other federal law, at the request of the Federal Government, of a *Land* government, or of one third of the Bundestag members;
3. In case of differences of opinion on the rights and duties of the Federation and the *Länder*, particularly in the execution of federal law by the *Länder* and in the exercise of federal supervision;
4. On other disputes involving public law, between the Federation and the *Länder*, between different *Länder* or within a *Land*, unless recourse to another court exists;
4a.** On complaints of unconstitutionality, which may be entered by any person who claims that one of his basic rights or one of his rights under paragraph (4) of Article 20, under Article 33, 38, 101, 103, or 104 has been violated by public authority;
4b.** On complaints of unconstitutionality, entered by communes or associations of communes on the ground that their

---

*As amended by federal law of 18 June 1968 (*Federal Law Gazette*, I, p. 657).

**Inserted by federal law of 29 January 1969 (*Federal Law Gazette*, I, p. 97).

right to self-government under Article 28 has been violated by a law other than a *Land* law open to complaint to the respective *Land* constitutional court;

5. In the other cases provided for in this Basic Law.

(2) The Federal Constitutional Court shall also act in such other cases as are assigned to it by federal legislation.

Article 94 (Federal Constitutional Court, composition). (1) The Federal Constitutional Court shall consist of federal judges and other members. Half of the members of the Federal Constitutional Court shall be elected by the Bundestag and half by the Bundesrat. They may not be members of the Bundestag, the Bundesrat, the Federal Government, nor of any of the corresponding organs of a *Land*.

(2) The constitution and procedure of the Federal Constitutional Court shall be regulated by a federal law which shall specify in what cases its decisions shall have the force of law.* Such law may require that all other legal remedies must have been exhausted before any such complaint of unconstitutionality can be entered, and may make provision for a special procedure as to admissibility.

Article 95** (Highest courts of justice of the Federation – Joint Panel). (1) For the purposes of ordinary, administrative, fiscal, labour, and social jurisdiction, the Federation shall establish as highest courts of justice the Federal Court of Justice, the Federal Administrative Court, the Federal Fiscal Court, the Federal Labour Court, and the Federal Social Court.

(2) The judges of each of these courts shall be selected jointly by the competent Federal Minister and a committee for the selection of judges consisting of the competent *Land* Ministers and an equal number of members elected by the Bundestag.

(3) In order to preserve uniformity of jurisdiction, a Joint Panel (*Senat*) of the courts specified in paragraph (1) of this Article shall be set up. Details shall be regulated by a federal law.

Article 96* (Federal courts). (1) The Federation may establish

*Inserted by federal law of 29 January 1969 (*Federal Law Gazette*, I, p. 97).
**As amended by federal law of 18 June 1968 (*Federal Law Gazette*, I, p. 657).

a Federal Court for matters concerning industrial property rights.

(2) The Federation may establish military criminal courts for the Armed Forces as federal courts. They shall exercise criminal jurisdiction while a state of defence exists, and otherwise only over members of the Armed Forces serving abroad or on board warships. Details shall be regulated by a federal law. These courts shall be within the competence of the Federal Minister of Justice. Their full-time judges must be persons qualified to exercise the functions of a judge.

(3) The highest court of justice for appeals from the courts mentioned in paragraphs (1) and (2) of this Article shall be the Federal Court of Justice.

(4)* The Federation may establish federal courts for disciplinary proceedings against, and for proceedings in pursuance of complaints by, persons in the federal public service.

(5)** In respect of criminal proceedings under paragraph (1) of Article 26 or involving the protection of the State, a federal law requiring the consent of the Bundesrat may provide that *Land* courts shall exercise federal jurisdiction.

Article 96a.***

Article 97 (Independence of the judges). (1) The judges shall be independent and subject only to the law.

(2) Judges appointed permanently on a full-time basis in established positions cannot against their will be dismissed or permanently or temporarily suspended from office or given a different function or retired before the expiration of their term of office except by virtue of a judicial decision and only on the grounds and in the form provided for by law. Legislation may set age

*As amended by federal law of 12 May 1969 (*Federal Law Gazette*, I, p. 363).

**Inserted by federal law of 26 August 1969 (*Federal Law Gazette*, I, p. 1357).

***The original Article 96 was repealed by federal law of 18 June 1968 (*Federal Law Gazette*, I, p. 658). The present Article 96 in the former Article 96a as inserted by federal law of 19 March 1956 (*Federal Law Gazette*, I, p. 111) and amended by federal laws of 6 March 1961 (*Federal Law Gazette*, I, p. 141), 18 June 1968 (*Federal Law Gazette*, I, p. 658), 12 May 1969 (*Federal Law Gazette*, I, p. 363), and 26 August 1969 (*Federal Law Gazette*, I, p. 1357).

limits for the retirement of judges appointed for life. In the event
of changes in the structure of courts or in districts of jurisdiction,
judges may be transferred to another court or removed from
office, provided they retain their full salary.

Article 98* (Legal status of judges). (1) The legal status of the
federal judges shall be regulated by a special federal law.

(2) If a federal judge, in his official capacity or unofficially, in-
fringes the principles of this Basic Law or the constitutional order
of a *Land*, the Federal Constitutional Court may decide by a two-
thirds majority, upon the request of the Bundestag, that the judge
be given a different function or retired. In a case of intentional
infringement, his dismissal may be ordered.

(3)* The legal status of the judges in the *Länder* shall be regulated by special *Land* laws. The Federation may enact general
provisions, in so far as paragraph (4) of Article 74a does not provide otherwise.

(4) *Länder* may provide that the *Land* Minister of Justice together with a committee for the selection of judges shall decide on
the appointment of judges in the *Länder*.

(5) The *Länder* may, in respect of *Land* judges, enact provisions
corresponding to those of paragraph (2) of this Article. Existing
Land constitutional law shall remain unaffected. The decision in
a case of impeachment of a judge shall rest with the Federal Constitutional Court.

Article 99 (Assignment of competencies to Federal Constitu-
tional Court and highest federal courts in matters involving *Land*
law).** The decision on constitutional disputes within a *Land* may
be assigned by *Land* legislation to the Federal Constitutional
Court, and the decision of last instance in matters involving the
application of *Land* law, to the highest courts of justice referred
to in paragraph (1) of Article 95.

Article 100 (Compatibility of statutory law with the Basic Law).
(1) If a court considers unconstitutional a law the validity of
which is relevant to its decision, the proceedings shall be stayed,

**As amended by federal law of 18 March 1971 (Federal Law Gazette, I,
p. 206).
**As amended by federal law of 18 June 1968 (Federal Law Gazette, I,
p. 658).*

and a decision shall be obtained from the *Land* court competent for constitutional disputes if the constitution of a *Land* is held to be violated, or from the Federal Constitutional Court if this Basic Law is held to be violated. This shall also apply if this Basic Law is held to be violated by *Land* law or if a *Land* law is held to be incompatible with a federal law.

(2) If, in the course of litigation, doubt exists whether a rule of public international law is an integral part of federal law and whether such rule directly creates rights and duties for the individual (Article 25), the court shall obtain a decision from the Federal Constitutional Court.

(3)* If the constitutional court of a *Land*, in interpreting this Basic Law, intends to deviate from a decision of the Federal Constitutional Court or of the constitutional court of another *Land*, it must obtain a decision from the Federal Constitutional Court.

Article 101 (Ban on extraordinary courts). (1) Extraordinary courts shall be inadmissible. No one may be removed from the jurisdiction of his lawful judge.

(2) Courts for special fields may be established only by legislation.

Article 102 (Abolition of capital punishment). Capital punishment shall be abolished.

Article 103 (Basic rights in the courts). (1) In the courts everyone shall be entitled to a hearing in accordance with the law.

(2) An act can be punished only if it was an offence against the law before the act was committed.

(3) No one may be punished for the same act more than once under general penal legislation.

Article 104 (Legal guarantees in the event of deprivation of liberty). (1) The liberty of the individual may be restricted only by virtue of a formal law and only with due regard to the forms prescribed therein. Detained persons may not be subjected to mental nor to physical ill-treatment.

(2) Only judges may decide on the admissibility or continuation of any deprivation of liberty. Where such deprivation is not

*As amended by federal law of 18 June 1968 (*Federal Law Gazette*, I, p. 658).

based on the order of a judge, a judicial decision must be obtained without delay. The police may hold no one on their own authority in their own custody longer than the end of the day after the day of apprehension. Details shall be regulated by legislation.

(3) Any person provisionally detained on suspicion of having committed an offence must be brought before a judge not later than the day following the day of apprehension; the judge shall inform him of the reasons for the detention, examine him, and give him an opportunity to raise objections. The judge must, without delay, either issue a warrant of arrest setting forth the reasons therefor or order his release from detention.

(4) A relative or a person enjoying the confidence of the person detained must be notified without delay of any judicial decision ordering or continuing his deprivation of liberty.

X. FINANCE

Article 104a* (Apportionment of expenditure, Financial assistance). (1) The Federation and the *Länder* shall meet separately the expenditure resulting from the discharge of their respective tasks in so far as this Basic Law does not provide otherwise.

(2) Where the *Länder* act as agents of the Federation, the Federation shall meet the resulting expenditure.

(3) Federal laws to be executed by the *Länder* and involving the disbursement of funds may provide that such funds shall be contributed wholly or in part by the Federation. Where any such law provides that the Federation shall meet one half of the expenditure or more, the *Länder* shall execute it as agents of the Federation. Where any such law provides that the *Länder* shall meet one quarter of the expenditure or more, it shall require the consent of the Bundesrat.

(4) The Federation may grant the *Länder* financial assistance for particularly important investments by the *Länder* or communes or associations of communes, provided that such investments are necessary to avert a disturbance of the overall economic equilibrium or to equalize differences of economic capacities

*Inserted by federal law of 12 May 1969 (*Federal Law Gazette*, I, p. 359).

within the federal territory or to promote economic growth. Details, especially concerning the kinds of investments to be promoted, shall be regulated by federal legislation requiring the consent of the Bundesrat, or by administrative arrangements based on the federal budget.

(5) The Federation and the *Länder* shall meet the administrative expenditure incurred by their respective authorities and shall be responsible to each other for ensuring proper administration. Details shall be regulated by a federal law requiring the consent of the Bundesrat.

Article 105 (Customs duties, Monopolies, Taxes – legislation). (1) The Federation shall have exclusive power to legislate on customs matters and fiscal monopolies.

(2)* The Federation shall have concurrent power to legislate on all other taxes the revenue from which accrues to it wholly or in part or where the conditions provided for in paragraph (2) of Article 72 apply.

(2a)** The *Länder* shall have power to legislate on local excise taxes as long and in so far as they are not identical with taxes imposed by federal legislation.

(3) Federal laws relating to taxes the receipts from which accrue wholly or in part to the *Länder* or communes or associations of communes shall require the consent of the Bundesrat.

Article 106*** (Apportionment of tax revenue). (1) The yield of fiscal monopolies and the revenue from the following taxes shall accrue to the Federation:

1. Customs duties,
2. Excise taxes in so far as they do not accrue to the *Länder* pursuant to paragraph (2) of this Article, or jointly to the Federation and the *Länder* in accordance with paragraph (3) of this Article, or to the communes in accordance with paragraph (6) of this Article,

---

*As amended by federal law of 12 May 1969 (*Federal Law Gazette*, I, p. 359).

**Inserted by federal law of 12 May 1969 (*Federal Law Gazette*, I, p. 359).

***As amended by federal laws of 23 December 1955 (*Federal Law Gazette*, I, p. 817), of 24 December 1956 (*Federal Law Gazette*, I, p. 1077), and of 12 May 1969 (*Federal Law Gazette*, I, p. 359).

3. The road freight tax,
4. The capital transfer taxes, the insurance tax and the tax on drafts and bills of exchange,
5. Non-recurrent levies on property, and contributions imposed for the purpose of implementing the equalization of burdens legislation,*
6. Income and corporation surtaxes,
7. Charges imposed within the framework of the European Communities.

(2) Revenue from the following taxes shall accrue to the *Länder*:

1. Property (net worth) tax,
2. Inheritance tax,
3. Motor-vehicle tax,
4. Such taxes on transactions as do not accrue to the Federation pursuant to paragraph (1) of this Article or jointly to the Federation and the *Länder* pursuant to paragraph (3) of this Article,
5. Beer tax,
6. Taxes on gambling establishments.

(3) Revenue from income taxes, corporation taxes and turn-over taxes shall accrue jointly to the Federation and the *Länder* (joint taxes) to the extent that the revenue from income tax is not allocated to the communes pursuant to paragraph (5) of this Article. The Federation and the *Länder* shall share equally the revenues from income taxes and corporation taxes. The respective shares of the Federation and the *Länder* in the revenue from turnover tax shall be determined by federal legislation requiring the consent of the Bundesrat. Such determination shall be based on the following principles:

1. The Federation and the *Länder* shall have an equal claim to coverage from current revenues of their respective necessary expenditures. The extent of such expenditures shall be determined with a system of pluri-annual financial planning;
2. The coverage requirements of the Federation and of the *Länder* shall be coordinated in such a way that a fair balance is struck,

*i.e. contributions imposed on persons having suffered no war damage and used to indemnify persons having suffered such damage.

any overburdening of taxpayers precluded, and uniformity of living standards in the federal territory ensured.

(4) The respective shares of the Federation and the *Länder* in the revenue from the turnover tax shall be apportioned anew whenever the relation of revenues to expenditures in the Federation develops substantially differently from that of the *Länder*. Where federal legislation imposes additional expenditures on, or withdraws revenue from, the *Länder*, the additional burden may be compensated by federal grants under federal laws requiring the consent of the Bundesrat, provided such additional burden is limited to a short period. Such laws shall lay down the principles for calculating such grants and distributing them among the *Länder*.

(5) A share of the revenue from income tax shall accrue to the communes, to be passed on by the *Länder* to their communes on the basis of income taxes paid by the inhabitants of the latter. Details shall be regulated by a federal law requiring the consent of the Bundesrat. Such law may provide that communes shall assess communal percentages of the communal share.

(6) Revenue from taxes on real property and businesses shall accrue to the communes; revenue from local excise taxes shall accrue to the communes or, as may be provided for by *Land* legislation, to associations of communes. Communes shall be authorized to assess the communal percentages of taxes on real property and businesses within the framework of existing laws. Where there are no communes in a *Land*, revenue from taxes on real property and businesses as well as from local excise taxes shall accrue to the *Land*. The Federation and the *Länder* may participate, by assessing an impost, in the revenue from the trade tax. Details regarding such impost shall be regulated by a federal law requiring the consent of the Bundesrat. Within the framework of *Land* legislation, taxes on real property and businesses as well as the communes' share of revenue from income tax may be taken as a basis for calculating the amount of such impost.

(7) An overall percentage, to be determined by *Land* legislation, of the *Land* share of total revenue from joint taxes shall accrue to the communes and associations of communes. In all other respects *Land* legislation shall determine whether and to

what extent revenue from *Land* taxes shall accrue to communes and associations of communes.

(8) If in individual *Länder* or communes or associations of communes the Federation causes special facilities to be established which directly result in an increase of expenditure or a loss of revenue (special burden) to these *Länder* or communes or associations of communes, the Federation shall grant the necessary compensation, if and in so far as such *Länder* or communes or associations of communes cannot reasonably be expected to bear such special burden. In granting such compensation, due account shall be taken of third-party indemnities and financial benefits accruing to the *Länder* or communes or associations of communes concerned as a result of the institution of such facilities.

(9) For the purpose of this Article, revenues and expenditures of communes and associations of communes shall be deemed to be *Land* revenues and expenditures.

Article 107* (Financial equalization). (1) Revenue from *Land* taxes and the *Land* share of revenue from income and corporation taxes shall accrue to the individual *Länder* to the extent that such taxes are collected by revenue authorities within their respective territories (local revenue). Federal legislation requiring the consent of the Bundesrat may provide in detail for the delimitation as well as the manner and scope of allotment of local revenue from corporation and wage taxes. Legislation may also provide for the delimitation and allotment of local revenue from other taxes. The *Land* share of revenue from the turnover tax shall accrue to the individual *Länder* on a *per capita* basis; federal legislation requiring the consent of the Bundesrat may provide for supplemental shares not exceeding one quarter of a *Land* share to be granted to *Länder* whose *per capita* revenue from *Land* taxes and from the income and corporation taxes is below the average of all the *Länder* combined.

(2) Federal legislation shall ensure a reasonable equalization between financially strong and financially weak *Länder*, due account being taken of the financial capacity and financial re-

---

*As amended by federal laws of 23 December 1955 (*Federal Law Gazette*, I, p. 817) and of 12 May 1969 (*Federal Law Gazette*, I, p. 359).

quirements of communes and associations of communes. Such legislation shall specify the conditions governing equalization claims of *Länder* entitled to equalization payments and equalization liabilities of *Länder* owing equalization payments as well as the criteria for determining the amounts of equalization payments. Such legislation may also provide for grants to be made by the Federation from federal funds to financially weak *Länder* in order to complement the coverage of their general financial requirements (complemental grants).

Article 108* (Fiscal administration). (1) Customs duties, fiscal monopolies, excise taxes subject to federal legislation, including the excise tax on imports, and charges imposed within the framework of the European Communities, shall be administered by federal revenue authorities. The organization of these authorities shall be regulated by federal legislation. The heads of authorities at the intermediate level shall be appointed in consultation with the respective *Land* governments.

(2) All other taxes shall be administered by *Land* revenue authorities. The organization of these authorities and the uniform training of their civil servants may be regulated by federal legislation requiring the consent of the Bundesrat. The heads of authorities at the intermediate level shall be appointed in agreement with the Federal Government.

(3) To the extent that taxes accruing wholly or in part to the Federation are administered by *Land* revenue authorities, those authorities shall act as agents of the Federation. Paragraphs (3) and (4) of Article 85 shall apply, the Federal Minister of Finance being, however, substituted for the Federal Government.

(4) In respect of the administration of taxes, federal legislation requiring the consent of the Bundesrat may provide for collaboration between federal and *Land* revenue authorities, or in the case of taxes under paragraph (1) of this Article for their administration by *Land* revenue authorities, or in the case of other taxes for their administration by federal revenue authorities, if and to the extent that the execution of tax laws is substantially improved or facilitated thereby. As regards taxes the revenue from which

*As amended by federal law of 12 May 1969 (*Federal Law Gazette*, I, p. 359).

accrues exclusively to communes or associations of communes, their administration may wholly or in part be transferred by *Länder* from the appropriate *Land* revenue authorities to communes or associations of communes.

(5) The procedure to be applied by federal revenue authorities shall be laid down by federal legislation. The procedure to be applied by *Land* revenue authorities or, as envisaged in the second sentence of paragraph (4) of this Article, by communes or associations of communes, may be laid down by federal legislation requiring the consent of the Bundesrat.

(6) The jurisdiction of fiscal courts shall be uniformly regulated by federal legislation.

(7) The Federal Government may issue pertinent general administrative rules which, to the extent that administration is incumbent upon *Land* revenue authorities or communes or associations of communes, shall require the consent of the Bundesrat.

Article 109* (Separate budgets for Federation and *Länder*). (1) The Federation and the *Länder* shall be autonomous and independent of each other in their fiscal administration.

(2) The Federation and the *Länder* shall take due account in their fiscal administration of the requirements of overall economic equilibrium.

(3)** By means of federal legislation requiring the consent of the Bundesrat, principles applicable to both the Federation and the *Länder* may be established governing budgetary law, responsiveness of the fiscal administration to economic trends, and financial planning to cover several years ahead.

(4) With a view to averting disturbances of the overall economic equilibrium, federal legislation requiring the consent of the Bundesrat may be enacted providing for:

1. Maximum amounts, terms and timing of loans to be raised by public administrative entities, whether territorial (*Gebietskörperschaften*) or functional (*Zweckverbände*), and

2. An obligation on the part of the Federation and the *Länder* to

*As amended by federal law of 8 June 1967 (*Federal Law Gazette*, I, p. 581).
**As amended by federal law of 12 May 1969 (*Federal Law Gazette*, I, p. 357).

247

maintain interest-free deposits in the German Federal Bank (reserves for counterbalancing economic trends).

Authorizations to enact pertinent ordinances having the force of law may be issued only to the Federal Government. Such ordinances shall require the consent of the Bundesrat. They shall be repealed in so far as the Bundestag may demand; details shall be regulated by federal legislation.

Article 110* (Budget of the Federation). (1) All revenues and expenditures of the Federation shall be included in the budget; in respect of federal enterprises and special funds, only allocations to or remittances from them need be included. The budget must be balanced as regards revenue and expenditure.

(2) The budget shall be established by means of a law covering one year or several fiscal years separately before the beginning of the first of those fiscal years. Provision may be made for parts of the budget to apply to periods of different duration, but divided into fiscal years.

(3) Bills within the meaning of the first sentence of paragraph (2) of this Article as well as bills to amend the budget law and the budget shall be submitted simultaneously to the Bundesrat and to the Bundestag; the Bundesrat shall be entitled to state its position on such bills within six weeks or, in the case of amending bills, within three weeks.

(4) The budget law may contain only such provisions as apply to revenues and expenditures of the Federation and to the period for which the budget law is being enacted. The budget law may stipulate that certain provisions shall cease to apply only upon the promulgation of the next budget law or, in the event of an authorization pursuant to Article 115, at a later date.

Article 111 (Payments before approval of the budget). (1) If, by the end of a fiscal year, the budget for the following year has not been established by law, the Federal Government may, until such law comes into force, make all payments which are necessary:

(a) To maintain institutions existing by law and to carry out measures authorized by law;

*As amended by federal law of 12 May 1969 (*Federal Law Gazette*, I, p. 357).

(b) To meet the Federation's statutory, contractual, and treaty obligations;

(c) To continue building projects, procurements, and other services, or to continue to grant subsidies for these purposes, provided that pertinent amounts have already been appropriated in the budget of a previous year.

(2) To the extent that revenues provided by specific legislation and derived from taxes or duties or any other charges or sources, or the working capital reserves, do not cover the expenditures referred to in paragraph (1) of this Article, the Federal Government may borrow the funds necessary for the conduct of current operations up to a maximum of one quarter of the total amount of the previous budget.

Article 112* (Expenditure in excess of budgetary estimates). Expenditures in excess of budgetary appropriations and extra-budgetary expenditures shall require the consent of the Federal Minister of Finance. Such consent may be given only in the case of an unforeseen and compelling necessity. Details may be regulated by federal legislation.

Article 113* (Increases in expenditure). (1) Laws increasing the budget expenditures proposed by the Federal Government or involving, or likely in future to cause, new expenditures shall require the consent of the Federal Government. This shall also apply to laws involving, or likely in future to cause, decreases in revenue. The Federal Government may require the Bundestag to postpone its vote on such bills. In this case the Federal Government shall state its position to the Bundestag within six weeks.

(2) Within four weeks after the Bundestag has adopted such a bill, the Federal Government may require it to vote on that bill again.

(3) If the bill has become a law pursuant to Article 78, the Federal Government may withhold its consent only within six weeks and only after having initiated the procedure provided for in the third and fourth sentences of paragraph (1) or in paragraph (2) of the present Article. Upon the expiry of this period such consent shall be deemed to have been given.

*As amended by federal law of 12 May 1969 (*Federal Law Gazette*, I, p. 357).

Article 114* (Rendering of accounts, Audit Office). (1) The Federal Minister of Finance shall, on behalf of the Federal Government, submit annually to the Bundestag and to the Bundesrat for their approval an account, covering the preceding fiscal year, of all revenues and expenditures as well as of property and debt.

(2) The Federal Audit Office, the members of which shall enjoy judicial independence, shall audit the account and examine the management of the budget and the conduct of business as to economy and correctness. The Federal Audit Office shall submit an annual report directly to the Federal Government as well as to the Bundestag and to the Bundesrat. In all other respects the powers of the Federal Audit Office shall be regulated by federal legislation.

Article 115* (Procurement of credit). (1) The borrowing of funds and the assumption of pledges, guarantees or other commitments, as a result of which expenditure may be incurred in future fiscal years, shall require federal legislative authorization indicating, or permitting computation of, the maximum amounts involved. Revenue obtained by borrowing shall not exceed the total of expenditures for investments provided for in the budget; exceptions shall be permissible only to avert a disturbance of the overall economic equilibrium. Details shall be regulated by federal legislation.

(2) In respect of special funds of the Federation, exceptions from the provisions of paragraph (1) of this Article may be authorized by federal legislation.

Xa.** STATE OF DEFENCE

Article 115a (Determination of a state of defence). (1) The determination that the federal territory is being attacked by armed force or that such an attack is directly imminent (state of defence) shall be made by the Bundestag with the consent of the Bundesrat.

*As amended by federal law of 12 May 1969 (*Federal Law Gazette*, I, p. 357).
**Entire section Xa inserted by federal law of 24 June 1968 (*Federal Law Gazette*, I, pp. 710–11).

Such determination shall be made at the request of the Federal Government and shall require a two-thirds majority of the votes cast, which shall include at least the majority of the members of the Bundestag.

(2) If the situation imperatively calls for immediate action and if insurmountable obstacles prevent the timely meeting of the Bundestag, or if there is no quorum in the Bundestag, the Joint Committee shall make this determination with a two-thirds majority of the votes cast, which shall include at least the majority of its members.

(3) The determination shall be promulgated in the *Federal Law Gazette* by the Federal President pursuant to Article 82. If this cannot be done in time, the promulgation shall be effected in another manner; it shall subsequently be printed in the *Federal Law Gazette* as soon as circumstances permit.

(4) If the federal territory is being attacked by armed force and if the competent organs of the Federation are not in a position at once to make the determination provided for in the first sentence of paragraph (1) of this Article, such determination shall be deemed to have been made and promulgated at the time the attack began. The Federal President shall announce such time as soon as circumstances permit.

(5) When the determination of the existence of a state of defence has been promulgated and if the federal territory is being attacked by armed force, the Federal President may, with the consent of the Bundestag, issue internationally valid declarations regarding the existence of such state of defence. Subject to the conditions mentioned in paragraph (2) of this Article, the Joint Committee shall thereupon deputize for the Bundestag.

Article 115b (Power of command during state of defence). Upon the promulgation of a state of defence, the power of command over the Armed Forces shall pass to the Federal Chancellor.

Article 115c (Legislative competence of the Federation during state of defence). (1) The Federation shall have the right to exercise concurrent legislation even in matters belonging to the legislative competence of the *Länder* by enacting laws to be applicable upon the occurrence of a state of defence. Such laws shall require the consent of the Bundesrat.

(2) Federal legislation to be applicable upon the occurrence of a state of defence to the extent required by conditions obtaining while such state of defence exists, may make provision for:

1. Preliminary compensation to be made in the event of expropriations, thus diverging from the second sentence of paragraph (3) of Article 14;

2. Deprivations of liberty for a period not exceeding four days, if no judge has been able to act within the period applying in normal times, thus diverging from the third sentence of paragraph (2) and the first sentence of paragraph (3) of Article 104.

(3)* Federal legislation to be applicable upon the occurrence of a state of defence to the extent required for averting an existing or directly imminent attack, may, subject to the consent of the Bundesrat, regulate the administration and the fiscal system of the Federation and the *Länder* in divergence from Sections VIII, VIIIa and X, provided that the viability of the *Länder*, communes and associations of communes is safeguarded, particularly in fiscal matters.

(4) Federal laws enacted pursuant to paragraph (1) or subparagraph (1) of paragraph (2) of this Article may, for the purpose of preparing for their execution, be applied even prior to the occurrence of a state of defence.

Article 115d (Shortened procedure in the case of urgent bills during state of defence). (1) While a state of defence exists, the provisions of paragraphs (2) and (3) of this Article shall apply in respect of federal legislation, notwithstanding the provisions of paragraph (2) of Article 76, the second sentence of paragraph (1) and paragraphs (2) to (4) of Article 77, Article 78, and paragraph (1) of Article 82.

(2) Bills submitted as urgent by the Federal Government shall be forwarded to the Bundesrat at the same time as they are submitted to the Bundestag. The Bundestag and the Bundesrat shall debate such bills in common without delay. In so far as the consent of the Bundesrat is necessary, the majority of its votes shall be required for any such bill to become a law. Details shall be

*As amended by federal law of 12 May 1969 (*Federal Law Gazette*, I, p. 359).

regulated by rules of procedure adopted by the Bundestag and requiring the consent of the Bundesrat.

(3) The second sentence of paragraph (3) of Article 115a shall apply *mutatis mutandis* in respect of the promulgation of such laws.

Article 115e (Status and functions of the Joint Committee). (1) If, while a state of defence exists, the Joint Committee determines with a two-thirds majority of the votes cast, which shall include at least the majority of its members, that insurmountable obstacles prevent the timely meeting of the Bundestag, or that there is no quorum in the Bundestag, the Joint Committee shall have the status of both the Bundestag and the Bundesrat and shall exercise their rights as one body.

(2) The Joint Committee may not enact any law to amend this Basic Law or to deprive it of effect or application either in whole or in part. The Joint Committee shall not be authorized to enact laws pursuant to paragraph (1) of Article 24 or to Article 29.

Article 115f (Extraordinary powers of the Federation during state of defence). (1) While a state of defence exists, the Federal Government may to the extent necessitated by circumstances:

1. Commit the Federal Border Guard throughout the federal territory;
2. Issue instructions not only to federal administrative authorities but also to *Land* governments and, if it deems the matter urgent, to *Land* authorities, and may delegate this power to members of *Land* governments to be designated by it.

(2) The Bundestag, the Bundesrat, and the Joint Committee, shall be informed without delay of the measures taken in accordance with paragraph (1) of this Article.

Article 115g (Status and functions of the Federal Constitutional Court during state of defence). The constitutional status and the exercise of the constitutional functions of the Federal Constitutional Court and its judges must not be impaired. The Law on the Federal Constitutional Court may not be amended by a law enacted by the Joint Committee except in so far as such amendment is required, also in the opinion of the Federal Constitutional Court, to maintain the capability of the Court to function. Pending the enactment of such a law, the Federal Constitutional Court may take such measures as are necessary to maintain the capability of the Court to carry out its work. Any decisions by the Federal Constitutional Court in pursuance of the second and third sentences of this Article shall require a two-thirds majority of the judges present.

Article 115h (Legislative terms and terms of office during state of defence). (1) Any legislative terms of the Bundestag or of *Land* Diets due to expire while a state of defence exists shall end six months after the termination of such state of defence. A term of office of the Federal President due to expire while a state of defence exists, and the exercise of his functions by the President of the Bundesrat in case of the premature vacancy of the Federal President's office, shall end nine months after the termination of such state of defence. The term of office of a member of the Federal Constitutional Court due to expire while a state of defence exists shall end six months after the termination of such state of defence.

(2) Should the necessity arise for the Joint Committee to elect a new Federal Chancellor, the Committee shall do so with the majority of its members; the Federal President shall propose a candidate to the Joint Committee. The Joint Committee can express its lack of confidence in the Federal Chancellor only by electing a successor with a two-thirds majority of its members.

(3) The Bundestag shall not be dissolved while a state of defence exists.

Article 115i (Extraordinary power of the *Land* governments). (1) If the competent federal organs are incapable of taking the measures necessary to avert the danger, and if the situation imperatively calls for immediate independent action in individual parts of the federal territory, the *Land* governments or the authorities or commissioners designated by them shall be authorized to take, within their respective spheres of competence, the measures provided for in paragraph (1) of Article 115f.

(2) Any measures taken in accordance with paragraph (1) of the present Article may be revoked at any time by the Federal Government, or in the case of *Land* authorities and subordinate federal authorities, by *Land* Prime Ministers.

Article 115k (Grade and duration of validity of extraordinary laws and ordinances having the force of law). (1) Laws enacted in accordance with Articles 115c, 115e, and 115g, as well as ordinances having the force of law issued by virtue of such laws, shall, for the duration of their applicability, suspend legislation contrary to such laws or ordinances. This shall not apply to earlier legislation enacted by virtue of Articles 115c, 115e, or 115g.

(2) Laws adopted by the Joint Committee, and ordinances having the force of law issued by virtue of such laws, shall cease to have effect not later than six months after the termination of a state of defence.

(3)* Laws containing provisions that diverge from Articles 91a, 91b, 104a, 106 and 107, shall apply no longer than the end of the second fiscal year following upon the termination of the state of defence. After such termination they may, with the consent of the Bundesrat, be amended by federal legislation so as to lead up to the settlement provided for in Sections VIIIa and X.

Article 115l (Repealing of extraordinary laws, Termination of state of defence, Conclusion of peace). (1) The Bundestag, with the consent of the Bundesrat, may at any time repeal laws enacted by the Joint Committee. The Bundesrat may request the Bundestag to make a decision in any such matter. Any measures taken by the Joint Committee or the Federal Government to avert a danger shall be revoked if the Bundestag and the Bundesrat so decide.

(2) The Bundestag, with the consent of the Bundesrat, may at any time declare the state of defence terminated by a decision to be promulgated by the Federal President. The Bundesrat may request the Bundestag to make a decision in any such matter. The state of defence must be declared terminated without delay when the prerequisites for the determination thereof no longer exist.

(3) The conclusion of peace shall be the subject of a federal law.

XI. TRANSITIONAL AND CONCLUDING PROVISIONS

Article 116 (Definition of 'German', Regranting of citizenship).
(1) Unless otherwise provided by law, a German within the meaning of this Basic Law is a person who possesses German citizenship or who has been admitted to the territory of the

*As amended by federal law of 12 May 1969 (*Federal Law Gazette*. I p. 359).

German Reich within the frontiers of 31 December 1937 as a refugee or expellee of German stock (*Volkszugehörigkeit*) or as the spouse or descendant of such person.

(2) Former German citizens who, between 30 January 1933 and 8 May 1945, were deprived of their citizenship on political, racial, or religious grounds, and their descendants, shall be regranted German citizenship on application. They shall be considered as not having been deprived of their German citizenship if they have established their domicile (*Wohnsitz*) in Germany after 8 May 1945 and have not expressed a contrary intention.

Article 117 (Temporary ruling for Article 3 and Article 11). (1) Law which conflicts with paragraph (2) of Article 3 shall remain in force until adapted to that provision of this Basic Law, but not beyond 31 March 1953.

(2) Laws which restrict the right of freedom of movement in view of the present housing shortage shall remain in force until repealed by federal legislation.

Article 118 (Reorganization of the *Länder* of Baden, Württemberg-Baden and Württemberg-Hohenzollern). The reorganization of the territory comprising the *Länder* of Baden, Württemberg-Baden, and Württemberg-Hohenzollern may be effected notwithstanding the provisions of Article 29, by agreement between the *Länder* concerned. If no agreement is reached, the reorganization shall be effected by federal legislation which must provide for a referendum.*

Article 119 (Refugees and expellees). In matters relating to refugees and expellees, in particular as regards their distribution among the *Länder*, the Federal Government may, with the consent of the Bundesrat, issue regulations having the force of law, pending the settlement of the matter by federal legislation. The Federal Government may in this matter be authorized to issue individual instructions for particular cases. Except where there is danger in delay, such instructions shall be addressed to the highest *Land* authorities.

Article 120 ** (Occupation costs and burdens as consequence of

*See footnote * to Article 23.
**As amended by federal laws of 30 July 1965 (*Federal Law Gazette*, I, p. 649) and of 28 July 1969 (*Federal Law Gazette*, I, p. 985).

the war). (1)* The Federation shall meet the expenditure for occupation costs and the other internal and external burdens caused as a consequence of the war, as provided for in detail by federal legislation. To the extent that these costs and other burdens have been provided for by federal legislation on or before 1 October 1969, the Federation and the *Länder* shall meet such expenditure between them in accordance with such federal legislation. In so far as expenditures for such of these costs and burdens as neither have been nor will be provided for by federal legislation have been met on or before 1 October 1965 by *Länder*, communes, associations of communes or other entities performing functions of *Länder* or communes, the Federation shall not be obliged to meet expenditure of that nature even if arising after that date. The Federation shall pay the subsidies towards the burdens of social insurance institutions, including unemployment insurance and public assistance to the unemployed. The distribution between the Federation and the *Länder* of costs and other burdens caused as a consequence of the war, as provided for in this paragraph, shall not affect any legislative settlement of claims for indemnification in respect of consequences of the war.

(2) The corresponding revenue shall pass to the Federation at the same time as the latter assumes responsibility for the expenditure referred to in this Article.

Article 120a ** (Implementation of equalization of burdens legislation).** (1) Laws concerning the implementation of the equalization of burdens legislation may, with the consent of the Bundesrat, stipulate that they shall be executed, as regards equalization benefits, partly by the Federation and partly by the *Länder* acting as agents of the Federation, and that the relevant powers vested in the Federal Government and the competent highest federal authorities by virtue of Article 85, shall be wholly or partly delegated to the Federal Equalization Office. In exercising these powers, the Federal Equalization Office shall not require the consent of the Bundesrat; with the exception of urgent cases, its in-

---

*As amended by federal law of 28 July 1969 (*Federal Law Gazette*, I, p. 985).

**Inserted by federal law of 14 August 1952 (*Federal Law Gazette*, I, p. 445).

structions shall be given to the highest *Land* authorities (*Land* Equalization Offices).

(2) The provisions of the second sentence of paragraph (3) of Article 87 shall not be affected hereby.

Article 121 (Definition of 'majority'). Within the meaning of this Basic Law, a majority of the members of the Bundestag and a majority of the members of the Federal Convention (Bundesversammlung) shall be the majority of the respective statutory number of their members.

Article 122 (Legislative competence hitherto existing). (1) From the date of the first meeting of the Bundestag, laws shall be enacted exclusively by the legislative organs recognized in this Basic Law.

(2) Legislative bodies and bodies participating in legislation in an advisory capacity, whose competence ends by virtue of paragraph (1) of this Article, are herewith dissolved with effect from that date.

Article 123 (Continued validity of old law and old treaties). (1) Law in force before the first meeting of the Bundestag shall remain in force in so far as it does not conflict with this Basic Law.

(2) Subject to all rights and objections of the interested parties, the treaties concluded by the German *Reich* concerning matters which, under this Basic Law, shall be within the competence of *Land* legislation, shall remain in force, if they are and continue to be valid in accordance with general principles of law, until new treaties are concluded by the agencies competent under this Basic Law, or until they are in any other way terminated pursuant to their provisions.

Article 124 (Old law affecting matters subject to exclusive legislation). Law, wherever applicable,* affecting matters subject to the exclusive legislative power of the Federation, shall become federal law.

Article 125 (Old law affecting matters subject to concurrent legislation). Law, wherever applicable,* affecting matters subject to the concurrent legislative power of the Federation, shall become federal law:

*i.e. *Land* or zonal law.

1. In so far as it applies uniformly within one or more zones of occupation;
2. In so far as it is law by which former *Reich* law has been amended after 8 May 1945.

Article 126 (Disputes regarding continued validity of old law). Disputes regarding the continuance of law as federal law shall be decided by the Federal Constitutional Court.

Article 127 (Legislation of the Bizonal Economic Administration). Within one year of the promulgation of this Basic Law the Federal Government may, with the consent of the governments of the *Länder* concerned, extend to the *Länder* of Baden, Greater Berlin, Rhineland-Palatinate and Württemberg-Hohenzollern any legislation of the Bizonal Economic Administration, in so far as it continues to be in force as federal law under Article 124 or 125.

Article 128 (Continuance of powers to give instructions). In so far as law continuing in force provides for powers to give instructions within the meaning of paragraph (5) of Article 84, these powers shall remain in existence until otherwise provided by law.

Article 129 (Continued validity of authorizations). (1) In so far as legal provisions which continue in force as federal law contain authorizations to issue ordinances having the force of law or to issue general administrative rules or to perform administrative acts, such authorizations shall pass to the agencies henceforth competent in the matter. In cases of doubt, the Federal Government shall decide in agreement with the Bundesrat; such decisions must be published.

(2) In so far as legal provisions which continue in force as *Land* law contain such authorizations, they shall be exercised by the agencies competent under *Land* law.

(3) In so far as legal provisions within the meaning of paragraphs (1) and (2) of this Article authorize their amendment or supplementation or the issue of legal provisions instead of laws, such authorizations have expired.

(4) The provisions of paragraphs (1) and (2) of this Article shall apply *mutatis mutandis* where legal provisions refer to regulations no longer valid or to institutions no longer in existence.

Article 130 (Corporate bodies under public law). (1) Administrative agencies and other institutions which serve the public administration or the administration of justice and are not based on *Land* law or treaties between *Länder*, as well as the Association of Management of South West German Railroads and the Administrative Council for the Postal Services and Telecommunications of the French Zone of Occupation, shall be placed under the Federal Government. The Federal Government shall provide, with the consent of the Bundesrat, for their transfer, dissolution, or liquidation.

(2) The highest disciplinary superior of the personnel of these administrations and institutions shall be the appropriate Federal Minister.

(3) Corporate bodies and institutions under public law not directly under a *Land* nor based on treaties between *Länder* shall be under the supervision of the appropriate highest federal authority.

Article 131 (Persons formerly employed in the public service). Federal legislation shall regulate the legal position of persons, including refugees and expellees, who, on 8 May 1945, were employed in the public service, have left the service for reasons other than those arising from civil service regulations or collective agreement rules, and have not until now been reinstated or are employed in a position not corresponding to their former one. The same shall apply *mutatis mutandis* to persons, including refugees and expellees, who, on 8 May 1945, were entitled to a pension and who no longer receive any such pension or any commensurate pension for reasons other than those arising from civil service regulations or collective agreement rules. Until the pertinent federal law comes into force, no legal claims can be made, unless otherwise provided by *Land* legislation.

Article 132 (Temporary revocation of rights of civil servants). (1) Civil servants and judges who, when this Basic Law comes into force, are appointed for life, may, within six months after the first meeting of the Bundestag, be placed on the retired list or waiting list or be given a different function with lower remuneration if they lack the personal or professional aptitude for their present function. This provision shall apply *mutatis mutandis* also to salaried public employees, other than civil servants or judges, whose service cannot be terminated by notice. If, however, such service can be terminated by notice, periods of notice in excess of the periods fixed by collective agreement rules may be cancelled within the six months referred to above.

(2) The preceding provision shall not apply to members of the public service who are not affected by the provisions regarding the Liberation from National Socialism and Militarism or who are recognized victims of National Socialism, except on important grounds in respect of their personality.

(3) Those affected may have recourse to the courts in accordance with paragraph (4) of Article 19.

(4) Details shall be specified by a regulation of the Federal Government requiring the consent of the Bundesrat.

Article 133 (Bizonal Economic Administration, succession to rights). The Federation shall succeed to the rights and obligations of the Bizonal Economic Administration.

Article 134 (*Reich* property to become federal property). (1) *Reich* property shall on principle become federal property.

(2) In so far as such property was originally intended to be used predominantly for administrative tasks which, under this Basic Law, are not administrative tasks of the Federation, it shall be transferred without compensation to the agencies now charged with such tasks, and to the *Länder* in so far as it is being used at present, and not merely temporarily, for administrative tasks which under this Basic Law are now within the administrative competence of the *Länder*. The Federation may also transfer other property to the *Länder*.

(3) Property which was placed at the disposal of the Reich by *Länder* or communes or associations of communes without compensation, shall again become the property of such *Länder* or communes or associations of communes, in so far as it is not required by the Federation for its own administrative tasks.

(4) Details shall be regulated by a federal law requiring the consent of the Bundesrat.

Article 135 (Property in the event of territorial changes). (1) If after 8 May 1945 and before the coming into force of this Basic Law an area has passed from one *Land* to another, the *Land* to which the area now belongs shall be entitled to the property located therein of the *Land* to which it belonged.

(2) Property of *Länder* or corporate bodies or institutions under public law which no longer exist shall pass, in so far as it was originally intended to be used predominantly for administrative tasks or is being used at present, and not merely temporarily, predominantly for administrative tasks, to the *Land* or the corporate body or institution under public law which now discharges these tasks.

(3) Real estate of *Länder* which no longer exist, including appurtenances, shall pass to the *Land* within which it is located, in so far as it is not included among property within the meaning of paragraph (1) of this Article.

(4) If an overriding interest of the Federation or the particular interest of an area so requires, a settlement in divergence from paragraphs (1) to (3) of this Article may be effected by federal legislation.

(5) In all other respects, the succession in title and the settlement of the property, in so far as it has not been effected before 1 January 1952 by agreement between the *Länder* or corporate bodies or institutions under public law concerned, shall be regulated by federal legislation requiring the consent of the Bundesrat.

(6) Interests of the former *Land* of Prussia in enterprises under private law shall pass to the Federation. A federal law, which may also be in divergence from this provision, shall regulate details.

(7) In so far as property which on the coming into force of this Basic Law would devolve upon a *Land* or a corporate body or institution under public law pursuant to paragraphs (1) to (3) of this Article, has been disposed of through or by virtue of a *Land* law or in any other manner by the party thus entitled, the transfer of the property shall be deemed to have taken place before such disposition.

Article 135a* (Discharging, wholly or partially, of certain liabilities of, *inter alia*, the Reich and the former *Land* of Prussia). The legislation reserved to the Federation in paragraph (4) of Article 134 and in paragraph (5) of Article 135 may also stipulate

*Inserted by federal law of 22 October 1957 (*Federal Law Gazette*, I, p. 1745).

that the following liabilities shall not be discharged, or not to their full extent:

1. Liabilities of the Reich or liabilities of the former *Land* of Prussia or liabilities of such corporate bodies and institutions under public law as no longer exist;
2. Such liabilities of the Federation or corporate bodies and institutions under public law as are connected with the transfer of properties pursuant to Articles 89, 90, 134 or 135, and such liabilities of these entities as arise from measures taken by the entities mentioned under item 1;
3. Such liabilities of *Länder* or communes or associations of communes as have arisen from measures taken by these entities before 1 August 1945 within the framework of administrative functions incumbent upon, or delegated by, the Reich to comply with regulations of occupying Powers or to remove a state of emergency due to the war.

Article 136 (First assembly of the Bundesrat). (1) The Bundesrat shall assemble for the first time on the day of the first meeting of the Bundestag.

(2) Until the election of the first Federal President his powers shall be exercised by the President of the Bundesrat. He shall not have the right to dissolve the Bundestag.

Article 137 (Right of civil servants to stand for election). (1)* The right of civil servants, of other salaried public employees, of professional soldiers, of temporary volunteer soldiers, or of judges, to stand for election in the Federation, in the *Länder*, or in the communes, may be restricted by legislation.

(2) The electoral law to be adopted by the Parliamentary Council shall apply to the election of the first Bundestag, of the first Federal Convention, and of the first Federal President of the Federal Republic.

(3) The function of the Federal Constitutional Court pursuant to paragraph (2) of Article 41 shall, pending its establishment, be exercised by the German High Court for the Combined Economic Area, which shall decide in accordance with its rules of procedure.

*As amended by federal law of 19 March 1956 (*Federal Law Gazette*, I, p. 111).

Article 138 (Notaries). Changes in the rules relating to notaries as they now exist in the *Länder* of Baden,* Bavaria, Württemberg-Baden,* and Württemberg-Hohenzollern,* shall require the consent of the governments of these *Länder*.

Article 139 (Liberation Law). The legislation enacted for the Liberation of the German People from National Socialism and Militarism shall not be affected by the provisions of this Basic Law.

Article 140 (Validity of Articles of the Weimar Constitution). The provisions of Articles 136, 137, 138, 139, and 141 of the German Constitution of 11 August 1919 shall be an integral part of this Basic Law.**

Article 141 ('Bremen Clause'). The first sentence of paragraph (3) of Article 7 shall not be applied in any *Land* in which different provisions of *Land* law were in force on 1 January 1949.

Article 142 (Basic rights in *Land* constitutions). Notwithstanding the provision of Article 31, such provisions of *Land* constitutions shall also remain in force as guarantee basic rights in conformity with Articles 1 to 18 of this Basic Law.

Article 142a* (Repealed).

Article 143** (Repealed).

Article 144 (Ratification of the Basic Law – Berlin representatives in the Bundestag and Bundesrat). (1) This Basic Law shall require ratification by the representative assemblies of two thirds of the German *Länder* in which it is for the time being to apply.

(2) In so far as the application of this Basic Law is subject to restrictions in any *Land* listed in Article 23 or in any part thereof, such *Land* or part thereof shall have the right to send representatives to the Bundestag in accordance with Article 38 and to the Bundesrat in accordance with Article 50.

Article 145 (Promulgation of the Basic Law). (1) The Parlia-

* See footnote * to Article 23.
** See Appendix to the Basic Law.
***Inserted by federal law of 26 March 1954 (*Federal Law Gazette*, I, p. 45) and repealed by federal law of 24 June 1968 (*Federal Law Gazette*, I, p. 714).
****Amended by federal law of 19 March 1956 (*Federal Law Gazette*, I, p. 111) and repealed by federal law of 24 June 1968 (*Federal Law Gazette*, I, p. 714).

mentary Council shall confirm in public session, with the participation of the deputies of Greater Berlin, the fact of ratification of
this Basic Law and shall sign and promulgate it.

(2) This Basic Law shall come into force at the end of the day
of promulgation.

(3) It shall be published in the *Federal Law Gazette*.

Article 146 (Duration of validity of the Basic Law). This Basic
Law shall cease to be in force on the day on which a constitution
adopted by a free decision of the German people comes into force.

APPENDIX TO THE BASIC LAW*

Article 136 (Weimar Constitution of 11 August 1919). (1) Civil
and political rights and duties shall be neither dependent on nor
restricted by the exercise of the freedom of religion.

(2) The enjoyment of civil and political rights and eligibility for
public office shall be independent of religious creed.

(3) No one shall be bound to disclose his religious convictions.
The authorities shall not have the right to inquire into a person's
membership of a religious body except to the extent that rights
or duties depend thereon or that a statistical survey ordered by
law makes it necessary.

(4) No one may be compelled to perform any religious act or
ceremony or to participate in religious exercises or to use a
religious form of oath.

Article 137 (Weimar Constitution). (1) There shall be no state
church.

(2) Freedom of association to form religious bodies is guaranteed. The union of religious bodies within the territory of the
Reich shall not be subject to any restrictions.

(3) Every religious body shall regulate and administer its affairs
independently within the limits of the law valid for all. It shall
confer its offices without the participation of the state or the
civil community.

(4) Religious bodies shall acquire legal capacity according to
the general provisions of civil law.

(5) Religious bodies shall remain corporate bodies under public

*See Article 140 above.

law in so far as they have been such heretofore. The other religious bodies shall be granted like rights upon application, if their constitution and the number of their members offer an assurance of their permanency. If several such religious bodies under public law unite in one organization, such organization shall also be a corporate body under public law.

(6) Religious bodies that are corporate bodies under public law shall be entitled to levy taxes in accordance with *Land* law on the basis of the civil taxation lists.

(7) Associations whose purpose is the cultivation of a philosophical ideology shall have the same status as religious bodies.

(8) Such further regulation as may be required for the implementation of these provisions shall be incumbent on *Land* legislation.

Article 138 (Weimar Constitution). (1) State contributions to religious bodies, based on law or contract or special legal title, shall be redeemed by means of *Land* legislation. The principles for such redemption shall be established by the Reich.

(2) The right to own property and other rights of religious bodies or associations in respect of their institutions, foundations and other assets destined for purposes of worship, education, or charity, are guaranteed.

Article 139 (Weimar Constitution). Sunday and the public holidays recognized by the state shall remain under legal protection as days of rest from work and of spiritual edification.

Article 141 (Weimar Constitution). To the extent that there exists a need for religious services and spiritual care in the army, in hospitals, prisons, or other public institutions, the religious bodies shall be permitted to perform religious acts; in this connection there shall be no compulsion of any kind.

[23 May 1949]

THE DECLARATION
OF THE RIGHTS OF MAN
AND THE CITIZEN
1789

THE Representatives of the French People constituted in National Assembly,

Considering that ignorance, forgetfulness or contempt of the rights of man are the sole causes of public misfortune and governmental depravity,

Have resolved to expound in a solemn declaration the natural, inalienable and sacred rights of man,

So that this declaration, perpetually present to all members of the body social, shall be a constant reminder to them of their rights and duties;

So that, since it will be possible at any moment to compare the acts of the legislative authority and those of the executive authority with the final end of all political institutions, those acts shall thereby be the more respected;

So that the claims of the citizenry, founded thenceforth on simple and uncontestable principles, shall always tend to the support of the constitution and to the common good.

Consequently the *National Assembly* recognizes and declares in the presence and under the auspices of the Supreme Being the following rights of man and of the citizen:

1. In respect of their rights men are born and remain free and equal. The only permissible basis for social distinctions is public utility.
2. The final end of every political institution is the preservation of the natural and imprescriptible rights of man. These rights are those of liberty, property, security and resistance to oppression.
3. The basis of all sovereignty lies, essentially, in the Nation. No corporation nor individual may exercise any authority that is not expressly derived therefrom.
4. Liberty is the capacity to do anything that does no harm to

others. Hence the only limitations on the individual's exercise of his natural rights are those which ensure the enjoyment of these same rights to all other individuals. These limits can be established only by legislation.

5. Legislation is entitled to forbid only those actions which are harmful to society. Nothing not forbidden by legislation may be prohibited nor may any individual be compelled to do anything that legislation has not prescribed.

6. Legislation is the expression of the general will. All citizens have a right to participate in shaping it either in person, or through their representatives. It must be the same for all, whether it punishes or it protects. Since all citizens are equal in its eyes, all are equally eligible for all positions, posts and public employments in accordance with their abilities and with no other distinctions than those provided by their virtues and their talents.

7. No individual may be accused, arrested or detained except in the cases prescribed by legislation and according to the procedures it has laid down. Those who solicit, further, execute or arrange for the execution of arbitrary commands must be punished; but every citizen charged or detained by virtue of legislation must immediately obey; resistance renders him culpable.

8. The only punishments established by legislation must be ones that are strictly and obviously necessary, and no individual may be punished except by virtue of a law passed and promulgated prior to the crime and applied in due legal form.

9. Since every individual is presumed innocent until found guilty, legislation must severely repress all use of force beyond that which is necessary to secure his person in those cases where it is deemed indispensable to arrest him.

10. Nobody must be persecuted on account of his opinions, including religious ones, provided that the manifestation of these does not disturb the public order established by legislation.

11. The free communication of thoughts and opinions is one of the most precious rights of man; hence every citizen may speak, write and publish freely, save that he must answer for

any abuse of such freedom according to the cases established by legislation.

12. In order to guarantee the rights of man and the citizen, a police force is necessary: it follows that such a force is established for the public weal and not for the private advantage of those to whom it is entrusted.

13. The upkeep of the police force and the expenses of public administration necessitate public taxation. This must be borne by all citizens equally, according to their means.

14. All citizens, individually or through their representatives, possess the right to assure themselves that a need for taxation exists, to accept it by free consent, to monitor the way it is being used and to prescribe the base, the allocation, collection and duration of the tax.

15. Society possesses the right to demand from every public servant an account of his administration.

16. A society in which rights are not secured nor the separation of powers established is a society without a constitution.

17. Since property is an inviolable and sacred right, no individual may be deprived of it unless some public necessity, legally certified as such, clearly requires it; and subject always to a just and previously determined compensation.

[26 August 1789]

The Preamble to
the Constitution of the

FOURTH FRENCH
REPUBLIC
1946

The National Constituent Assembly has adopted,
The French people has approved,
The President and the Provisional Government of the Republic promulgate the Constitution which runs as follows:

PREAMBLE

On the morrow of the victory won by the free peoples over the régimes which have sought to enslave and degrade the human personality, the French people, once again, proclaims that all human beings without distinction of race, religion or belief possess inalienable and sacred rights.

It solemnly reaffirms the Rights and Liberties of Man and the Citizen hallowed by the Declaration of Rights of 1789 and the fundamental principles recognized by the laws of the Republic.

It proclaims, in addition, as particularly necessary to our time the following political, economic and social principles:

1. The laws shall guarantee to women, in every sphere, equal rights with men.
2. Every individual who is the victim of persecution by reason of his activities in favour of freedom shall possess the right of asylum within the territories of the Republic.
3. Every individual has the duty to work and the right to employment. Nobody shall be allowed to suffer injury in respect of his work or occupation by reason of his origins, his opinions or his beliefs.
4. Every individual shall have the right to defend his rights and his interests by trade-union activities and to join the trade union of his choice.
5. The right to strike shall be exercised within the framework of the laws which govern this.
6. Every worker shall participate through his delegates in the

collective arrangement of work-conditions as well as in the running of the firm.

7. Every resource or enterprise the working of which has acquired or is in the process of acquiring the characteristics of a public national service or, effectively, a monopoly, must pass into public ownership.

8. The Nation shall assure to the individual and the family the conditions necessary for their development.

9. It shall guarantee to everybody and notably to children, mothers and elderly workpeople, health care, material security, rest and leisure. Every human being who by reason of age, physical or mental condition, or economic situation is incapable of working shall have the right to obtain the means of subsistence from the community.

10. The Nation proclaims the solidarity and the equality of all the members of the French people when faced with the responsibilities arising from a national calamity.

11. The Nation guarantees to children and adults equal access to education, professional training and culture. The organization of free, public and secular instruction at all levels is a duty incumbent upon the state.

12. The French Republic, faithful to its traditions, shall conform to the rules of international public law. It will never engage in wars of conquest nor use force against the freedom of any people.

13. Subject to reciprocity, France will consent to such limitations upon her sovereignty as are necessary for the organization and defence of peace.

14. France and her overseas peoples make up a union founded on the equality of rights and duties without distinction of race or religion.

15. The French Union comprises nations and peoples who pool or coordinate their resources and efforts in order to develop their individual civilizations, increase their well-being, and ensure their security.

16. Faithful to her traditional mission France intends to guide the peoples under her care to the self-administration of their affairs; rejecting any systems of colonization founded on

arbitrary rule, she guarantees everybody equal access to public employments, and the individual or collective exercise of the rights and the liberties proclaimed or confirmed above.

[27 October 1946]

The Constitution of the

FIFTH FRENCH
REPUBLIC
1958

CONTENTS

PREAMBLE

The French people solemnly proclaims its attachment to the Rights of Man and the principles of national sovereignty as defined by the Declaration of 1789, reaffirmed and completed by the Preamble of the Constitution of 1946.

By virtue of these principles and that of the free determination of peoples, the Republic offers to those Overseas Territories which express the desire to adhere to them, new institutions founded on the common ideal of liberty, equality and fraternity and conceived with a view to their democratic evolution.

Article 1. The Republic and the peoples of the Overseas Territories who, by an act of free determination, adopt the present Constitution thereby institute a Community.

The Community shall be based on the equality and the solidarity of the peoples composing it.

TITLE I. ON SOVEREIGNTY

Article 2. France is a Republic, indivisible, secular, democratic and social. It shall ensure the equality of all citizens before the law, without distinction of origin, race or religion. It shall respect all beliefs.

The national emblem is the tricolour flag, blue, white and red.

The national anthem is the *Marseillaise.*

The motto of the Republic is 'Liberty, Equality, Fraternity'.

Its principle is government of the people, by the people, and for the people.

Article 3. National sovereignty belongs to the people, which shall exercise it through its representatives and by way of referendums.

No section of the people, nor any individual, may attribute to themselves or himself the exercise thereof.

The suffrage may be direct or indirect under the conditions stipulated by the Constitution. It shall always be universal, equal and secret.

All French citizens of either sex who have reached their majority and who enjoy civil and political rights may vote, under the conditions determined by legislation.

Article 4. Political parties and groups shall play a part in the exercise of the right to vote. They shall be formed, and shall carry on their activities, freely. They are obliged to respect the principles of national sovereignty and democracy.

TITLE II. THE PRESIDENT OF THE REPUBLIC

Article 5. The President of the Republic shall watch to see that the Constitution is respected. He shall ensure, by his arbitrament (sc. *arbitrage*), the regular functioning of the public authorities, as well as the continuity of the state.

He shall be the protector of the independence of the nation, of the integrity of its territory, and of respect for Community agreements and for treaties.

Article 6. The President of the Republic shall be elected for seven years by direct universal suffrage.

The procedures implementing the present Article shall be determined by an organic law.

Article 7. The President of the Republic shall be elected by an absolute majority of the votes cast. If this is not obtained on the first ballot, there shall be a second ballot on the second Sunday following. Only the two candidates who received the greatest number of votes on the first ballot shall present themselves, having taken into account that candidates with even more votes may have nevertheless withdrawn.

The voting shall begin at the time fixed by the Government.

The election of the new President shall take place not less than twenty days and not more than thirty-five days before the expiry of the powers of the President in office.

Should the Presidency of the Republic fall vacant for any cause whatsoever, or, if the Constitutional Council has formally certified on the request of the Government and by an absolute majority of its members that there is an impediment to the functioning of the Presidency, the functions of the President of the Republic, except for those provided for by Articles 11 and 12 below, shall be temporarily exercised by the President of the Senate, and, if the latter in his turn suffer impediment in the exercise of these functions, by the Government.

In the case of a vacancy, or, when the impediment is declared by the Constitutional Council to be permanent, the voting for the election of a new President shall take place, except in the case of duress certified officially by the Constitutional Council, not less than twenty days and not more than thirty-five days after the beginning of the vacancy or of the declaration of the permanent character of the impediment.

If, in the seven days preceding the latest date for the lodging of candidatures, one of the persons who, at least thirty days prior to that date, publicly announced his decision to be a candidate dies or suffers impediment, the Constitutional Council can decide to postpone the election.

If, before the first ballot, one of the candidates dies or suffers impediment, the Constitutional Council shall order the postponement of the election.

If, before any candidates have withdrawn, one of the two candidates who received the greatest number of votes in the first ballot shall have died or suffered impediment, the Constitutional Council shall declare that the electoral procedure must be repeated in full; the same shall apply in the event of the death or impediment of one of the two candidates standing for the second ballot.

All cases shall be referred to the Constitutional Council under the conditions laid down in Article 61 (second paragraph) below, or under those determined for the presentation of candidates by the organic law provided for in Article 6 above.

The Constitutional Council can extend the periods stipulated in the third and fifth paragraphs [of this Article] above, provided that polling shall not take place more than thirty-five days after the date of the decision of the Constitutional Council. If the implementation of the provisions of this paragraph results in the postponement of the election beyond the expiry of the powers of the President in office, the latter shall remain in office until his successor is proclaimed.

Neither Articles 49 and 50, nor Article 89 of the Constitution, may be applied during the vacancy of the Presidency of the Republic or during the period that elapses between the declaration of the permanent character of the impediment of the President and the election of his successor.

Article 8. The President of the Republic shall appoint the Prime Minister. He shall terminate the functions of the Prime Minister when the latter tenders the resignation of the Government.

On the proposal of the Prime Minister he shall appoint and dismiss the other members of the Government.

Article 9. The President of the Republic shall preside over the Council of Ministers.

Article 10. The President of the Republic shall promulgate laws within fifteen days following the transmission to the Government of the law as finally adopted.

He may, before the expiry of this time limit, ask Parliament to reconsider the law or certain of its articles. Such reconsideration cannot be refused.

Article 11. The President of the Republic may, on the proposal of the Government during the sessions of Parliament or on the joint motion of its two Houses, published in the *Journal Officiel*, submit to a referendum any Bill dealing with the organization of the public authorities, entailing approval of a Community agreement, or providing for authorization to ratify a treaty which, without being contrary to the Constitution, would affect the functioning of [existing] institutions.

Should the referendum have decided in favour of the Bill, the President of the Republic shall promulgate it within the time limit stipulated in the preceding Article.

Article 12. The President of the Republic may, after consultation with the Prime Minister and the Presidents of the two Houses, declare the dissolution of the National Assembly.

General elections shall take place not less than twenty days and not more than forty days after the dissolution.

The National Assembly shall convene by right on the second Thursday following its election. If this meeting takes place outside the periods provided for ordinary sessions, a session shall, as of right, be held for a fifteen-day period.

No further dissolution may take place within a year following these elections.

Article 13. The President of the Republic shall sign the ordinances and decrees decided upon in the Council of Ministers.

He shall make appointments to the civil and military posts of the state.

Councillors of State, the Grand Chancellor of the Legion of Honour, ambassadors and envoys-extraordinary, Master Councillors of the Court of Accounts, prefects, representatives of the Government in the Overseas Territories, general officers, rectors of academies and *directeurs* of central government departments shall be appointed in the Council of Ministers.

An organic law shall determine the other posts to be filled in the Council of Ministers, as well as the conditions under which the power of the President of the Republic to make appointments to office may be delegated by him and exercised in his name.

Article 14. The President of the Republic shall accredit ambassadors and envoys-extraordinary to foreign powers; foreign ambassadors and envoys-extraordinary shall be accredited to him.

Article 15. The President of the Republic shall be the head of the Armed Forces. He shall preside over the Higher Councils and Committees of National Defence.

Article 16. When the institutions of the Republic, the independence of the nation, the integrity of its territory or the fulfilment of its international commitments are threatened in a grave and immediate manner, and when the regular functioning of the constitutional public authorities is interrupted, the President of the Republic shall take the measures demanded by these circumstances after official consultation with the Prime Minister, the Presidents of the two Houses and the Constitutional Council.

He shall inform the nation of these measures by a message.

These measures must be prompted by the desire to ensure to the constitutional public authorities, in the shortest possible time, the means of fulfilling their assigned function. The Constitutional Council shall be consulted with regard to such measures.

Parliament shall convene as of right.

The National Assembly may not be dissolved during the exercise of the emergency powers.

Article 17. The President of the Republic shall enjoy the right of pardon.

Article 18. The President of the Republic shall communicate with the two Houses of Parliament by means of messages, which he shall cause to be read, and which are not debatable.

If Parliament is not sitting, it shall be convened especially for this purpose.

Article 19. The acts of the President of the Republic, other than those provided for under Articles 8 (first paragraph), 11, 12, 16, 18, 54, 56 and 61, shall be countersigned by the Prime Minister and, where required, by the appropriate Ministers.

TITLE III. THE GOVERNMENT

Article 20. The Government shall determine and conduct the policy of the nation.

It shall have at its disposal the Administration and the Armed Forces.

It shall be responsible to Parliament under the conditions and in accordance with the procedures stipulated in Articles 49 and 50.

Article 21. The Prime Minister shall direct the operation of the Government. He shall be responsible for national defence. He shall ensure the execution of the laws. Subject to the provisions of Article 13, he shall exercise regulation-making power, and shall make appointments to civil and military posts.

He may delegate certain powers to the Ministers.

Should the occasion arise, he shall deputize for the President of the Republic as chairman of the councils and committees provided for under Article 15.

In exceptional circumstances he may deputize for him as the Chairman of a meeting of the Council of Ministers, by virtue of an explicit delegation of authority and for a specific agenda.

Article 22. The acts of the Prime Minister shall be countersigned, where required, by the Ministers responsible for their execution.

Article 23. The duties of a member of the Government shall be incompatible with the holding of any parliamentary mandate, with the holding of any office at national level in business, professional or labour organizations, and with any public employment or professional activity.

An organic law shall determine the conditions under which the holders of such mandates, duties or employments shall be replaced.

The replacement of members of Parliament shall take place in accordance with the provisions of Article 25.

TITLE IV. THE PARLIAMENT

Article 24. Parliament consists of the National Assembly and the Senate.

The Deputies of the National Assembly shall be elected by direct suffrage.

The Senate shall be elected by indirect suffrage. It shall ensure the representation of the territorial units of the Republic. Frenchmen living outside France shall be represented in the Senate.

Article 25. An organic law shall lay down the term for which each House is elected, the number of its members, their emoluments, the conditions of eligibility and non-eligibility, and the offices incompatible with membership of the Houses.

It shall likewise lay down the conditions under which, in the case of a vacancy in either House, persons shall be elected to replace the Deputy or the Senator whose seat has been vacated, until the holding of new general or partial elections to the House in which the vacancy has occurred.

Article 26. No member of Parliament may be prosecuted, sought out, arrested, held in custody or tried as a result of the opinions or votes expressed by him in the exercise of his duties.

No member of Parliament may, during parliamentary sessions, be prosecuted or arrested for criminal or minor offences without the authorization of the House of which he is a member, except when apprehended *in flagrante delicto.**

When Parliament is not in session, no member of Parliament may be arrested without the authorization of the Bureau of the House of which he is a member, except in the case of *flagrante delicto*, or authorized prosecution, or of final conviction.

The holding in custody, or the prosecution, of a member of Parliament shall be suspended if the House of which he is a member so demands.

Article 27. All binding instructions from outside bodies** on members of Parliament shall be null and void.

The right to vote of the members of Parliament shall be exercised in person.

*i.e. caught in the act (Fr. *flagrant délit*).
**Tout mandat impératif est nul.*

An organic law may, by way of exception, authorize the delegation of a vote. In such a case no member may cast more than one delegated vote.

Article 28. Parliament shall convene as of right in two ordinary sessions per year.

The first session shall open on 2 October and last for eighty days.

The second session shall open on 2 April and shall not last for more than ninety days.

If the 2 October or the 2 April be a public holiday the session shall open on the first working day thereafter.

Article 29. Parliament shall convene in extraordinary session, at the request of the Prime Minister or of the majority of the members of the National Assembly, to consider a specific agenda.

When an extraordinary session is held at the request of the members of the National Assembly, the closure decree shall take effect as soon as Parliament has completed the agenda for which it was convened, and at the latest, twelve days from the date of its meeting.

Only the Prime Minister may ask for a new session before the end of the month following the closure decree.

Article 30. Apart from the cases where Parliament meets as of right, extraordinary sessions shall be opened and closed by decree of the President of the Republic.

Article 31. The members of the Government shall have access to the two Houses. They shall be heard when they so request.

They may be assisted by Government commissioners.

Article 32. The President of the National Assembly shall be elected for the duration of the legislature. The President of the Senate shall be elected after each partial renewal (of the Senate).

Article 33. The meetings of the two Houses shall be public. A verbatim report of the debates shall be published in the *Journal Officiel*.

Each House may sit in secret committee at the request of the Prime Minister or of one tenth of its members.

TITLE V. RELATIONS BETWEEN PARLIAMENT AND THE GOVERNMENT

Article 34. Legislation* shall be passed by Parliament.

Legislation shall establish the rules concerning:

Civil rights and the fundamental guarantees granted to citizens for the exercise of their public liberties; the obligations imposed on citizens in respect to their persons and property for reasons of national defence.

Nationality, status and legal capacity of persons, matrimony, inheritance and gifts.

Determination of crimes and misdemeanours and also the penalties imposed therefor; criminal procedure; amnesty; the creation of new orders of jurisdiction; and the status of the magistracy.

The basis of assessment, the rate and the modes of collecting taxes of all kinds; the currency system.

Legislation shall likewise establish rules concerning:

The electoral systems for the Houses of Parliament and for local councils.

The creation of categories of public organizations.

The fundamental guarantees granted to the civil and military personnel of the state.

The nationalization of enterprises and the transfer of the property of enterprises from the public to the private sector.

Legislation shall lay down the basic principles of:

The general organization of national defence.

The free administration of local authorities, the scope of their jurisdiction, and their resources.

Education.

Property rights, real-estate rights, civil and commercial contracts.

Labour, trade-union and social-security law.

*The French text gives, '*La loi est votée par le Parlement*'. The translation of '*la loi*' gives rise to certain difficulties. Elsewhere in this document it is translated as 'the law' or 'laws', according to context. In the present context it seems to me that the exact translation must be '*legislation*', since, as will be seen, Article 37 draws a fundamental distinction between '*la loi*', and '*matières . . . d'un caractère réglementaire*', i.e. regulations.

Financial legislation shall determine the financial resources and obligations of the state under the conditions and with the qualifications to be provided for by an organic law.

Programme-laws shall determine the objectives of the economic and social action of the state.

The provisions of the present Article may be developed in detail and amplified by an organic law.

Article 35. Parliament shall authorize the declaration of war.

Article 36. The State of Siege shall be decreed in a meeting of the Council of Ministers.

Its prolongation beyond twelve days may be authorized by Parliament alone.

Article 37. Matters other than those that fall within the domain of legislation shall have the character of regulations.

Legislative texts concerning such matters may be modified by decree issued after consultation with the Council of State. Those legislative texts which shall have come into existence only after the present Constitution has become operative shall only be modified by decree if the Constitutional Council has declared that they have the character of regulations as defined in the preceding paragraph.

Article 38. In order to carry out its programme the Government may ask Parliament to authorize it, for a limited period, to take measures which are normally within the domain of legislation, by means of ordinances.

The ordinances shall be made in meetings of the Council of Ministers after consultation with the Council of State. They shall come into force upon their publication but expire if the Bill for their ratification is not submitted to Parliament by the date set by the enabling Act.

At the expiry of the time limit referred to in the first paragraph of the present Article, the ordinances in those matters which fall within the domain of legislation may be modified only by legislation.

Article 39. The Prime Minister and the members of Parliament shall each have the right to initiate legislation.

Government Bills shall be discussed in the Council of Ministers after consultation with the Council of State and shall be filed with the Bureau of one of the two Houses. Finance Bills shall be submitted first to the National Assembly.

Article 40. Bills and amendments introduced by members of Parliament shall be out of order when their adoption would result either in a diminution of public revenue or the creation or increase of public expenditure.

Article 41. If in the course of legislative procedure it shall appear that a Private Member's Bill or an amendment is outside the domain of legislation or is counter to a delegation of authority granted by virtue of Article 38, the Government may declare it out of order.

In the case of dispute between the Government and the President of the House concerned, the Constitutional Council, upon the request of either party, shall give a ruling within eight days.

Article 42. In the first of the two Houses of Parliament to which a Government Bill has been referred, the discussion shall take place on the text presented by the Government.

A House which has been given a text passed on by the other House shall debate on the basis of the text transmitted to it.

Article 43. Government and Private Member's Bills shall, at the request of the Government or of the House concerned, be sent for consideration to committees especially established for this purpose.

Government and Private Member's Bills for which such a request has not been made shall be sent to one of the permanent committees, the number of which shall be limited to six in each House.

Article 44. Members of Parliament, and the Government, shall each have the right of amendment.

Once the debate has opened, the Government may oppose the consideration of any amendment which has not been previously submitted to committee.

If the Government so requests, the House concerned shall accept or reject all or part of the text under discussion, including only the amendments proposed or accepted by the Government, in one single vote.

Article 45. Every Government or Private Member's Bill shall be considered successively in the two Houses of Parliament with a view to the adoption of an identical text.

When, as a result of disagreement between the two Houses, it has become impossible to adopt a Government or a Private Member's Bill after two readings by each House or (if the Government has declared the matter urgent) after a single reading by each of them, the Prime Minister shall have the right to have a joint committee meet, composed of an equal number from each House and instructed to put forward a text on the provisions still in dispute.

The text drafted by the joint committees may be submitted by the Government to the two Houses for their approval. No amendment shall be in order except by agreement with the Government.

If the joint committee fails to arrive at a common text, or if this text is not adopted under the conditions set forth in the preceding paragraph, the Government may, after a new reading by the National Assembly and by the Senate, ask the National Assembly to make a final decision. In this event, the National Assembly may reconsider either the text put forward by the joint committee or the last one adopted by itself, modified, if necessary, by one or any of the amendments made by the Senate.

Article 46. Laws characterized as organic by the Constitution shall be passed and amended in the following ways:

A Government or Private Member's Bill shall be sent for deliberation and vote of the first House to which it is passed only at the end of a period of fifteen days from its introduction.

The procedure of Article 45 shall apply. Nevertheless, in the absence of agreement between the two Houses, the text may be adopted by the National Assembly, at its final reading, only by an absolute majority of its members.

The organic laws relating to the Senate must be passed by the two Houses on the same terms.

Organic laws may be promulgated only after the Constitutional Council has declared them constitutional.

Article 47. Parliament shall pass finance Bills by a procedure to be stipulated by an organic law.

Should the National Assembly fail to reach a decision on first reading within a time limit of forty days from the introduction of the Bill, the Government shall refer the Bill to the Senate, which must reach a decision within fifteen days. Thereafter the procedure set forth in Article 45 shall be followed.

Should Parliament fail to reach a decision within seventy days, the provisions of the Bill may be put into force by ordinance.

Should the finance Bill establishing the revenue and expenditures of a fiscal year not be introduced in time for it to be promulgated before the beginning of that fiscal year, the Government shall request Parliament as a matter of urgency for authorization to levy taxes and shall make available by decree the funds needed to meet commitments already sanctioned.

The time limits stipulated in the present Article are suspended when Parliament is not in session.

The Court of Accounts shall assist Parliament and the Government in supervising the carrying out of the finance Acts.

Article 48. The discussion of Government Bills or of Private Member's Bills agreed to by the Government shall have priority on the agenda of the Houses, in the order laid down by the Government.

Priority is given at one sitting a week to questions asked by members of Parliament and the Government's replies.

Article 49. The Prime Minister, after deliberation by the Council of Ministers, may pledge the responsibility of the Government before the National Assembly in respect to the Government's programme or a declaration of its general policy, as the case may be.

The National Assembly may challenge the responsibility of the Government by passing a motion of censure. Such a motion shall be in order only if signed by at least one tenth of the members of the National Assembly. The vote may not take place until forty-eight hours after the motion was tabled; the only votes counted shall be those in favour of the motion of censure, which may be adopted only by a majority of all the members comprising the Assembly. Should the motion of censure be rejected, its signatories may not introduce another motion in the course of the same session except in the case provided for in the next paragraph.

The Prime Minister may, after deliberation by the Council of Ministers, pledge the responsibility of the Government before the National Assembly on the passing of a legislative text, or motion. In this event, the legislative text or motion shall be considered as adopted unless a motion of censure, tabled within the succeeding twenty-four hours, is voted under the conditions provided for in the previous paragraph.

The Prime Minister shall be entitled to seek the Senate's approval for a general policy declaration.

Article 50. When the National Assembly passes a vote of censure, or when it rejects the programme or general policy declaration of the Government, the Prime Minister must tender the resignation of the Government to the President of the Republic.

Article 51. The closure of ordinary or extraordinary sessions shall be postponed as of right, where the necessity arises, in order to permit the application of the provisions of Article 49.

TITLE VI. TREATIES AND INTERNATIONAL AGREEMENTS

Article 52. The President of the Republic shall negotiate and ratify treaties.

He shall be informed of all negotiations leading to the conclusion of an international agreement not subject to ratification.

Article 53. Peace treaties, commercial treaties, treaties or agreements concerning international organizations, those that imply a commitment for the finances of the state, those that modify provisions with a legislative character, those concerning personal status, those that call for cession, exchange or addition of territory, may only be ratified or approved by way of legislation.

They shall take effect only after having been ratified or approved.

No cession, no exchange, no addition of territory shall be valid without the consent of the populations concerned.

Article 54. If the Constitutional Council, the matter having been referred to it by the President of the Republic, by the Prime Minister or by the President of one or the other Houses, shall declare that an international commitment contains a clause contrary to the Constitution, the authorization to ratify or approve this commitment may be given only after the amendment of the Constitution.

Article 55. Treaties or agreements duly ratified or approved shall, upon their publication, have an authority superior to that of [domestic] legislation, subject, for each separate agreement or treaty, to reciprocal application by the other party.

TITLE VII. THE CONSTITUTIONAL COUNCIL

Article 56. The Constitutional Council shall consist of nine members, whose term of office shall last nine years and shall not be renewable. One third of the membership of the Constitutional Council shall be renewed every three years. Three of its members shall be appointed by the President of the Republic, three by the President of the National Assembly, three by the President of the Senate.

In addition to the nine members provided for above, former Presidents of the Republic shall be *ex officio* life-members of the Constitutional Council.

The President shall be appointed by the President of the Republic. He shall have the casting vote in the case of a tie.

Article 57. The office of member of the Constitutional Council shall be incompatible with that of Minister or member of Parliament. Other incompatibilities shall be laid down by an organic law.

Article 58. The Constitutional Council shall keep watch to secure the regularity of the election of the President of the Republic.

It shall consider objections and shall announce the results of the vote.

Article 59. The Constitutional Council shall pronounce, in disputed cases, on the regularity of the election of deputies and senators.

Article 60. The Constitutional Council shall keep watch to secure the regularity of the procedures for referendums and shall announce the results thereof.

Article 61. Organic laws before their promulgation, and standing orders of the Houses of Parliament before they come into application, must be submitted to the Constitutional Council, which shall pronounce on their constitutionality.

To the same end, legislation may be submitted to the Constitutional Council, before its promulgation, by the President of the Republic, the Prime Minister, the President of the National Assembly, the President of the Senate, or sixty Deputies or sixty Senators.

In the cases provided for by the two preceding paragraphs, the Constitutional Council must make its decision within one month. Notwithstanding, at the request of the Government, in cases of urgency, this period shall be reduced to eight days.

In these same cases, referral to the Constitutional Council shall suspend the time-limit for promulgation.

Article 62. A provision declared unconstitutional may not be promulgated or implemented.

The decisions of the Constitutional Council are not subject to appeal. They are binding on the public authorities and on all administrative and judicial authorities.

Article 63. An organic law shall determine the rules of the organization and functioning of the Constitutional Council, the procedure to be followed before it, and in particular the periods of time allowed for laying disputes before it.

TITLE VIII. THE JUDICIARY

Article 64. The President of the Republic shall be the custodian of the independence of the judiciary.

He shall be assisted by the Higher Council of the Judiciary.

An organic law shall lay down the status of the judiciary.

Judges shall be irremovable.

Article 65. The Higher Council of the Judiciary shall be presided over by the President of the Republic. The Minister of Justice shall be its Vice-President *ex officio*. He may deputize for the President of the Republic.

The Higher Council shall, in addition, include nine members

appointed by the President of the Republic in conformity with the conditions to be laid down by an organic law.

The Higher Council of the Judiciary shall present nominations for judges of the Court of Cassation and for the First Presidents of Courts of Appeal. It shall give its opinion, under the conditions to be laid down by an organic law, on proposals of the Minister of Justice relative to the nomination of the other judges. It shall be consulted on questions of reprieves under conditions to be laid down by an organic law.

The Higher Council of the Judiciary shall act as the disciplinary council for judges. In such cases, it shall be presided over by the First President of the Court of Cassation.

Article 66. No one may be arbitrarily detained.

The judiciary, guardian of individual liberty, shall ensure respect for this principle under conditions stipulated by legislation.

TITLE IX. THE HIGH COURT OF JUSTICE

Article 67. A High Court of Justice shall be established.

It shall be composed of members of Parliament, elected in equal number and from within the National Assembly and the Senate after each general or partial election to these Houses. It shall elect its President from among its members.

An organic law shall lay down the composition of the High Court, its rules, and also the procedure to be followed before it.

Article 68. The President of the Republic shall not be held accountable for actions performed in the exercise of his office except in the case of high treason. He can only be indicted by the two Houses ruling by identical vote in open balloting and by an absolute majority of the members of the two Houses. He shall be tried by the High Court of Justice.

Members of the Government shall be criminally liable for actions performed in the exercise of their office and classed as crimes or misdemeanours at the time they were committed. The procedure defined above shall be applied to them, as well as to their accomplices, in the case of a conspiracy against the security of the state. In the cases provided for by the present paragraph, the High Court shall be bound by the definition of crimes and misdemeanours as well as by the rules concerning penalties, as established by the criminal laws in force when the acts were committed.

TITLE X. THE ECONOMIC AND SOCIAL COUNCIL

Article 69. The Economic and Social Council, at the request of the Government, shall give its opinion on the Government Bills, draft ordinances and decrees as well as on the Private Member's Bills that are submitted to it.

A member of the Economic and Social Council may be designated by it to present the Houses of Parliament with the Council's opinion on the Government or Private Member's Bills that have been submitted to it.

Article 70. The Economic and Social Council may likewise be consulted by the Government on any economic or social problem concerning the Republic or the Community. Any plan or any programme-bill of an economic or social character shall be submitted to it for its opinion.

Article 71. The composition of the Economic and Social Council and the rules of its procedure shall be laid down by an organic law.

TITLE XI. TERRITORIAL UNITS

Article 72. The territorial units of the Republic are the Communes, the Departments and the Overseas Territories. Other territorial units may be created by legislation.

These units shall be free to govern themselves through elected councils and under the conditions to be stipulated by legislation.

In the Departments and the Territories, the delegate of the Government shall be responsible for the national interest, for administrative supervision and for seeing that the laws are respected.

Article 73. The legislative system and administrative organization of the Overseas Departments may be modified as required by their peculiar circumstances.

Article 74. The Overseas Territories of the Republic shall have a special organization which takes into account their local interests within the general interests of the Republic. This organization shall be defined and modified by legislation after consultation with the relevant Territorial Assembly.

Article 75. Citizens of the Republic who do not enjoy ordinary civil status, the only status to which Article 34 refers, shall retain their personal status so long as they have not renounced it.

Article 76. The Overseas Territories may retain their status within the Republic.

If they express the desire to do so by a decision of their Territorial Assemblies taken within the time-limit set in the first paragraph of Article 91, they shall become Overseas Departments of the Republic or Member States of the Community, either as single units or grouped together.

TITLE XII. THE COMMUNITY

Article 77. In the Community established by the present Constitution, the states shall enjoy autonomy; they shall administer themselves and manage their own affairs democratically and freely.

There shall be only one citizenship in the Community.

All citizens shall be equal before the law, whatever their origin, their race and their religion. They shall have the same duties.

Article 78. The Community's jurisdiction shall extend over foreign policy, defence, currency, common economic and financial policy, as well as over policy on strategic raw materials.

It shall include, in addition, except in the case of specific agreements, the supervision of the administration of justice, higher education, the general organization of external transportation, and transportation within the Community as well as telecommunications.

Special agreements may establish other common jurisdictions or provide any transfer of jurisdiction from the Community to one of its members.

Article 79. The Member States shall come within the provisions of Article 77 as soon as they have exercised the choice provided for in Article 76.

Until the measures required for the implementation of the present Title come into force, matters of common jurisdiction shall be managed by the Republic.

Article 80. The President of the Republic shall preside over and represent the Community.

The institutional organs of the Community shall be an Executive Council, a Senate, and a Court of Arbitration.

Article 81. The Member States of the Community shall participate in the election of the President according to the conditions stipulated in Article 6.

The President of the Republic, in his capacity as President of the Community, shall be represented in each state of the Community.

Article 82. The Executive Council of the Community shall be presided over by the President of the Community. It shall consist of the Prime Minister of the Republic, the heads of Government of each of the Member States of the Community, and the Ministers responsible for common affairs on behalf of the Community.

The Executive Council shall organize the cooperation of members of the Community at the government and administrative levels.

The organization and procedure of the Executive Council shall be determined by an organic law.

Article 83. The Senate of the Community shall be composed of delegates whom the Parliament of the Republic and the legislative assemblies of the other members of the Community shall choose from among their own memberships. The number of delegates of each state shall be determined so as to take account of its population and the responsibilities it assumes in the Community.

The Senate of the Community shall hold two sessions a year which shall be opened and closed by the President of the Community and may not last longer than one month each.

The Senate of the Community, when called upon by the President of the Community, shall deliberate upon the common

economic and financial policy before laws on these matters are
voted upon by the Parliament of the Republic and, should
circumstances so require, by the legislative assemblies of the
other members of the Community.

The Senate of the Community shall examine the acts, treaties
and international agreements that are specified in Articles 35 and
53, and which commit the Community.

The Senate of the Community shall make binding decisions in
the domains in which it has received delegation of power from the
legislative assemblies of the members of the Community. These
decisions shall be promulgated in the same form as the legislation within the territory of each of the states concerned.

An organic law shall lay down the composition of the Senate
and its rules of procedure.

Article 84. A Court of Arbitration of the Community shall rule
on disputes among members of the Community.

Its composition and its jurisdiction shall be determined by an
organic law.

Article 85. Notwithstanding the procedure provided for in
Article 89, the provisions of the present Title that concern the
functioning of the common institutions shall be amendable by
identically phrased legislation passed by the Parliament of the
Republic and the Senate of the Community.

The provisions of the present Title may also be amended by
agreements concluded between all the states of the Community;
the new provisions shall be applied under the conditions specified
by the constitution of each state.

Article 86. A change of status of a Member State of the Community may be requested, either by the Republic or by a resolution of the legislative assembly of the State concerned, and
confirmed by a local referendum, the organization and supervision of which shall be ensured by the institutions of the
Community. The procedures governing this change shall be
determined by an agreement approved by the Parliament of the
Republic and the legislative assembly concerned.

In the same manner, a Member State of the Community may
become independent. It shall thereby cease to belong to the
Community.

A Member State of the Community may also, by means of agreements, become independent without thereby ceasing to belong to the Community.

An independent state not a member of the Community may, by means of agreements, join the Community without ceasing to be independent.

The position of these states within the Community shall be determined by agreements concluded to this end, in particular the agreement mentioned in the preceding paragraphs as well as, should the occasion arise, the agreements provided for in the second paragraph of Article 85.

Article 87. The special agreements made for the implementation of the present Title shall be approved by the Parliament of the Republic and the legislative assembly concerned.

TITLE XIII. AGREEMENTS OF ASSOCIATION

Article 88. The Republic or the Community may make agreements with states that wish to associate themselves with the Community in order to develop their cultures.

TITLE XIV. AMENDMENT

Article 89. The initiative for amending the Constitution shall pertain both to the President of the Republic, on the proposal of the Prime Minister, and to the members of Parliament.

The Government's, or the Private Member's Bill for amendment must be passed by the two Houses in identical terms. The amendment shall become effective after approval by referendum.

Nevertheless, the proposed amendment shall not be submitted to a referendum should the President of the Republic decide to submit it to Parliament convened as Congress; in this case, the proposed amendment shall be approved only if it is adopted by a three-fifths majority of the votes cast. The Bureau of the Congress shall be that of the National Assembly.

No amendment procedure may be undertaken or followed when the integrity of the territory is in jeopardy.

The Republican form of government shall not be subject to amendment.

TITLE XV. TEMPORARY PROVISIONS

Article 90. The ordinary session of Parliament is suspended. The term of office of the members of the present National Assembly shall expire on the day that the Assembly elected under the present Constitution is convened.

Until this meeting, the Government alone shall have the authority to convene Parliament.

The term of office of the members of the Assembly of the French Union shall expire at the same time as that of the members of the present National Assembly.

Article 91. The institutions of the Republic, provided for by the present Constitution, shall be established within four months of its promulgation.

This time-limit shall be extended to six months for the institutions of the Community.

The powers of the President of the Republic now in office shall expire only when the results of the election provided for in Articles 6 and 7 of the present Constitution are proclaimed.

The Member States of the Community shall participate in this first election under the conditions derived from their status at the date of the promulgation of this Constitution.

The established authorities shall continue to exercise their functions in these states according to the laws and regulations applicable when the Constitution becomes operative, until the authorities provided for by their new régimes are set up.

Until it is definitely constituted, the Senate shall consist of the present members of the Council of the Republic. The organic laws that lay down the definitive composition of the Senate must be passed before 31 July 1959.

The powers conferred upon the Constitutional Council by Articles 58 and 59 of the Constitution shall be exercised, until this council is set up, by a committee composed of the Vice-President of the Council of State, as Chairman, the First President of the Court of Cassation, and the First President of the Court of Accounts.

The peoples of the Member States of the Community shall continue to be represented in Parliament until the measures necessary to the implementation of Title XII have been put into effect.

Article 92. The legislative measures necessary for establishing the institutions and, until they are set up, the functioning of the public authorities, shall be taken in meetings of the Council of Ministers, after consultation with the Council of State, in the form of ordinances having the force of law.

During the time-limit set in the first paragraph of Article 91, the Government shall be authorized to lay down, by ordinances having the force of law and passed in the same form, the system of election to the Houses provided for by the Constitution.

During the same period and under the same conditions, the Government may also take such measures in all matters as it deems necessary for the life of the nation, the protection of the citizens or the preservation of liberties.

The present law shall be applied as the Constitution of the Republic and of the Community.

[4 October 1958]

INDEXES

NOTE ON THE PRESENTATION
OF THE INDEXES

THE five constitutions printed above are laid out in different ways. Thus the 1936 (Stalin) Constitution of the USSR is divided, first, into chapters and then into Articles, which sometimes subdivide into clauses, whereas the 1977 (Brezhnev) Constitution is divided into nine major parts, then into chapters, then into Articles, which may be further subdivided. The German Constitution is divided into twelve main parts or chapters, then into Articles, which are further subdivided into clauses. The French document is divided into fifteen titles (*titres*), then into Articles, which are often subdivided into *alinéas*, or paragraphs. The US Constitution, however, is divided into seven major Articles (chapters, in effect) which are subdivided into Sections, and these are often subdivided into clauses.

The building-block in each of these constitutions is the element which is called Article in all but the US Constitution, where it is called Section. So the method of correlating the constitutions is to align them on this element, which produces the following table of equivalents:

United States	Soviet (1936)	Soviet (1977)	German	French
—	—	Part	—	—
Article	Chapter	Chapter	Chapter	Title
Section	Article	Article	Article	Article
Clause	Clause	Clause	Clause	*Alinéa* (= paragraph)

Consequently, the index entries contain four figures, each of which corresponds to one of the horizontal bands shown in the above table. To help in identification, Article numbers are printed in bold type, as they are in the constitutions themselves.

A further complication arises from the way in which the texts subdivide the Articles (or, in the American case, the Sections). In the German Constitution clauses in the text are numbered, in the Soviet constitutions some are numbered, some merely indicated by paragraphing. In the French Constitution, the *alinéas* or paragraphs are indicated only by paragraph indentation, and this is so for the original text of the American Constitution also. However, for the purposes of this edition I have used, for the latter, the text as printed in House Document No. 93–215 (of the 93rd Congress), and in this edition the clauses into which the Sections are divided are numbered.

Accordingly, I have adopted the following convention: where the text as printed numbers the clauses, these are listed as a fourth and last figure in the index entry. Where the text as printed simply starts a new line to indicate the existence of a fresh clause or paragraph, these divisions are recorded in the index by letters A, B, C etc., and also listed last in the entry. No *alinéas* are numbered in the French text, and therefore all appropriate entries in column 4 appear as letters A, B, C and so on.

In addition, there are a number of abbreviations:

'Preamble' refers to the Preamble to the existing text; but in the French case, the expression '1946 Preamble' refers to the Preamble to the 1946 Constitution, which is referred to in the Preamble to the 1958 Constitution, and has some juridical significance.

'Amdt' stands for Amendment and 'App.' (in the German case) for Appendix. 'RMC' stands for the Declaration of the Rights of Man and the Citizen, 1789, also referred to by the Preamble to the 1958 French Constitution.

Finally, the two Soviet constitutions are distinguished by 'USSR(S)' for the 1936 Stalin Constitution and 'USSR(B)' for the Brezhnev Constitution. As in the Introduction, I refer throughout to the Federal Republic of Germany as, simply, 'GERMANY'.

Plan of the Analytical Index

Constitutions

    I. Amendment of: (1) Method of; (2) Unamendable provisions
    II. Scope and duration of
    III. Legal status of: (1) Organs signalling constitutionality or otherwise of legislation; (2) Consequences of pronouncement of unconstitutionality of legislation

Federations

    I. Constituent units of: (1) Designation and nomenclature; (2) Boundaries of
    II. The division of powers
        (1) Powers exclusive to the federation
            (a) Common-market provisions: (i) Taxing and borrowing; (ii) Foreign and internal commerce; (iii) Bankruptcy; (iv) Coinage, currency and credit; (v) Postal service; (vi) Copyright; (vii) Debts; (viii) Other
            (b) External affairs, defence, war, security: (i) General supremacy clause; (ii) Treaties and ambassadors; (iii) Armed forces; (iv) Declaration of war; (v) Invasions and security; (vi) Asylum to foreign nationals
            (c) Common citizenship
            (d) Capital city, admission of new states, state boundaries
            (e) Miscellaneous social matters
            (f) Juridical
            (g) Other
        (2) Powers exclusive to the constituent units
        (3) Concurrent, i.e. alternative, powers
        (4) Collaboration between federation and constituent units
        (5) Federal, deconcentration to constituent units
        (6) Revenues, division of
        (7) Federal/constituent unit obligations: (a) Federal obligation to the units; (b) Units' obligations to the federation; (c) Reciprocal obligations
        (8) The conflict of laws
        (9) Federal enforcement powers
        (10) Form of government in the constituent units

Local Government

Dependencies

The Legislative Branch

  I. Generalia
    (1) Structure and competence of
    (2) Members of: (a) Credentials, recognition of; (b) Rights and duties of members; (c) Disqualifications for membership; (d) Immunities of members; (e) Payment to members; (f) Publicity of proceedings; (g) Sessions of
  II. Upper chambers: (1) Composition of; (2) Officers of; (3) Membership, qualifications for; (4) Procedure; (5) Term of office
  III. Lower chambers: (1) Composition of; (2) Officers of; (3) Membership, qualifications for; (4) Procedure; (5) Term of office
  IV. Respective powers of upper and lower Houses
  V. Relationship to executive branch *see* Executive Branch
  VI. Relationship to judicial branch *see* Judicial Branch
  VII. Legislation
  VIII. 'Pro-legislatures'
  IX. Advisory councils

The Executive Branch

  I. Heads of state: (1) Election; (2) Disqualifications; (3) Deputization for; (4) Payment of; (5) Oath of office; (6) Term of office; (7) Re-eligibility; (8) Removal of; (9) Powers of
  II. Chief executives: (1) Election; (2) Disqualifications; (3) Deputization for; (4) Term of office; (5) Removal of; (6) Powers of
  III. Governments and cabinets
  IV. Ministers individually: (1) Appointment and removal; (2) Disqualifications; (3) Powers and duties
  V. Civil servants

The Judicial Branch

  I. The system of courts generally
  II. Constitutional courts
  III. The French High Court of Justice
  IV. Extraordinary courts
  V. Judges: (1) Appointment of judges; (2) The independence of judges; (3) The accountability of judges; (4) The procuracy (USSR)

Emergency Powers

  I. Circumstances of emergency: (1) Circumstances short of war; (2) War
  II. Emergency powers

External Affairs and Defence

  I. Conduct of external affairs
  II. Defence and war

ANALYTICAL INDEX

CONSTITUTIONS

FEDERATIONS

LOCAL GOVERNMENT

DEPENDENCIES

FRANCE — XI 72-6

THE LEGISLATIVE BRANCH

I. Generalia
(1) Structure and competence of

USA	—	1	1	—
	—	1	9	1-3
	—	1	9	5-7
Amdt I-IX				
Amdt XIX				
Amdt XXVI				

USSR(S)	—	III	30-35

USSR(B)
System of Soviets, generally

	IV	12	89-94
Supreme Soviet	V	15	108-9
	V	15	110	A

FRANCE	—	IV	24
	—	V	35
	—	V	37

(2) Members of
(a) Credentials, recognition of

USA	—	I	5	1

USSR(S)	—	III	50

USSR(B)	V	15	110	D

GERMANY (*Bundestag only*)

	—	III	41

FRANCE	—	VII	59

(b) Rights and duties of members

USA	—	VI	—	3

USSR(S)	—	XI	142	—

USSR(B)	IV	13	102
	IV	14	103-7

GERMANY	—	III	38	(1)

FRANCE	—	IV	27

(c) Disqualifications for
membership

USA	—	I	6	2
	Amdt	XIV	3	—

USSR(B)	IV	13	101	B

FRANCE	—	III	23	A
	—	IV	25	A

(d) Immunities of members

USA	—	I	6	1

USSR(S)	—	III	52	—
	—	XI	142	—

USSR(B)	IV	14	106
	V	15	118

GERMANY	—	III	38	(2)
	—	III	46-8	—

FRANCE	—	IV	26

(e) Payment to members

USA	—	I	6	1

USSR(B)	IV	14	104

II. Chief executives

For the USA, see I. Heads of state *above. For the USSR, see* III. Governments and cabinets *below*

THE JUDICIAL BRANCH

EMERGENCY POWERS

EXTERNAL AFFAIRS AND DEFENCE

FRANCE 1946 Preamble 12–16
Preamble.
— — 1
— XII 77–88

V. Flags, symbols etc.

USSR(S)	—	XII	143–5
USSR(B)	VIII	—	169–71
GERMANY	—	II	22
FRANCE	—	II	2 B, C, D

IV. International law, status of

GERMANY	—	II	25	
	—	IX	100	(2)
FRANCE	—	VI	55	

CITIZENS AND THE STATE

I. Citizenship

USA	—	IV	2	1
	Amdt	XIV	1	
USSR(S)	—	II	21	
USSR(B)	II	6	33	
	II	7	39	
GERMANY	—	XI	116	
FRANCE	—	V	34	A
	—	XI	75	

II. Sovereignty
(1) The location of sovereignty

USA	Preamble		
	Amdt	IX	
	Amdt	X	
USSR(S)	—	I	1–3
USSR(B)	I	1	1–2
GERMANY	—	II	20 (1), (2)
FRANCE	RMC	3	
	RMC	6	
	—	I	3 A, B

(2) The mode of exercise of sovereignty
(a) Elections

USA	—	I	2	1
	—	I	4	1
	—	II	1, 2, 3	—
	Amdt	XII	
	Amdt	XV	
	Amdt	XVII	
	Amdt	XIX	
	Amdt	XXIV	
	Amdt	XXVI	
USSR(S)	—	XI	134–42
USSR(B)	I	1	3
	IV	13	95–102
GERMANY	—	II	28	(1)
	—	III	38	
FRANCE	—	I	3	C, D

(b) 'Participation'

USSR(B)	I	1	7–9

(c) Political parties

USSR(S)	—	X	126
	—	XI	141

ALPHABETICAL INDEX

SUPPLEMENTARY PAGES TO
THE INDEXES

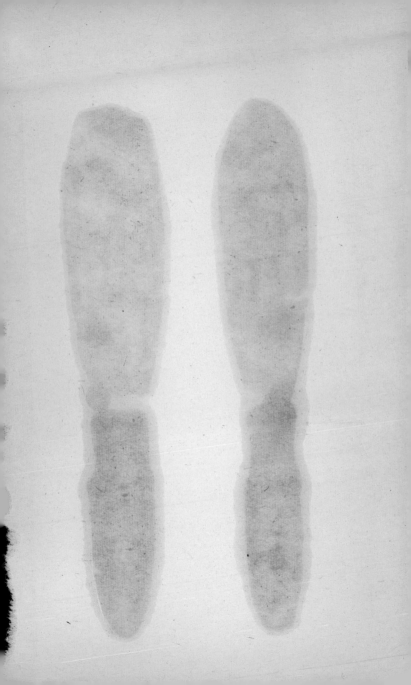